The Gentle Needle Arts

CAVENDISH HOUSE

Edited by Yvonne Deutch
Designed by Linda Cole

Published by Marshall Cavendish Books Limited
58 Old Compton Street
London W1V 5PA

© Marshall Cavendish Limited 1971-79, 1983

First printing 1977
Second printing 1979
Third printing 1983

Printed and bound by Koon Wah Printing Pte Ltd,

ISBN 0 85685 267 8

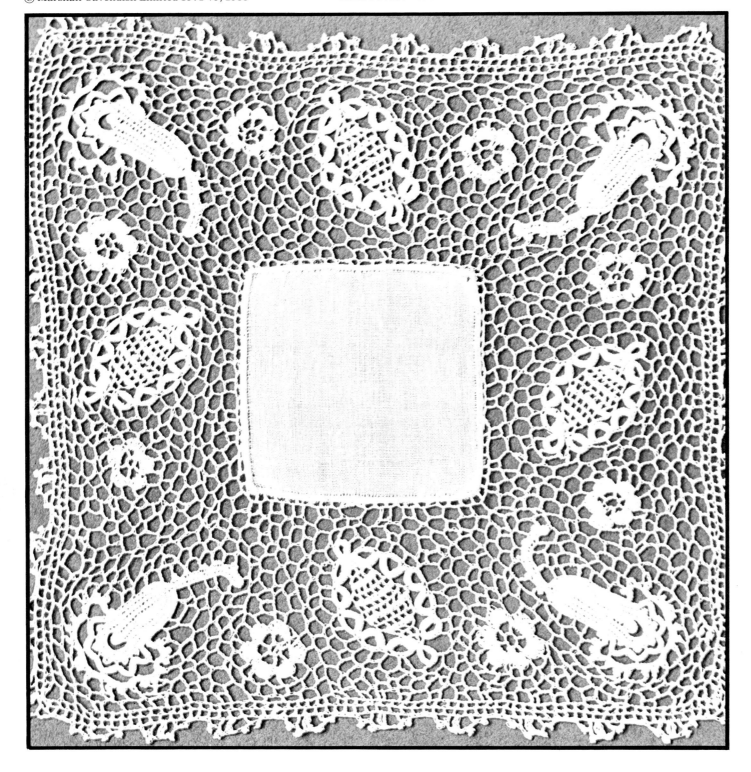

Introduction

Think of cobwebs, filigree patterns, delicate traceries, filmy clouds and tiny, perfect flowers. All these are fragile motifs for the designs in *The Gentle Needle Arts*. If you enjoy the texture of hand-made lace, or the intricacy of fine stitches, then you'll discover hours of pleasure and creativity. Skills such as lace-making, tatting, Irish crochet, netting and dainty embroidery are translated into gorgeous home and fashion accessories in traditional and modern styles.

The projects are all planned and written by experts, and there are clear step-by-step instructions for every pattern. In addition the basic techniques of the less familiar needlecrafts such as tatting and lace-making are explained with the help of useful diagrams and sumptuous illustrations, so you can't go wrong. Choose from a wide variety of patterns, ranging in scope from an exquisite border on a tiny handkerchief to a fabulous door curtain in filigree crochet. Many of the items are of heirloom quality, and make wonderful gifts, and if you're feeling in a more down-to-earth mood you might like to try a sturdy hammock or some macramé pot holders.

Generations of women have created these stitches as they sewed for themselves and their families. You can join this great tradition yourself, and *The Gentle Needle Arts* will be a constant source of inspiration, as well as a collection you'll be proud to own.

Contents

Daisywork

How to wind the loom

To make the larger daisies, both the inner and the outer rings of pegs on the loom are used. The smaller daisies are worked on the inner ring only.

Work with the loom on a flat surface and position space number 1 at the top. Begin with the large outer petals. Place the end of the yarn in space 7 and fasten with clear adhesive tape. Take the yarn across to space 1, round the outer peg to space 12, back across to space 6, round the outer peg to space 7 (fig.1). Wind the yarn round the same pegs the number of times required so that each petal has several loops.

Continuing with the yarn at space 7, take it across to space 2, (fig.2), round the outer peg to space 1, across to space 7, round the outer peg to space 8 (fig.3). Wind the yarn round the same pegs the number of times required.

Continue in this way in an anti-clockwise direction until all pegs have been used and there are 12 petals in all, ending with the yarn in space 6. Cut about 12mm (½in) of yarn beyond the loom and secure with clear adhesive tape.

To work the small petals, secure the end of the yarn at space 7, take it across to space 1, round the inner peg to space 12, across to space 6, round the inner peg to space 7. Wind the yarn round the same pegs the required number of times.

Continuing with the yarn at space 7, take it across to space 2, round the inner peg to space 1 (fig.4), across to space 7, round the inner peg to space 8. Wind the yarn round the same pegs the required number of times.

Continue to wind the inner pegs in this way until there are 12 petals in all, ending with the yarn in space 6. Cut the yarn leaving about 20.5cm (8in) for fastening off. Thread the end into a blunt-ended needle, pass round the inner peg to space 7 and push the needle through to the back at the centre, taking care not to split the yarn (fig.5) and fasten off at the centre back.

Cut a piece of yarn about 40.5cm (16in) long and join in at centre back. Bring the needle up through space 12, pull tightly against the centre back of the flower, push the needle through to the back between the strands in space 6. Bring the needle through to the front again at space 1 and push it through to the back at space 7. Continue working the star in an anti-clockwise direction until every space has been used, keeping the stitch as firm as possible. End with the yarn at the back of the loom in space 5.

Gently remove the flower from the loom and fasten the end securely on the wrong side. Trim the loose ends close to the centre of the flower to make a neat finish.

Daisy baby quilt

Once you have discovered how to make daisies with closed centres (see previous page) you can begin to be more ambitious. The daisies can be worked with open centres which in themselves can be decorated with beads.

The edges of the daisies, too, lend themselves to decoration although it is not essential to edge single daisies, especially if you like a random petal effect. The lock stitch edging shown here makes for a neater and more stylized finish which holds the petals firmly in their original shape and if you want to make the daisies into a trimming this edging is part of the basic method.

Open centres

Thread needle with tail of yarn. Put needle into centre of daisy and pull it through between any two petals. Put needle into centre again and bring it out between the next two petals, working clockwise. Continue overcasting, working an extra (13th) stitch to make the centre complete. Finish off by threading the needle through the loop of the 13th stitch before pulling it tight. Then thread the needle under the overcasting to hide the knot.

Decorative centres

There's no end to the ways you can decorate daisies. Add a pearl or rhinestone to the centre for evening daisies or coloured wooden or glass beads, buttons (the smooth, rounded ones which have a shank at the back for sewing to the fabric) or even sunflower seeds. When you finish overcasting, push the needle up through the centre, thread it through the pearl or rhinestone then sew through the opposite side of the hole. Make another overcasting stitch there to secure the bead then draw the needle through the loop of the next stitch and finish off as for the open centre daisy.

Lock stitch edging

1 Make a daisy in the usual way but leave a tail 36cm (14in) long when you begin. Then, keeping the daisy on the the daisy maker, thread up with the tail of wool. Take the needle upwards through the centre of a petal to the left of the spoke. Thread the needle through again, to the right of the spoke, leaving a loop.

2 Thread needle through this loop from right to left and pull tight with a gentle jerk so that the knot locks below the spoke. Stitch each petal in turn in the same way, leaving a fairly loose thread between each spoke. When circle is complete, take end of thread back to the centre and finish off. Release the daisy from the daisy maker.

To join daisies

3 Make one daisy complete with lock stitch edging. Make a second, without the edging, and leave it on the daisy maker. Taking the completed daisy, place it wrong side up to cover the daisy on the daisy maker. Begin the lock stitch edging, going through two petals only of both top and bottom daisy.

4 Turn back the top daisy and finish edging the bottom daisy as described.

To make a pretty trimming or edging for a dress make and join together in the way just described as many daisies as you require.

Square daisies

Place adapter on the loom. Wind wool across adapter from daisy to daisy following instructions for round daisy. However, wool will lie across opening of each post. Make two windings, overcast stitches in

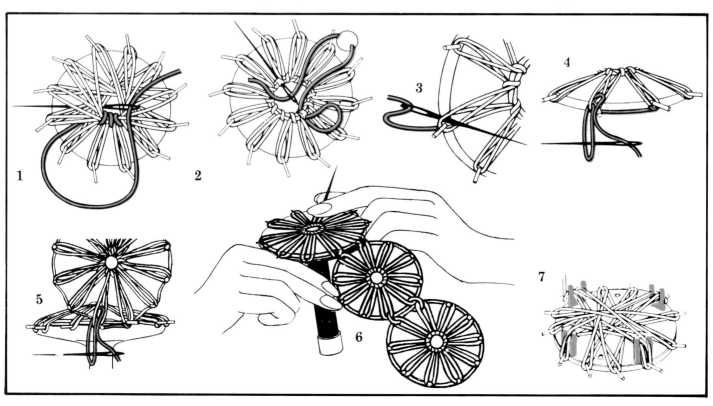

Above: Make up lots of daisies so that they can be joined together to make this delightful coverlet for the pram or crib. Some of the daisies have been embroidered.
1. Overcasting open centre
2. Decorating centre with bead
3. Lock stitch step 1
4. Lock stitch step 2
5. Joining two daisies
6. Working a chain of daisies
7. Square daisy on adapter

centre, and lock-stitch edging according to instructions for round daisy.

Joining square daisies
When joining square daisies, work same as for round daisy except that you join 4 petals of top square to 4 petals of bottom square by starting joining at one post of adapter, working following two spokes, finishing joining at 2nd post of adapter (one complete side of square).

After releasing, square may appear to be cup-shaped. Take square in both hands and stretch gently to bring corners out to true square shape.

Daisy babies
Making a pram coverlet is a perfect way to start joining daisies together. It's small enough for the individual daisies to retain their importance, is quick to finish and lends itself to pretty decoration. Here the centres of some of the daisies have been embroidered to emphasise their 'daisy-ness', but you could apply a few separate daisies instead, or attach a pom-pon to each corner, or make the sewn-together daisies in a patchwork of colours.

Materials
9 x 20g (6oz) balls Bri-Nylon Double Knitting yarn [double knitting yarn in 100% orlon] and 2 balls of contrast yarn (nylon for washability).

The coverlet consists of 11 rows of 15 [orlon] square daisies. Follow instructions for making and joining these. When the first row is completed add each individual daisy working lock stitch edging to form the next row joining to the previous row as well as to one another. Oversew centres of daisies round the edge with contrast yarn and also a ring of centres in the middle of the coverlet.

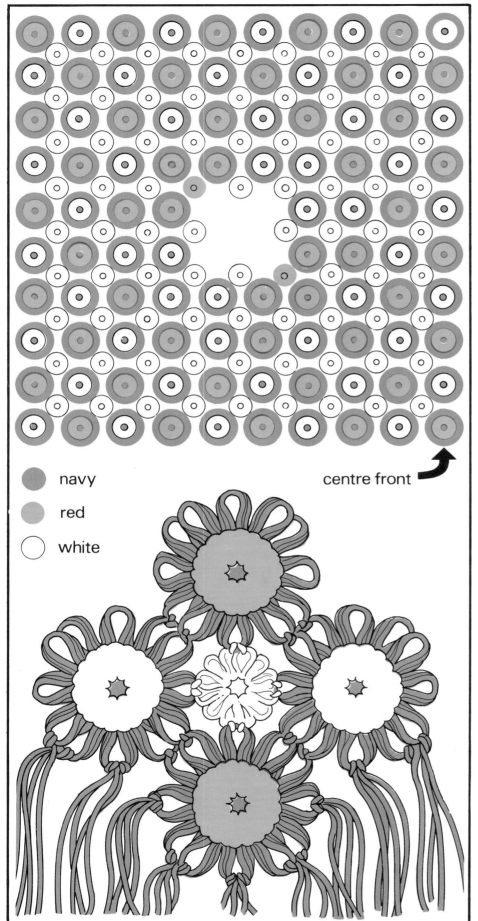

Poncho

Tension
Each flower motif measures about 7.5cm *(3in)* diameter

Materials
Double knitting wool [knitting worsted]
8 x 50g (2oz) [4 x 100g (4oz)] balls A, navy
8 x 25g (1oz) [2 x 100g (4oz)] balls B, white
4 x 25g (1oz) [1 x 100g (4oz)] balls C, red
Multi-Fleur Loom [Lazy Daisy Winder] Medium size crochet hook.

Large flowers
Using the full loom, make 48 flowers with three loops in A on the outer ring and two loops in B on the inner ring. Work the centre in A.
Using the full loom, make 48 flowers with three loops in A on the outer ring and two loops in C on the inner ring. Work the centre in A.

Small flowers
Using the inner ring only, make 78 flowers with three loops in each petal in B. Work the centre in B.
Using the inner ring only, make two flowers with three loops in each petal in C. Work the centre in C.

Joining the flowers
Using A and small overcasting stitches, join large flowers as shown in the chart with two petals on each flower at each join, taking in all three loops of each petal, and missing one petal between each joining.
Using B, join in the small B flowers as shown on the chart, sewing two small petals to the one large petal left free between the previous joins.
Using C, join in the two small C flowers in the same way.
Cut remaining A yarn into lengths of 30.5cm *(12in)* each and taking two strands together throughout, knot with the crochet hook into two petals together all round work, except at the corners, where there are seven free petals, knot into one petal, two petals together, then one petal. Trim fringe.

Top: Pattern chart for poncho
Left: Joining flowers to fringes
Opposite: The completed poncho

navy

red

white

centre front

Daisy bedspread

Tension
Each flower measures about 9cm
(3½in) across

Materials
Any 4 ply yarn in 25g (1oz) balls
[4 ply sport weight yarn]
17 balls in red [equivalent U.S.
weight]
15 balls in coral [equivalent U.S.
weight]
8 balls in green [equivalent U.S.
weight]
Multi-Fleur Loom [Lazy Daisy
Winder]
One No. 2.50 crochet hook
[Aluminium crochet hook B]

Large flowers
Using the full loom, work outer
petals in red, winding the yarn six
times round each peg, then using the
inner circle of pegs only, make the
smaller petals in coral winding the
yarn round each peg three times.
Work the centre in green.
Make 328 large flowers altogether.

Small flowers
Using only the inner ring of the
loom, work with green, winding the
yarn three times round each peg.
Work the centres with coral.
Make 290 small flowers in all.

Joining the flowers
Using green and small overcasting
stitches, join the top two petals of
each large flower to the corresponding two petals on the next flower as
illustrated. Join eight rows of 23
flowers, then along each long edge
add one row of 21 flowers, one row of
19, one row of 17 and one row of 15.
Using green, and a small overcasting stitch, sew the small flowers
between the large ones.

Edging
Using crochet hook and green,
attach with a slip stitch between
any two daisies along the outer
edge. *Make 6 chain, 1 double
[single] crochet into the next petal,
repeat from * all round edge of
bedspread, ending with 1 double
[single] crochet into first slip stitch.
Fasten off end of yarn.

Right: Detail of the pattern

Needle-made lace

Needle-made lace is very pretty and easy to make. Alpine girls with plenty of time to spare use fine yarn and produce delicate results. This particular form of needle-made lace is called Puncetto (pronounced poon-che-toe) and comes from a word in the dialect of Northern Italy meaning stitch. But we are going to present Puncetto in a more modern form which is easier and quicker to make because it is made with thicker threads which give a bold, bright effect.

Steps to lace-making

Puncetto lace is easy to make. It's simply needle-made knots worked in rows from left to right and back again. You can use it as an edging on a piece of material, or base it on supporting thread. It must always be worked on the right side of the cloth.

Threads to use Firm, tightly twisted yarns such as fine crochet cotton are best, although for a chunky effect Pearl Cotton and Crysette can be used. Of course, the thicker the thread, the faster the work grows. Use a blunt needle like a tapestry needle.

The basic method

When starting off, hold the material on which the edging is to be worked in the left hand. Work either on a selvedge, or make a small hem. Always secure the thread with a couple of tiny back stitches on the wrong side of the work and bring the needle out on the edge. It is most important to keep the stitches of the first row of equal depth and distance from each other, and each knot of uniform tension, or the edging will be spoilt.

First row Working from left to right, bring the needle upward under the edge of the cloth, two or three threads in from the edge. Take the working thread in the right hand and wind it round the needle once. (Take it from left to right and back, passing it in front of the needle first.) Pull the needle up, tightening the knot you've made. Continue in this way making as many knots as required along the edge, taking care to space them evenly.

Second row Work the second row from right to left. Bring the needle upwards through the space between the last two knots of the preceding row. Wind the thread round the needle (from right to left and back, passing in front of the needle first) then pull it up, tightening the knot. Continue to the end of the row, keeping the tension even.

Following rows Repeat the first and second rows as many times as necessary, to make a solid border. Go on practising this for a while to get the stitches even and then you will be ready to tackle the scalloped, trellissed and other lacy motifs which are to come.

Pyramid border

This simple border consists of a series of triangles, which look very pretty edging a baby's pillow, cuffs or a collar. In very coarse thread it makes an unusual and effective edging for a roller blind or lampshade. Using the instructions for the basic method, work as many knots as required to form the base of the first triangle and then turn, working one knot less at the end of each row. Continue until the triangle is completed. Then overcast along the side to bring the thread back to the foundation line, ready to start the next triangle.

Top left: Starting first row.
Top right: Working second row from fileft to right.
Bottom left: By third row, lace begins to build up.
Bottom right: Pyramid border. Overcast along the edge.

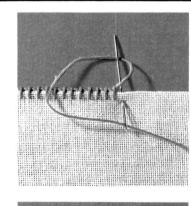
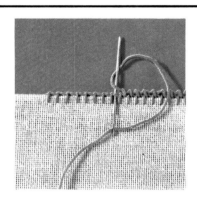
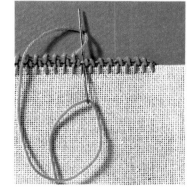

Lacy borders

Once you've got the knack of making rows of needle-made lace, you can start building up all sorts of lacy borders, or you can use it to join two pieces of fabric with a decorative insertion.

Trellises
Work from left to right. Make two rows of edging on the material finishing at the left. At the beginning of the third row start the first square by missing two foundation knots and making a knot. Insert the needle upwards through the next space but before tightening it, measure out enough thread with the needle to form three sides of a small square (the fourth side is provided by the base). Tighten the knot and make three or four knots round the thread which forms the third side, ending with the needle facing upwards. Continue forming the other squares in the same way, missing two foundation knots and measuring out the thread to obtain the two sides of the next square. Complete this row of foundation squares. Work from right to left and cover the foundation squares with a row of knots, working three knots for each square. Continue to the required length.
Cover this thread with a row of knots worked from right to left, working about three knots for each length of thread.

Loophole border
Build up basic edging to the depth required, then work solid sections alternating with loopholes as follows. Work a section of knots in rows from left to right and back again until you reach the depth you want. To make the loophole, miss two or three foundation knots and make a square with the thread as already explained for square trellises. Make a knot at the base of the square, then work a section of knots in rows from left to right and back again to match the first. At the end of each row on the square side, make the last knot round the thread which forms the third side of the square.

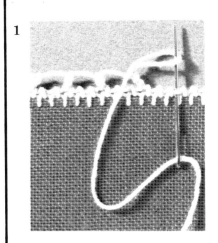
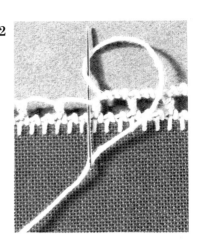
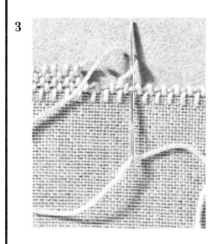
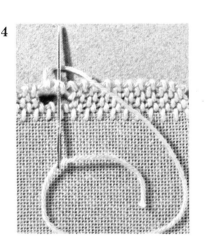
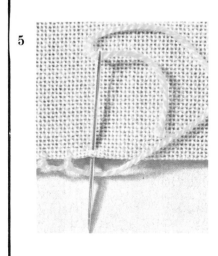
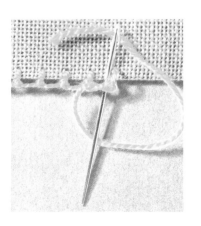

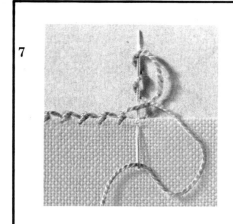

7

8

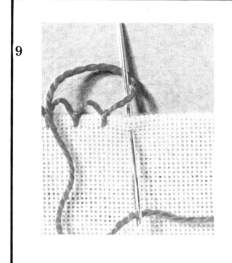

9

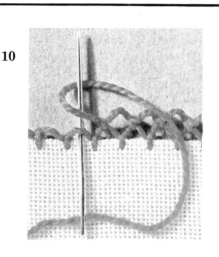

10

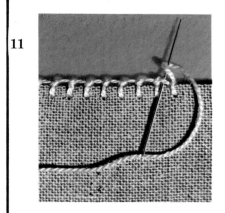

11

12

1. First row of trellis border.
2. Work back along trellis with a row of knots.
3. For loophole border, work solid row of knots to desired depth.
4. Work knots over top of the square loophole.
5. Work simple lace with blanket stitch along fabric edge.
6. Secure each stitch with knot.
7. First row of double knot lace.
8. Form knot in each loop for second row of double knot lace.
9. Leave the thread loose between knots for lace arches.
10. Work second row same way.
11. Bar lace is worked in the same way as lace arches.
12. Bar lace quickly builds up into a border, producing a very attractive woven effect.

Over the top of the square, work the same number of knots as you missed at the base. Continue building the border to the required depth.

Simple lace

Hold the work downwards, and work from left to right. Insert the needle downwards through the material, and passing it over the thread, make a small loop or blanket stitch. Finish the loop by securing it with a knot by passing the needle from left to right through the loop and tightening it.

Double knot lace

Work from left to right fastening off the thread at the end of each row. Insert the needle upwards.

1st row Pass the thread coming from the cloth over the needle to the right. Wind the thread from the eye of the needle twice round the point from right to left. Pull the needle through tightening the knot. Continue along the border, leaving about 6mm ($\frac{1}{4}in$) between each stitch.

2nd row Work from left to right. Insert the needle through the first loop and wind thread twice round needle. Pull needle through, forming a knot.

Lace arches

1st row Work from left to right making knots, and as in ordinary needle-made lace, leaving the thread loose between them to form small loops. If you find it difficult to keep loops even, a pencil or knitting needle used as a gauge will help.

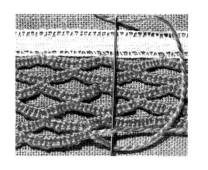

2nd row Work from right to left, in the same way, using the previous row of loops as a base.

Bar lace

In this lace, bars are formed between the knots. Work the rows from left to right fastening off the thread at the end of each row.

1st row Insert the needle upwards. Make knots as for the first row of lace arches leaving bars.

2nd row Make knots and bars from left to right by inserting the needle through the previous row of bars. Repeat these two movements.

Small buttonhole scallops

1st row Work groups of four buttonhole stitches and loops.

2nd row As for first row working buttonhole stitches into the loops.

Large buttonhole scallops

1st row Work a row of loops.

2nd row Work over loops in buttonhole stitch.

3rd row Work loops from the centre of each preceding loop to the centre of the next and work over in buttonhole stitch. Repeat.

Lace edgings

These lace edgings are perfect for decorating handkerchiefs, small napkins, fine underclothes and baby linen: thicker yarn makes them suitable for guest towels, tablecloths and sheets. The best yarn to use is crochet cotton because it runs easily and is tightly twisted and gives the lace a consistent appearance: it is also very hard wearing. And, of course, all these edgings can be as narrow or as deep as you wish.

Right border

Make three rows of bar lace. Work the fourth row with one looped stitch for every two. Work over each loop with six simple lace stitches.

Centre border

Work three rows of double knot lace.

Left border

1st and 2nd row Work as for lace arches.

3rd row Work as for your lace arches, over every four stitches of the previous row.

4th row Work over the loops with simple lace stitch. Repeat the last two rows, joining the loops to make scallops.

Take care to keep the loops fairly flat or the edge may look untidy. The curves become pronounced as you work them.

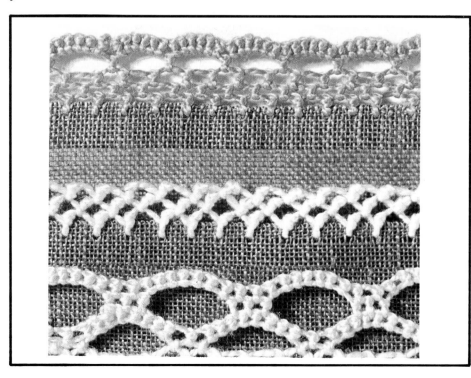

Web motif

Once you have learned the basic knots and borders, it is very easy to become your own designer and build them up into patterns to suit the particular article you have in mind.

The border and insert shown here are two such designs derived from a combination of basic knots, bars, pyramids and scallops.

Triangular inserts

First snip out the areas to be filled. Turning the raw edge under, make a base with one row of basic edging. Fill in the spaces with a variety of buttonhole bars and pyramids. Work the centre with a circle of plain bar lace.

Pyramid and scallop border

1st row Make a base with one row of basic edging.
2nd row Work a row of trellises with one bar to every four stitches.
3rd row Overwork the bars in buttonhole stitch.
4th row Using two bars as a base each time, work two buttonhole scallops, then two pyramids. Repeat to the end of the row.

The web motif

Web motifs are very popular in needle-made lace and although they are not difficult to do, they can be worked up into quite complex insets and borders.

To work an individual web motif, first prepare the usual foundation border with several rows of basic edging. Begin the web with a left to right row.

1st row Work four knots, miss two foundation knots forming the thread into a loop over them. Work one knot into the next one. Cover the right hand side of the loop with knots, bringing the needle out at the top. Miss two more foundation knots and once again looping the thread, make one knot into the next one. Make three more knots (fig.1).

2nd row Working from right to left, make four knots, cover the two loops with knots, then end with four knots.

3rd row Working from left to right, make four knots and work backwards and forwards over these until the work is high enough for the threads to be laid for the horizontal bar of the web. Make a bar across to the central column and fasten in the centre with three knots. Work rest of the bar leaving the thread loose (fig.2) so that the right-hand rows from left to right and back can be worked, taking in the thread as well, up to the level of the horizontal bar. Finish with a complete row from right to left, making knots on

Below: Trellises, pyramids and scallops combine to make a pretty and unusual edging.
Bottom: Inserts can be filled using a variety of stitches.
Each triangle is filled with a different pattern.

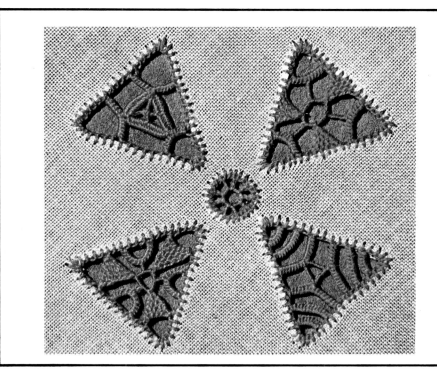

17

Left: The four stages followed in making a web motif.
1. Completing the first row
2. Building up side of the web
3. Levelling off the two sides
4. Finishing the top border

the horizontal bars.

Work rows backwards and forwards over the first four knots. Then fasten the thread in the centre with two knots to form a loop. Leave another loop and work several rows on the right-hand knots to build up level with the left (fig.3).

Next row Working from right to left, cover the loops with knots.

Next row Working from left to right, work four knots then fasten the thread to the centre of the web to form the central column. Work up this with three or four knots. Make the second half of the loop and work the last four knots.

Go back over the loops with a row of knots (fig.4) and then work backwards and forwards to border the top side of the web.

Web insert

Once you have learned to work a single web motif you will be able to work this beautiful insert, following the illustration. Cut out the square and turning under the edges, work several rows of basic edging. First work the webs in the corners, then the rows of three webs and finally the centre. Work in whatever thickness of yarn you wish, depending on the fabric and the finished effect desired.

Right: Use the illustration to make up an attractive insert based on the single web motif which has been described above. Experiment with different threads for a variety of effects.

Æmilia-Ars lace

Aemilia-Ars lace originally came from Bologna and was famous for its delicacy and the variety of its designs. Then for a long time it was neglected until, at the end of the nineteenth century, the Aemilia-Ars Society revived this form of needle-made lace. So it is to this society that we owe the re-appearance of this beautiful lace and its name. Aemilia-Ars lace is intricate and requires great patience, but the results more than justify the effort. Unlike other forms of needle-made lace, most of which are built up as edgings or inserts onto the fabric itself. Aemilia-Ars lace is built up over its own skeleton lattice base which is prepared by a special technique.

Preparing the design

Choose a design and copy it carefully onto stiff paper fixed to a thin card, or even to a piece of cardboard such as the back of a writing pad.

Make pinholes where the lines of the motif touch the line of the surround. Using a strong thread, such as buttonhole thread, make tiny bars by threading the needle through each hole and taking it outside the outline. For the design given in this chapter, make a cross with two bars at the centre where the diagonals meet.

Working the design

Starting at the bottom right-hand corner, lay the thread you have chosen for the lace round the edges of the square, passing the thread under the prepared bars. Repeat once more round the outside edge then lay one of the diagonals under the central cross, under the bar in the top left-hand corner taking in the thread of the frame, and then back to the starting point. Repeat once more to make a diagonal three threads thick. Working down from the corner, cover the first part of the diagonal in cording (wrapping the thread round and round the core) as far as the first

1. The design has already been traced onto card with some support stitches already in place.

2. Lay the thread around the outline of the motif and begin working on the first corner.

3. After completing first corner and cording first diagonal, begin working the second corner.

4. Lay the base for the central star after you have completed three corners and three diagonals.

5. Outline the central square with buttonhole stitch then lay the outline for each of the star points.

6. The points of the star are filled in with buttonhole stitch. The last corner remains to fill.

cross bar. Make this bar by laying a padding thread over and under the thread of the surround to the left, right, then to the left again. Work back to the diagonal covering the first half of the bar in buttonhole stitch.

Lay the third padding thread as described previously for the second half of the bar, and then work back to the centre, covering the padding with buttonhole stitch.

Continue cording along the diagonal as far as the second bar. Work this in the same way as the first one. Cover the diagonal in cording as far as the centre. Lay part of the second diagonal from here into the bottom left-hand corner and back to the centre. Then take it out to the opposite corner to lay the second half, then back to the bottom left-hand corner. Work back to the centre as for the previous diagonal and cross bars.

Take the thread out to the top right-hand corner, thus laying the third thread, and work the corner in the same way as the previous two. Complete by cording back into the centre again.

From the centre, cord along the remaining diagonal until you reach the point where it crosses the central square. Outline the square with two padding threads and cover them in buttonhole stitch. Next lay a single base thread for the star, fixing all the points to the surrounding square, starting with the right-hand point and working anti-clockwise.

The points of the star are filled in entirely in buttonhole stitch. Work from the centre outwards, decreasing one stitch on each row. Work in the same anti-clockwise direction, threading through back of work to bring thread to centre after each point is completed. When you have finished filling in the star, complete the fourth diagonal. Cord out from the centre to the corner and work the pattern the same as the others.

Finishing off
Finish off the framework by overcasting it. Fasten off securely then take the motif off the card by cutting the small thread bars. A number of motifs can be joined together by a fine overcasting stitch.

Joining motifs together
To join Aemilia-Ars motifs together,

place two right sides together, edge to edge, and neatly oversew through the threads so that the stitches are hidden at the back of the work once the seam is opened out. Alternatively, work cording over the two edges, completely covering the framework of the motifs.

Strengthen the outer edges of the completed article with buttonhole stitch or cording. If your choice is buttonhole stitch, picots can be added for further decoration.

Once the article is completed, pin the motifs out to their correct size and shape on a clean, flat surface and using rustless pins. Cover with a damp cloth and leave until completely dry.

Inserting motifs into fabric
To insert Aemilia-Ars motifs into fabric, first lightly mark the outline of the lace onto the material either in pencil or with dressmakers carbon. Make sure that the straight edges of the design follow the weave of the fabric.

Fix the motif in place on the outline

Above: The completed Aemilia Ars lace motif has been enlarged to show every detail of the stitches. Before removing the motif from the card, the framework should be finished off with overcasting stitches. A single motif can be used as a fabric insert or a number can be joined together to make a mat or a lacy insert.

Right: This modern lace sampler is composed of several types of lace making. Most of the outer motifs are done in needle-made lace, the centre is bobbin lace, and all the motifs are joined with lace ribbon.

and secure with small tacking stitches at the centre and also round the edges. Work buttonhole stitch or cording all round the edges of the motif.

Once this is completed, free the central tacking stitches and then cut away the fabric within the outline using small, sharp scissors and taking care not to cut the lace. Trim close to the stitches.

Sampler motifs

Add these Aemilia-Ars motifs to your repertoire. All of them include stitches and techniques you have already learnt. With practice, it is possible to work straight from an illustration without guide lines. Begin designing your own motifs by interchanging parts of these, such as the corner of the star with the petal centre, gradually introducing new ideas until a completely original motif evolves.

Making motifs without patterns

Once you have mastered the techniques of Aemilia-Ars lace, it is possible to make motifs by following photographs like these.

If a basic skeleton of the design is not provided, make one from the illustration and then work the motif by following the basic steps given already.

Broadly speaking, the simplest method is to work the corners first with their diagonals, starting at the top left-hand corner, followed by the bottom left-hand corner, then the top right-hand corner. Next, work the centre motifs from the middle outwards and finish with the last remaining corner. It is usually possible, in this way, to avoid breaking the thread at any stage.

Each of the three motifs given in this chapter has a pretty, snowflake effect. The charts of the basic outlines are used actual size working with DMC Coton Perlé No.8 [Pearl Cotton] or they can be en-

larged for thicker yarn. The designs are mostly worked in cording and buttonhole stitch enriched with picots. The spokes of the lace star motif are worked in spaced buttonhole stitch. The illustrations are enlarged to make the stitches clearer.

Once the motif is completed, remove it from the supporting bars and either sew several together or insert it in fabric using buttonhole stitch.

Above: Highly enlarged, these Aemilia Ars lace motifs show the variety of designs that can be created from the basic stitches and techniques. The designs are mostly worked in cording and buttonhole stitch.

Above: This is the actual size trace pattern which is used to work the lacy star motif shown on the facing page. Work the corners first, with their diagonals, starting from the top left hand corner.

Above: Another motif is the wheel star, which is illustrated in enlarged form at the top of the page, in the centre. The trace pattern here is actual size, and produces yet another variation on the basic snowflake effect.

Above: The final motif is used to create a flowery petal effect. It is illustrated in enlarged form at the top of the page on the right. Use this actual size trace pattern to work from, following the basic techniques and stitches.

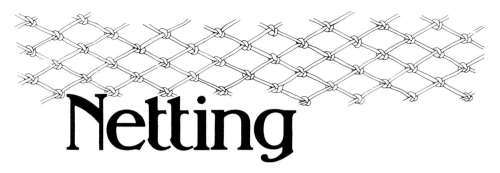

Netting

Netting, the traditional craft of fishermen, can be used to create all kinds of attractive and useful items, from shopping bags to hammocks. It is an easy craft to learn and an absorbing hobby.

Materials
String Ordinary cotton string is perfectly suitable but it is interesting to experiment with coloured and synthetic strings and with macramé twine.

Netting needle This is the string holder and is usually made of flexible plastic. Netting needles come in varying widths.

Mesh stick This determines the size of the mesh and ensures that the meshes are all equal in size. The mesh stick must always be wider than the needle so that the loaded needle passes comfortably through the meshes. Mesh sticks can be improvised from rulers but ideally they should be made from plastic, 15cm to 20.5cm *(6in to 8in)* and rectangular in shape.

Loading the needle
Cut the length of string required. Hold the needle in the left hand with the point upwards. Hold the end of the string anywhere on the body of the needle with the left thumb. Run the string up the body, round the prong and down the same side of the body to trap the starting end of the string. Take the string round the bottom or heel of the needle between the two projections. Turn the needle back to front, still with the point upwards, and continue loading by repeating the same process.

The netting knot
Practise with two pieces of fairly thick string, each about 46cm *(18in)* long. Tie one piece into a loop and attach it to a working surface as a foundation loop.
Using the second piece of string,

pass all except the last 5cm *(2in)* through from the back of the foundation loop and hold at the intersection with the thumb and forefinger of the left hand.
Holding the long end of the string (the working end) in the right hand, throw an open loop over to the left. Take care not to allow a twist in this loop. With the right hand, take the end of the string to the right across the front of the foundation loop, round the back and out to the front through the thrown loop. Keeping the left thumb and finger firmly in position until the last moment, pull the knot firm. Make sure to seat the knot correctly round the bottom of the foundation loop and not let it slip below.

Diamond mesh netting
For a first practice piece, use a medium netting needle and a 4cm *(1½in)* wide mesh stick. Make a foundation loop with a piece of string about 46cm *(18in)* long. Load the needle and fasten the foundation loop to the working surface. Attach the working string to the loop as before with a netting knot.
First row Hold the mesh stick from

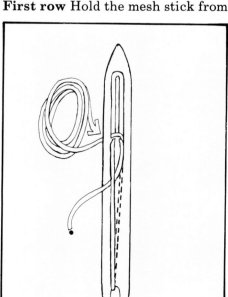

below with the left hand, thumb at the front. Lay the working string over the front of the mesh stick, taking it round below and up behind the stick and out through the foundation loop from the back. Pull the needle downwards with the right hand and the mesh stick will be hauled, pulley-fashion, up to the bottom of the foundation loop. With the left-hand thumb at the front and index finger at the back, hold the string and the foundation loop where they cross at the top of the mesh stick. Form the knot and draw it firm.
The mesh stick remains in position, encircled by this first loop and held in the left hand. The needle and working string should automatically be over the front of the mesh stick and ready to continue by repeating the process. Always make sure that the knot is made close to the top of the mesh stick so that the meshes are uniform.
Keeping the mesh stick in position with the left hand, repeat twice so that there are three loops on the mesh stick. Do not count the knots at the top but the bottom of the loops formed on the mesh stick.

Left: Loading the netting needle.
Opposite: The stages in making the netting knot and meshing.
1. Pass through loop from back
2. Throw loop across to left
3. Go behind loop and across front
4. Pull end to make knot firm
5. The correct seating of knot
6. Wrong seating of knot
7. Lay string over mesh stick at the front
8. Forming the first loop
9. Fixing mesh with netting knot
10. Mesh stick with two loops
11. Making first loop on second row
12. Detail of a piece of diamond netting.

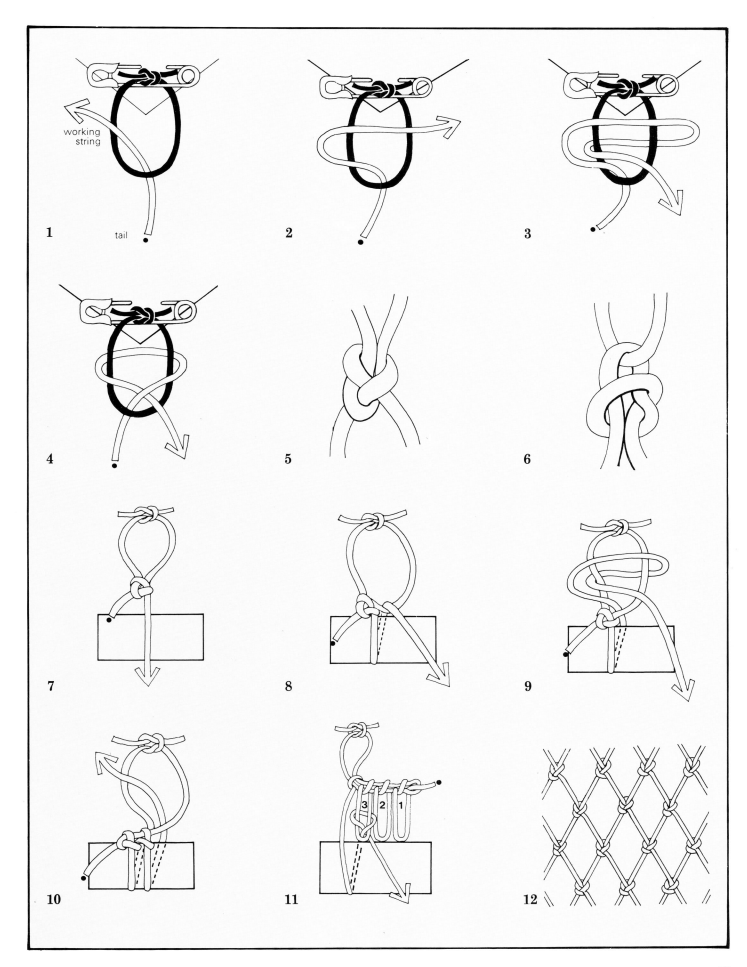

1

working string

tail

2

3

4

5

6

7

8

9

10

11

3 2 1

12

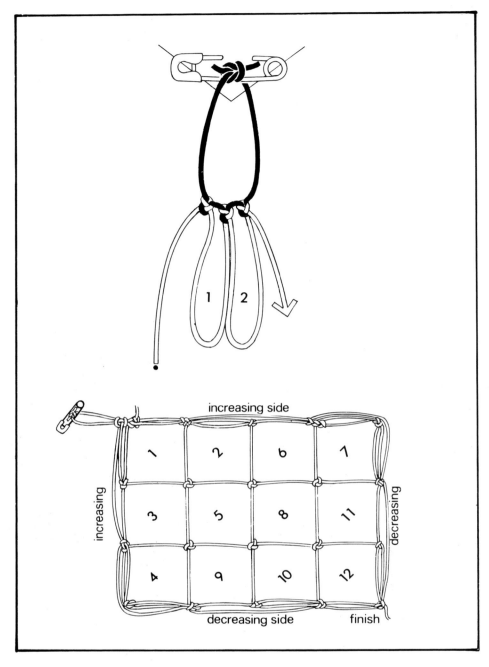

increasing side

increasing

decreasing

decreasing side   finish

always leave one loop on the stick. Continue the row in this way.

Square mesh netting
Make a 7cm *(3in)* foundation loop and attach it to the working surface as before.
Leaving a 7cm *(3in)* tail, attach the working string with a netting knot.
First row Make two loops over the mesh stick and into the foundation loop. Remove the mesh stick and turn the work.
Second row Mesh into the first loop and increase by meshing twice into second loop (three meshes). If the work is opened out at this point the first complete square mesh can be seen, and at each side the double string of the selvedge which will make the side of the end meshes of the next row.
Third to fifth rows Mesh into each loop, increasing in the last loop of each row (six meshes).

Turning the corner The corner is turned when one more row has been worked than the number of squares required (i.e. having worked five rows before turning the corner there will be four squares across the top of the net). The corner is turned by meshing all except the last two meshes and decreasing by meshing the last two together (five meshes).
Lengthening The net can be continued indefinitely by increasing at the end of alternate rows and decreasing at the end of the other rows. This develops the net diagonally, the increases further increasing the long side and decreases forming the opposite side.
Next row Mesh into each loop, increasing in last one (six meshes).
Next row Mesh all except the last two meshes and decrease by meshing the last two together (five meshes).
Continue in this way until the long side is one mesh longer than the required length. It is at this point that the last corner is turned.

To finish Decrease at the end of every row until only two meshes remain. Tie these two together with a netting knot but without making the normal mesh round the mesh stick. Remove the beginning of the net from the foundation loop, and with the 7cm *(3in)* tail tie together the first two loops with a netting knot as for the last two.

Top: The foundation loop used for square mesh netting.
Above: Detail of a piece of square mesh netting showing the way in which the net is worked diagonally and the meshes are formed.

Second row Remove the mesh stick. With the left hand turn the three newly made loops so that the last made loop is on the left ready to be used in the second row. As before, form a loop round the mesh stick and knot the first loop. Take care not to include the descending strand on the left as well as the two strands of the first loop. To avoid this, hold the intersection with the thumb and second finger of the left hand and use the left index finger to mark the space between the descending strand and the first loop, the space in fact through which the needle will pass as it comes round the back of the loop.
This makes the first full mesh. Each loop forms a half mesh. Keep the mesh stick in position and mesh into the remaining two loops.
Third and subsequent rows
Remove the mesh stick only at the end of each row and continue meshing successive rows, always working left to right.
For a piece of work with more than three loops, work until the mesh stick is full then slide it along, but

Netted shopping bags

These matching string shopping bags for mother and daughter are fun to make and very useful.

Materials
Twine in two colours
Large bag only One pair cane handles, 10cm *(4in)* diameter
18mm *(¾in)* mesh stick
Medium netting needle
Small bag only One pair cane handles, 7cm *(3in)* diameter
15mm *(⅝in)* mesh stick
Fine netting needle

Large bag
Casting on
Leaving a length of twine 122cm *(48in)* long, make a clove hitch onto one handle. Using the 18mm *(¾in)* mesh stick, cast on 24 loops with a clove hitch over the handle between each loop and securing each clove hitch by 'crowning' with an added half hitch.

Main section
Remove the mesh stick at the end of the row and reverse the work so that the next row is also worked from left to right.
Net 27 rows or an odd number of rows so that after casting off, there will be a length of twine at the opposite side to the length left before casting on.

Casting off
Make a clove hitch onto the second handle, then make a netting knot into the first mesh of the last row.
Continue alternately making a clove hitch over the handle and 'crowning' it and netting into successive meshes, ending with a clove hitch.
Leave a 122cm *(48in)* length of twine.

Drawing up the sides
Tie the end of this 122cm *(48in)* length to the same handle using a clove hitch so that it becomes a loop. Lace this loop through the outside meshes. Repeat with the length at the other end down the opposite side.
Draw up both sides to about 35cm *(14in)* between the handles and secure the doubled twine to the opposite handle with a clove hitch.

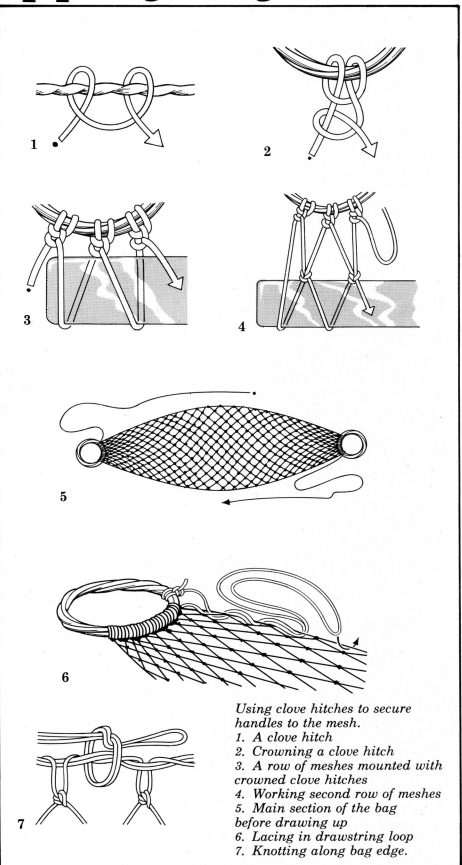

Using clove hitches to secure handles to the mesh.
1. A clove hitch
2. Crowning a clove hitch
3. A row of meshes mounted with crowned clove hitches
4. Working second row of meshes
5. Main section of the bag before drawing up
6. Lacing in drawstring loop
7. Knotting along bag edge.

Do not trim.
Using the remainder of the loop, work along the edge, knotting over both the side meshes and the double draw-string and evenly spacing two or three knots on each mesh. Fasten off using a crowned clove hitch over the handle and trim. Repeat along the other side to correspond.

Tassels
Loop 25cm (*10in*) lengths of contrast twine over one bar of the central mesh on the bottom row and secure by working a Turk's Head in main colour as shown in the diagrams:
Fig 1 Using 38cm (*15in*) length, tie round core as shown, then turn the core towards you as indicated by the arrow at the right of the diagram.
Fig 2 Holding the working end to the left as shown, cross the two threads at the top of the core left over right as indicated by the small

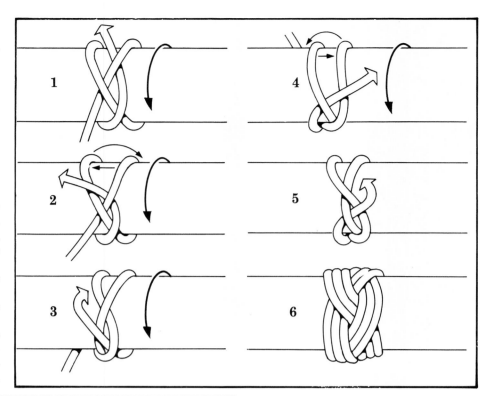

arrows, then turn the core towards you as indicated.
Fig 3 Pass the working end under the left-hand thread and up between it and the right-hand thread. Turn the core towards you as indicated.
Fig 4 Pass the working end over the right-hand thread, then cross the two threads again, this time right over left as indicated by the small arrows. Turn the core towards you.
Fig 5 Pass the working end under the right-hand thread and up between it and the left-hand thread as indicated.
Fig 6 Follow through again until the knot has three strands all round. Trim tassel if necessary. Position four other tassels half way up the bag, using 12 20cm (*8in*) lengths and securing each with a Turk's Head.

Small bag
Using the fine netting needle and 15mm (⅝*in*) mesh stick, cast on 16 loops in the same way as given for large bag. Work 23 rows of meshes, drawing up the sides to about 20cm (*8in*) with single thread and knotting thread along the edges.
Complete as given for large bag.

Top: Stages in making the tassels
Left: Matching shopping bags are fun for mother and daughter.

Cat net

Materials
To fit an average size pram 45m (50yd) nylon or cotton twine
one 18mm (¾in) netting needle
one 4cm (1½in) mesh stick
2.3m (2½yd) round elastic

Casting on
Using a 30cm (12in) length of twine, make a foundation loop and attach it to the working surface.

Load the needle with twine. Leaving a tail of about 10cm (4in), attach the working twine to the foundation loop with a netting knot.

First row Make two loops over the mesh stick and into the foundation loop. Remove the mesh stick and turn the work.

2nd row Mesh into the first loop but also taking in the outer strand to give a firm selvedge, then increase by meshing twice into the second loop (three meshes). If work is opened out at this point, the first complete square mesh can be seen and at each side the double string of the selvedge, which will make the side of the end meshes of the next row.

3rd to 15th rows Continue as given for second row, always beginning row by including the outer strand into the first netting knot, and increasing by working two meshes in the last loop of each row (16 meshes).
Note When the needle has been re-loaded, always join the new length of twine at the edge of the work, using a netting knot to join the new length to the old, and thread the ends into the neighbouring knots.

Turning the corner
16th row Work this row as before, but decrease at the end by meshing the last two loops together as one (15 meshes). Attach a coloured marker at the end of this row as a reminder that this is the decrease side.

17th row Work as before but increase at the end of the row (16 meshes).

18th row Work as before but decrease at the end of the row (15 meshes).

19th to 26th rows Continue in this way increasing and decreasing alternately.

Turning the second corner
27th row Work as before but decrease at the end of the row (14 meshes).

28th to 39th rows Continue as before but decreasing at the end of every row (two meshes).

To finish Without using the mesh stick, net the two remaining meshes as one. Cut twine and thread through neighbouring knot, then trim.

Remove the beginning of the net from the foundation loop and with the 10cm (4in) tail, tie together the first two loops with a netting knot. Thread the end into the neighbouring knot, then trim.

Tie the end of the elastic firmly at the end of one of the short sides of the net. Thread the elastic through the knots, then stretch to the width of the pram and tie to the next corner.

Continue threading the elastic through the knots to the centre point of the long edge. Stretch the elastic and tie just before the centre netting knot. Make a loop with the elastic and tie on the other side of the centre knot.

Continue to thread the elastic through the knots to the next corner, stretch and tie.

Work the second two sides of the net to correspond with the first two.

Below: A cat net is an easy netting project for the beginner, and can be made either in nylon or cotton twine. Designed to fit an average sized pram, it is an effective way of keeping baby safe.

Hammock for your garden

Nothing can be more luxurious than idling away an afternoon, indoors or out, in a gently swaying hammock. This one is not difficult to make, and netting is fun to do and gives very speedy results.

Materials

450g *(1lb)* No. 15 braided Polythene twine [heavy weight synthetic twine]
2 plastic 7cm *(3in)* thimbles
1 large netting needle
4cm *(1½in)* mesh stick
2 pieces strong wood each 76cm x 4cm x 18mm *(30in x 1½in x ¾in)*
2 pieces strong rope each about 183 *(72in)* long.

Hammock body

Tie a length of string between two firm points such as the legs of an upturned chair. Load the netting needle with as much twine as the needle will comfortably hold and attach the twine to the left end of the string with a clove hitch.

Hold the mesh stick from below with the left hand, thumb at the front. Lay the twine over the front of the mesh stick, taking it round below and up behind the stick to work a clove hitch round the string. This forms the first loop. Cast on 32 loops in all, sliding the mesh stick along as it fills up, but always leaving at least two loops on.

Remove the mesh stick and reverse the work so that the next row will also be worked left to right. Hold the mesh stick immediately below the loops, take the twine over the front of the stick, taking it round below and up behind the stick and out through the foundation loop from the back. Pull the needle downwards with your right hand and the mesh stick will be hauled by pulley effect hard up to the bottom of the foundation loop. With the left thumb at the front and index finger at the back, hold the string and the foundation loop where they cross at the top of the mesh stick. Throw a loop with the twine across to the left over the foundation loop. Take the twine to the right across the front of the foundation loop, round the back and out to the front through the thrown loop. Keeping the left thumb and finger

firmly in position until the last moment, pull the knot firm, making sure that it seats correctly round the bottom of the foundation loop and not letting it slip below.

Take care at the beginning of each row not to make the netting knot round the string carried down from the previous row as well as the first loop.

Continue along the row, making a netting knot into each loop.

Reverse the work at the end of each row and net the required number of rows:

48 rows draw up to 175cm *(69in)*
50 rows draw up to 183cm *(72in)*
54 rows draw up to 198cm *(78in)*

After about six rows, the foundation string can be removed and the clove hitches will fall out, leaving complete meshes. Slot the first row of meshes onto a loop of string to continue working.

At each end of the work, make one row of 16 extra-large meshes by passing the twine three times round the mesh stick and then taking the needle through two loops before working the knot.

Spreaders

These are the bars of wood positioned at the ends of the hammock. On the broad face of each, mark off 18 holes. Place the outer holes 18mm *(¾in)* from each end, the next one in 2.5cm *(1in)* along and the next 14 at 4cm *(1½in)* intervals.

Drill each hole wide enough to take one large end mesh. There will be less wear on the twine if the holes are counter-sunk at each end.

Making the nettles

Leave the hole at each end free and pass the large meshes one through each of the central 16 holes.

Position the thimble with the point towards the spreader at a distance of about 43cm *(17in)* from the centre large mesh.

Using a fully loaded needle, lay the twine round the thimble and make a netting knot in the end loop. Pass the twine round the thimble before netting into the mesh at the opposite end of the spreader. Pass the twine over the thimble again and net into the next mesh, following the sequence illustrated.

Continue in this manner until all meshes have been knotted.

Double a 609cm *(240in)* length of twine and pass the doubled end through one of the vacant holes in the spreader, pass the double thread round the thimble and through the other vacant hole so that there is a loop of about 15cm *(6in)* at one side and the remaining length of double twine at the other – this should be at least the length of the hammock.

Work the second spreader in the same way except that the double twine should be arranged so that the loop at one end is at the same side as the double length at the other end.

Making the clew

Pass a length of twine round the thimble and position the thimble so that it lies exactly at the centre of the length of twine.

Pass one end over the first double thread (the double thread is called a 'nettle'), under the next and so on across. Weave the other end of the twine from the opposite side over and under the same threads. Pull the ends in opposite directions to draw it tight. Repeat this, weaving over the nettles previously gone under and under the nettles previously worked over. Draw tight. Repeat this process once more, alternating the nettles again in the same way.

Continue weaving in this way, but on the next row omit one nettle at each side. Continue to omit the end nettles on each row until only two nettles remain. Using these as a core, work three flat knots over them with the weaving strands. Fasten off.

Whipping the thimbles

To ensure that all the strands re-

Right: This luxurious hammock is ideal for spending lazy summer days in your garden. The basic technique is easy, although the size of the project will mean that you will take rather longer to make up the hammock than some of the other netting patterns. The kind of twine used to make up the hammock ensures that it will be waterproof in rainy weather.

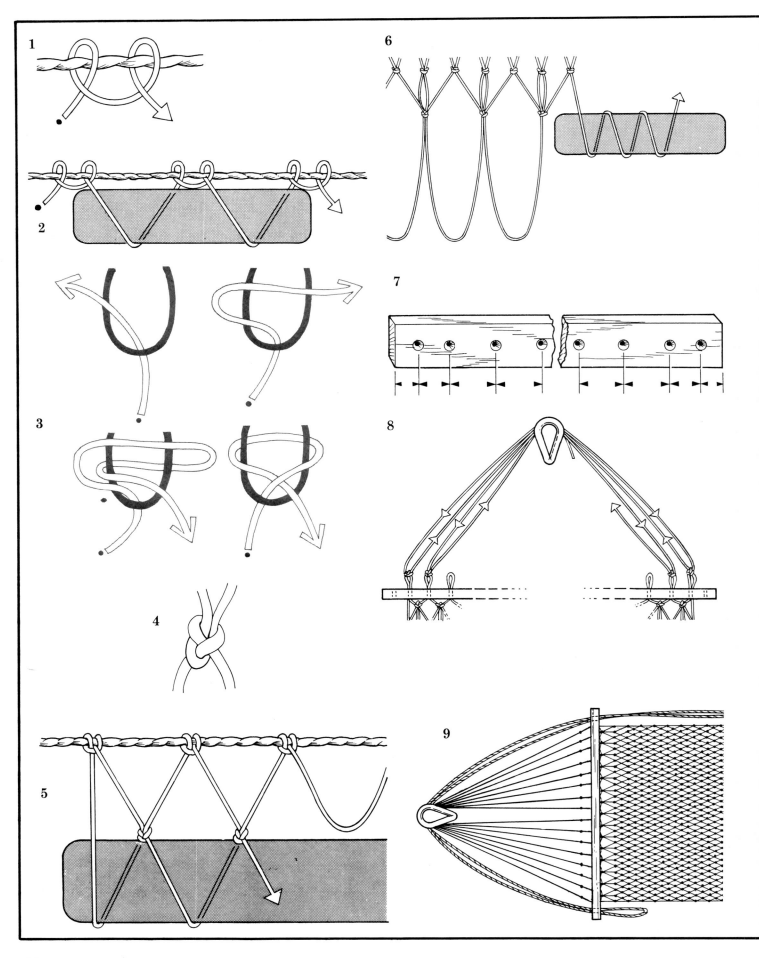

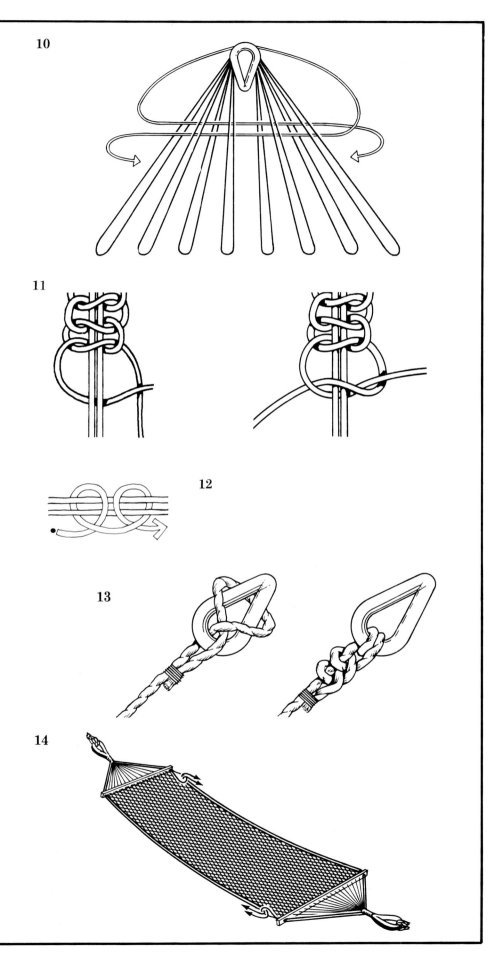

main in the hollow of the thimble, it is important to cover it with twine.

Use half hitches with the knot positioned over the centre of the hollow. Fasten the ends off by weaving into the clew.

Attaching the ropes

Into the rounded end of the thimble and using the strong rope, work either a netting knot or a round turn and two half hitches.

Bind the end of the rope securely to the main section of the rope by winding very tightly round it with a length of either fine string or thick linen thread.

Drawing up

Thread the long length of double twine through each mesh along the side of the hammock, then through the looped end of the other doubled thread at the end of the spreader.

Work the second doubled thread in the same way. Draw up the sides to give the required length and dip to the hammock and knot securely in position.

1. A clove hitch
2. A row of meshes mounted with clove hitches
3. Making the basic netting knot
4. Correct seating of knot
5. Making a row with the mesh stick in place
6. Making extra-large meshes
7. Position of holes in the spreaders
8. Making the nettles
9. Position of doubled twine through the spreader
10. Making the clew with thimble at centre of twine
11. Weaving over nettles
12. Whipping the thimbles
13. Attaching the ropes
14. Drawing the threads.

Mesh stole

A simple rectangular length of diamond mesh netting makes a warm and pretty scarf or stole. Use an attractive random yarn as illustrated, or alternatively you could use two different colours.

Size
Length 193cm *(76in)*, excluding fringe
Width 48cm *(19in)*
Fringe 10cm *(4in)*
Note These measurements are over work unstretched, but the meshes can be pulled considerably wider.

Materials
Jaeger Spiral-Spun Double Knitting 3 x 50g *(2oz)* balls, random blue [Knitting worsted, 2 x 100g *(4oz)* balls]
18mm *($\frac{3}{4}in$)* netting needle
21mm *($\frac{7}{8}in$)* mesh stick
4cm *($1\frac{1}{2}in$)* mesh stick

Loading the needle
The yarn is used double throughout. The netting needle will hold about 7.5m *(8yd)* double yarn.
Measure a 15m *(16yd)* length. Tie the two ends together with a reef knot to make a continuous length. Hook the yarn over the prong of the needle, positioning the knot about 7cm *(3in)* down from the prong (the ends of the reef knot can be trimmed once the scarf is completed), and load with the double strands evenly. Hold the needle in the left hand with the point upwards. Hold the double yarn against the body of the needle with the left thumb. Take the double yarn round the bottom or 'heel' of the needle between the two projections. Turn the needle back to front, still with the point upwards, and take the double yarn up the body of the needle, round the prong and down the same side of the needle. Take the double yarn round the heel of the needle, turn the needle back to front and continue in this way by repeating the same process.

Joining new lengths
Because the yarn is a continuous

length, it always ends in a loop.
Load the next length onto the needle as before, pass the looped end of the new yarn behind the old loop and through to the front, then pass the netting needle through the new loop from right to left and pull tight before continuing the work.

Casting on
Make a foundation cord by tying a length of string between two firm points, such as the legs of an up-turned chair. Join in the double yarn with a clove hitch.

1st row Using the 4cm *(1½in)* mesh stick, hold the mesh stick with the top edge against the foundation cord. Take the double yarn across the front and up the back of the mesh stick twice, then make a second clove hitch on the foundation cord. Make 17 double meshes more. Remove the mesh stick and shake out the meshes to their full length. Turn the work so that the working thread is at the left.

2nd row Using the 21mm *(⅞in)* mesh stick, work into each of the loops with a netting knot, taking the yarn round the mesh stick once only.

3rd to 82nd rows Work as given for second row, always starting from left. After about the 12th row, the work can be removed from the foundation cord. Tie a length of about 75cm *(30in)* into a loop with a reef knot. Hitch the loop round one complete row of the work about four rows back from the next row to be worked, using the same knot as for joining the double lengths. The other end of the loop can be fixed to some secure base.

83rd row Using the 4cm *(1½in)* mesh stick, work as given for first row, winding yarn twice round mesh stick but using a netting knot.

To finish Remove the work from foundation cord or securing loop. Cut through the loops at either end to make the fringe, trimming the first row to match the last as it will be fractionally longer.

The basic stages in making up the mesh for the stole.
1. A reef knot
2. Hooking loop onto the prong
3. Loading the needle
4. Joining in new yarn
5. Casting on double loops
6–9. Working the first row
10. Working the second row
11. Cutting the fringe loops.

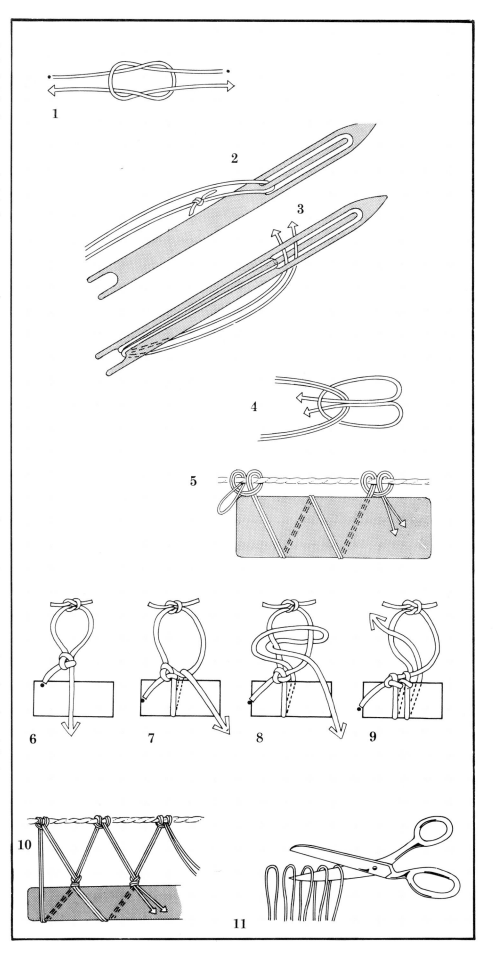

Knitted lace

Knitted lace is both simple to do and lovely to look at. Here are some tips for suitable yarns and casting on methods and two pretty edgings to work for hankerchief hems.

Suitable materials

The finer the thread used the daintier and more gossamer the lace will be. Some really beautiful shawls are made in one ply wool, but for household linens and fine edgings Coats Mercer Crochet is one of the most successful yarns. It has a crisp neat finish and can be as dainty and fine as required.

Edgings are usually made on a pair of needles and worked across the edging so that the required length is obtained by repeating the pattern. Table mats and larger areas of lace are usually worked on circular needles or sets of needles to avoid seams.

If a mat is worked from the centre outwards, it is necessary to begin at the centre with only a few stitches on each needle. As the work progresses and the stitches increase, some workers may find it easier to transfer all the stitches onto a circular needle for the remainder of the work.

Needles must be fine. If too large a needle is used, perhaps in the mistaken hope of making the work grow more quickly, the solid areas will not be as regular as they should be and will not contrast as well against the openwork areas.

Casting on for lace

Hard, thick lines must be avoided whether caused by seaming or by casting on or off as they immediately spoil the continuity of the lace.

The least noticeable cast on edge is a two-needle method in which the right-hand needle is inserted into the last stitch on the left-hand needle, the yarn passed round the needle point and drawn through to form the new stitch.

This is similar to the two-needle method normally used, except that the new stitch is drawn through the stitch instead of between the stitches.

For edgings which are to be worked lengthwise, normal cast on and off edges will spoil the look of the work and it is best to cast on using spare yarn which can later be withdrawn. This allows the casting on to be removed so that the first and last rows can be grafted together for an invisible finish.

Begin with these two simple designs for beautiful handkerchief edgings.

U.K. technique
Bird's eye edging

Size
It is possible to work any length required.

Tension
18mm (¾in) wide

Materials
Coats Mercer Crochet No.20 1 ball
One pair No.14 needles
One handkerchief

To make the edging
Using No.14 needles, cast on 7 sts.

1st row K1, K2 tog, y2rn, K2 tog, y2rn, K2.

2nd row Sl 1, K2, P1, K2, P1, K2.

3rd row K1, K2 tog, y2rn, K2 tog, K4.

4th row Cast off 2 sts, K3, P1, K2.

Repeat these 4 rows for length required, allowing a little fullness for corners. Cast off.

Leaf edging

Size
It is possible to work any length required

Tension
2.5cm (1in) wide

Materials
Coats Mercer Crochet No.60 1 ball
One pair No.16 needles
One handkerchief

To make the edging
Using No.16 needles, cast on 10 sts.

1st row K3, (yfwd, K2 tog) twice,

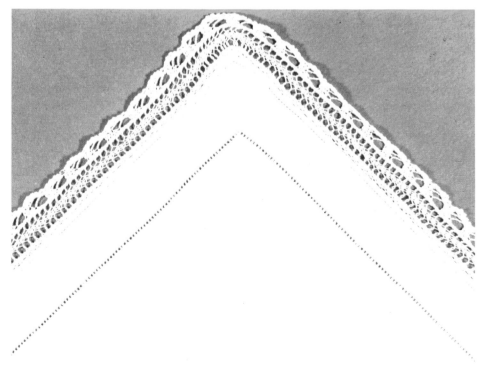

36

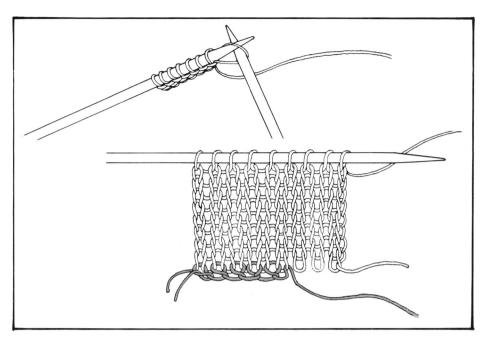

y2rn, K2 tog, K1.

2nd row K3, P1, K2, (yfwd, K2 tog) twice, K1.

3rd row K3, (yfwd, K2 tog) twice, K1, y2rn, K2 tog, K1.

4th row K3, P1, K3, (yfwd, K2 tog) twice, K1.

5th row K3, (yfwd, K2 tog) twice, K2, y2rn, K2 tog, K1.

6th row K3, P1, K4, (yfwd, K2 tog) twice, K1.

7th row K3, (yfwd, K2 tog) twice, K6.

8th row Cast off 3 sts, K4, (yfwd, K2 tog) twice, K1. Repeat these eight rows until required length. Cast off.

To finish Pin edging out in perfect shape to correct measurements, wrong side up and press with a damp cloth and a warm iron.

Slip stitch, neatly and securely, to handkerchief hem using fine sewing cotton. Seam cast on and cast off edges as invisibly as possible. Repress.

Top: Casting on with same thread
Above: Casting on with separate thread to be removed later

Far left: Bird's eye edging
Left: Detail of leaf edging

U.S. technique
Bird's eye edging
Size
It is possible to work any length required.
Tension
18mm ($\frac{3}{4}in$) wide
Materials
#20 mercerized crochet cotton 1 ball
One pair No.00 needles
One handkerchief

To make the edging
Using No.00 needles, cast on 7 sts.
1st row K1, K2 tog, yo twice, K2 tog, yo twice, K2.
2nd row Sl 1, K2, P1, K2, P1, K2.
3rd row K1, K2 tog, yo twice, K2 tog, K4.
4th row Cast off 2 sts, K3, P1, K2.
Repeat these 4 rows for length required, allowing a little fullness for corners. Cast off.

Leaf edging
Size
It is possible to work any length required
Tension
2.5cm (*1in*) wide

Materials
#60 mercerized crochet cotton 1 ball
One pair No.00 needles
One handkerchief

To make the edging
Using No.00 needles, cast on 10 sts.
1st row K3, (yo, K2 tog) twice, yo twice, K2 tog, K1.
2nd row K3, P1, K2, (yo, K2 tog) twice, K1.
3rd row K3, (yo, K2 tog) twice, K1, yo twice, K2 tog, K1.
4th row K3, P1, K3, (yo, K2 tog) twice, K1.
5th row K3, (yo, K2 tog) twice, K2, yo twice, K2 tog, K1.
6th row K3, P1, K4, (yo, K2 tog) twice, K1.
7th row K3, (yo, K2 tog) twice, K6.
8th row Cast off 3 sts, K4, (yo, K2 tog) twice, K1. Repeat these 8 rows until required length. Cast off.

To finish Pin edging out in perfect shape to correct measurements, wrong side up and press with a damp cloth and a warm iron.
Slip stitch, neatly and securely, to handkerchief hem using fine sewing cotton. Seam cast on and cast off edges as invisibly as possible. Repress.

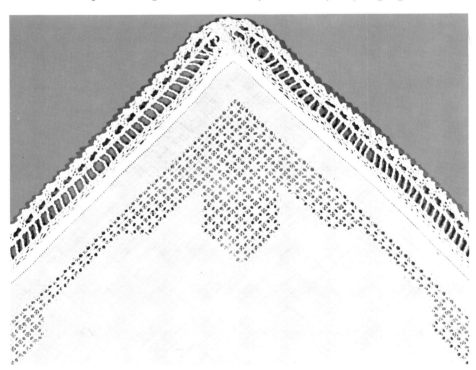

Pillowcase border

This edging is not difficult to work and can be used to edge bed linen, table linen or lampshades.

The size is determined by the yarn and needles used. This table gives an approximate guide to the possibilities.

Using Coats Mercer Crochet No.5, work on No. 11 needles.

For No.10 use No.12 needles.
For No.20 use No.14 needles.
For No.40 use No.15 needles.
For No.60 use No.16 needles.

The pillowcase edging illustrated is worked on No.14 needles using No.20 cotton. Each repeat requires 16 stitches plus 5 extra stitches for the borders. The repeat measures about 46cm by 6cm (*18in by 2½in*) deep. For border five repeats were worked, thus the required number to cast on was 5 × 16 + 5 = 85 sts.

Length
46cm (*18in*)
Tension
About 6cm (*2½in*) deep
Materials
Coats Mercer Crochet No.20
One pair No.14 needles
One No.1.00 crochet hook

U.K. technique
Edging
Using No.14 needles, cast on 85 sts.
1st row K2, *yfwd, K2 tog, yfwd, sl 1, K1, psso, K1, (K1, yfwd, K1, yfwd, K2) twice, K2 tog, yfwd, K1, rep from * to last 3 sts, yfwd, K2 tog, K1.
2nd row K1, P1, *yrn, P2 tog, P18, rep from * to last 3 sts, yrn, P2 tog, K1.
3rd row K2, *yfwd, K2 tog, yfwd, K1, (yfwd, sl 1, K2 tog, psso) 5 times, (yfwd, K1) twice, rep from * to last 3 sts, yfwd, K2 tog, K1.
4th row K1, P1, *yrn, P2 tog, P16, rep from * to last 3 sts, yrn, P2 tog, K1.
5th row K2,* yfwd, K2 tog, K1, yfwd, K2, yfwd, sl 1, K1, psso, K2, yfwd, K1, yfwd, K2, K2 tog, (yfwd, K2) twice rep from * to last 3 sts, yfwd, K2 tog, K1.
6th row K1, P1, *yrn, P2 tog, P20, rep from * to last 3 sts, yrn, P2 tog, K1.
7th row K2, *yfwd, K2 tog, K2, yfwd, K3, (yfwd, sl 1, K2 tog, psso) 3 times, (yfwd, K3) twice, rep from * to last 3 sts, yfwd, K2 tog, K1.

8th row K1, P1, *yrn, P2 tog, P20, rep from * to last 3 sts, yrn, P2 tog, K1.
9th row K2, *yfwd, K2 tog, K7, yfwd, sl 1, K1, psso, K1, K2 tog, yfwd, K8, rep from * to last 3 sts, yfwd, K2 tog, K1.
10th row K1, P1, *yrn, P2 tog, P20, rep from * to last 3 sts, yrn, P2 tog, K1.
11th row K2, *yfwd, K2 tog, K8, yfwd, sl 1, K2 tog, psso, yfwd, K9, rep from * to last 3 sts, yfwd, K2 tog, K1.
12th row As 10th.
13th row As 11th.
14th row As 10th.
15th row As 11th.
16th row As 10th.
17th row K2, *yfwd, K2 tog, K6, K2 tog, yfwd, K3, yfwd, sl 1, K1, psso, K7, rep from * to last 3 sts, yfwd, K2 tog, K1.
18th row As 10th.
19th row K2, *yfwd, K2 tog, K5, K2 tog, yfwd, K1, yfwd, sl 1, K2 tog, K1, yfwd, sl 1, K1, psso, K6, rep from * to last 3 sts, yfwd, K2 tog, K1.
20th row As 10th.
21st row K2, *yfwd, K2 tog, K4, K2 tog, yfwd, K3, yfwd, K1, yfwd, K3, sl 1, K1, psso, K5, rep from * to last 3 sts, yfwd, K2 tog, K1.
22nd row K1, P1, *yrn, P2 tog, P22, rep from * to last 3 sts, yrn, P2 tog, K1.
23rd row K2, *yfwd, K2 tog, K3, K2 tog, yfwd, K1, (yfwd, sl 1, K2 tog, psso) 3 times, yfwd, K1, yfwd, sl 1, K1, psso, K4, rep from * to last 3 sts, yfwd, K2 tog, K1.
24th row As 10th.
25th row K2, *yfwd, K2 tog, K2, K2 tog, yfwd, K3, yfwd, (K1, yfwd, K3, yfwd) twice, sl 1, K1, psso, K3, rep from * to last 3 sts, yfwd, K2 tog, K1.
26th row K1, P1, *yrn, P2 tog, P24, rep from * to last 3 sts, yrn, P2 tog, K1.
27th row K2, *yfwd, K2 tog, K1, K2 tog, yfwd, K1, (yfwd, sl 1, K2 tog, psso) 5 times, yfwd, K1, yfwd, sl 1, K1, psso, K2, rep from * to last 3 sts, yfwd, K2 tog, K1.
28th row As 10th.
29th row K1, K3 tog, *K2 tog, yfwd, K3, (yfwd, K1, yfwd, K3) 3 times, yfwd, sl 1, K1, psso, K3 tog, rep from * to last st, K1.

30th row K1, P to last st, K1.
31st row K1, K2 tog, *yfwd, K1, (yfwd, sl 1, K2 tog, psso) 7 times, yfwd, K1, yfwd, sl 1, K2 tog, psso, rep from * to last 2 sts, K2 tog.
Complete edging using crochet hook as follows:
Last row With WS of work facing, insert hook into first 2 sts and work 1dc, *7ch, 1dc into next st, 7ch, insert hook into next 3 sts and work 1dc, rep from * until all sts have been worked off. Finish off ends.

To make up Block out to shape and press. Stitch securely to edge of pillowcase.

Finishing off lace
Lace is not usually starched, but hand knitted lace in cotton or linen thread is made for everyday use and is better lightly starched. Only table mats or articles which are to be fully supported by tray or table require stiff starching.

Washing lace
Wash lace when finished in warm mild suds, rinsing carefully until the water is clear. Starch as required and leave aside wet until ready for blocking out to size.

Blocking out
The exact size of the article should be drawn out on brown or white paper which will not stain when damp. Whatever the shape of the article, the method is the same. Pin

Above: Blocking out a piece of lace. The basic idea is to pin the work out flat while it is still wet so that it dries to the correct, original shape.

Right: Knitted lace makes an exquisite border for a fine cotton pillowcase. Use the idea for table linen too.

out to the correct size working on opposite corners. If the mat is rectangular, pin each corner and half way along each side. Once the mat is positioned, divide each section by placing more pins to draw the mat to the required size.

If the edging has tiny points of crochet or knitting, the final stage must be to pin each point separately so that the shape is perfect.

Leave pinned until completely dry. Remove pins and press carefully without pulling out of shape.

U.S. technique

This edging is not difficult to work and can be used to edge bed linen, table linen or lampshades.

The size is determined by the yarn and needles used. This table gives an approximate guide to the possibilities.

Using #5 mercerized crochet cotton work on No.2 needles.

For No.10 use No.1 needles.
For No.20 use No.00 needles.
For No.40 use No.00 needles.
For No.60 use No.00 needles.

The pillowcase edging illustrated is worked on No.00 needles using No.20 cotton. Each repeat requires 16 stitches plus 5 extra stitches for the borders. The repeat measures about 46cm by 6cm *(18in by 2½in)* deep. For border five repeats were worked, thus the required number to cast on was 5×16+5=85 sts.

Length
46cm *(18in)*
Tension
About 6cm *(2½in)* deep
Materials
#20 mercerized crochet cotton
One pair No.00 Aero needles
Steel crochet hook #2
One pillowcase

Edging

Using No.00 needles, cast on 85sts.
1st row K2, *yo, K2 tog, yo, sl 1, K1, psso, K1, (K1, yo, K1, yo, K2) twice, K2 tog, yo, K1, rep from * to last 3 sts, yo, K2 tog, K1.
2nd row K1, P1, *yo, P2 tog, P18, rep from * to last 3 sts, yo, P2 tog, K1.
3rd row K2, *yo, K2 tog, yo, K1, sl 1, K2 tog, psso) 5 times, (yo, K1) twice, rep from * to last 3 sts, yo, K2 tog, K1.
4th row K1, P1, *yo, P2 tog, P16, rep from * to last 3 sts, yo, P2 tog, K1.
5th row K2, * yo, K2 tog, K1, yo, K2, yo, sl 1, K1, psso, K2, yo, K1, yo, K2, K2 tog, (yo, K2) twice rep from * to last 3 sts, yo, K2 tog, K1.
6th row K1, P1, *yo, P2 tog, P20, rep from * to last 3 sts, yo, P2 tog, K1.
7th row K2, *yo, K2 tog, K2, yo, K3, (yo, sl 1, K2 tog, psso) 3 times, (yo, K3) twice, rep from * to last 3 sts, yo, K2 tog, K1.
8th row K1, P1, *yo, P2 tog, P20, rep from * to last 3 sts, yo, P2 tog, K1.
9th row K2, *yo, K2 tog, K7, yo, sl 1, K1, psso, K1, K2 tog, yo, K8, rep from * to last 3 sts, yo, K2 tog, K1.
10th row K1, P1, *yo, P2 tog, P20, rep from * to last 3 sts, yo, P2 tog, K1.
11th row K2, *yo, K2 tog, K8, yo, sl 1, K2 tog, psso, yo, K9, rep from * to last 3 sts, yo, K2 tog, K1.
12th row As 10th.
13th row As 11th.
14th row As 10th.
15th row As 11th.
16th row As 10th.
17th row K2, *yo, K2 tog, K6, K2 tog, yo, K3, yo, sl 1, K1, psso, K7, rep from * to last 3 sts, yo, K2 tog, K1.
18th row As 10th.
19th row K2, *yo, K2 tog, K5, K2 tog, yo, K1, yo, sl 1, K2 tog, yo, K1, yo, sl 1, K1, psso, K6, rep from * to last 3 sts, yo, K2 tog, K1.
20th row As 10th.
21st row K2, *yo, K2 tog, K4, K2 tog, yo, K3, yo, K1, yo, K3, yo, sl 1, K1, psso, K5 rep from * to last 3 sts, yo, K2 tog, K1.
22nd row K1, P1, *yo, P2 tog, P22, rep from * to last 3 sts, yo, P2 tog, K1.
23rd row K2, *yo, K2 tog, K3, K2 tog, yo, K1, (yo, sl 1, K2 tog, psso) 3 times, yo, K1, yo, sl 1, K1, psso, K4, rep from * to last 3 sts, yo, K2 tog, K1.
24th row As 10th.
25th row K2, *yo, K2 tog, K2, K2 tog, yo, K3, yo, (K1, yo, K3, yo) twice, sl 1, K1, psso, K3, rep from * to last 3 sts, yo, K2 tog, K1.
26th row K1, P1, *yo, P2 tog, P24, rep from * to last 3 sts, yo, P2 tog, K1.
27th row K2, *yo, K2 tog, K1, K2 tog, yo, K1, (yo, sl 1, K2 tog, psso) 5 times, yo, K1, yo, sl 1, K1, psso, K2, rep from * to last 3 sts, yo, K2 tog, K1.
28th row As 10th.
29th row K1, K3 tog, *K2 tog, yo, K3, (yo, K1, yo, K3) 3 times, yo, sl 1, K1, psso, K3 tog, rep from * to last st, K1.
30th row K1, P to last st, K1.
31st row K1, K2 tog, *yo, K1, (yo, sl 1, K2 tog, psso) 7 times, yo, K1, yo, sl 1, K2 tog, psso, rep from * to last 2 sts, K2 tog.
Complete edging using crochet hook as follows:
Last row With WS of work facing, insert hook into first 2 sts and work 1dc, *7ch, 1dc into next st, 7ch, insert hook into next 3 sts and work 1dc, rep from * until all sts have been worked off. Finish off ends.

To make up Block out to shape and press. Stitch securely to edge of pillowcase.

Finishing off lace

Lace is not usually starched, but hand knitted lace in cotton or linen thread is made for everyday use and is better lightly starched. Only table mats or articles which are to be fully supported by tray or table require stiff starching.

Washing lace

Wash lace when finished in warm mild suds, rinsing carefully until the water is clear. Starch as required and leave aside wet until ready for blocking out to size.

Blocking out

The exact size of the article should be drawn out on brown or white paper which will not stain when damp. Whatever the shape of the article, the method is the same. Pin out to the correct size working on opposite corners. If the mat is rectangular, pin each corner and half way along each side. Once the mat is positioned, divide each section by placing more pins to draw the mat to the required size.

If the edging has tiny points of crochet or knitting, the final stage must be to pin each point separately so that the shape is perfect.

Leave pinned until completely dry. Remove pins and press carefully without pulling out of shape to give the final smooth finish.

Small table mat

This beautiful circular lace coffee table mat is achieved by graduating from a set of four needles to a slightly larger size and so on to a circular needle. In this way it is possible to cope with the ever increasing circumference.

U.K. technique
Size
57cm *(23in)* diameter

Tension
8 sts and 9 rows to 2.5cm *(1in)* over st st worked on No.11 needles

Materials
Coats Mercer Crochet No.20 3 balls
One No.1.25 crochet hook
One No.11 circular needle 61cm *(24in)* long.
Set of four No.12 double pointed needles
Set of four No.11 double pointed needles

Using set of No.12 needles, cast on 10 sts, 3 sts on each of first and second needles and 4 sts on third needle.
1st round K.
2nd round *Yfwd, K1, rep from * to end. 20 sts.
3rd, 4th and 5th rounds K.
6th round *Yfwd, K2, rep from * to end. 30 sts.
7th round K.
8th round *Yfwd, K3, rep from * to end. 40 sts.
9th and following 5 alt rounds K.
10th round *Yfwd, K4, rep from * to end. 50 sts.
12th round *Yfwd, K5, rep from * to end. 60 sts.
14th round *Yfwd, K6, rep from * to end. 70 sts.
16th round *Yfwd, K7, rep from * to end. 80 sts.
18th round *Yfwd, K8, rep from * to end. 90 sts.
20th round *Yfwd, K9, rep from * to end. 100 sts.
21st round *Yfwd, K1, yfwd, K8, K2 tog, K9, rep from * to end. 105 sts.
22nd round *Yfwd, K3, yfwd, sl 1, K1, psso, K16, rep from * to end. 110 sts.
23rd round *Yfwd, K1, yfwd, sl 1, K2 tog, psso, yfwd, K1, yfwd, K15, K2 tog, rep from * to end. 115 sts.
24th round *Yfwd, K3, yfwd, K1, yfwd, K3, yfwd, sl 1, K1, psso, K14, rep from * to end. 130 sts.
25th round *Yfwd, sl 1, K1, psso, K1, K2 tog, yfwd, K1, yfwd, sl 1, K1, psso, K1, K2 tog, yfwd, K15, rep from * to end. 130 sts.
26th round *Yfwd, K1, yfwd, sl 1, K2 tog, psso, yfwd, K3, yfwd, sl 1, K2 tog, psso, yfwd, K1, yfwd, sl 1, K1, psso, K11, K2 tog, rep from * to end. 130 sts.
27th round *Yfwd, K3, yfwd, K1, yfwd, sl 1, K1, psso, K1, K2 tog, yfwd, K1, yfwd, K3, yfwd, K13, rep from * to end. 150 sts.
28th round *Yfwd, (sl 1, K1, psso, K1, K2 tog, yfwd, K1, yfwd) twice, sl 1, K1, psso, K1, K2 tog, yfwd, sl 1, K1, psso, K9, K2 tog, rep from * to end. 140 sts.
29th round *Yfwd, K1, (yfwd, sl 1, K2 tog, psso, yfwd, K3) twice, yfwd, sl 1, K2 tog, psso, yfwd, K1, yfwd, K11, rep from * to end. 150 sts.
30th round *Yfwd, K3, (yfwd, K1, yfwd, sl 1, K1, psso, K1, K2 tog) twice, yfwd, K1, yfwd, K3, yfwd, sl 1, K1, psso, K7, K2 tog, rep from * to end. 160 sts.
31st round *Yfwd, K1, (yfwd, sl 1, K2 tog, psso, yfwd, K3) 3 times, yfwd, sl 1, K2 tog, psso, yfwd, K1, yfwd, sl 1, K1, psso, K5, K2 tog, rep from * to end. 160 sts.
32nd round *Yfwd, K3, (yfwd, K1, yfwd, sl 1, K1, psso, K1, K2 tog) 3 times, yfwd, K1, yfwd, K3, yfwd, sl 1, K1, psso, K3, K2 tog, rep from * to end. 170 sts.
33rd round *Yfwd K1, (yfwd, sl 1, K2 tog, psso, fywd, K3) 4 times, yfwd, sl 1, K2 tog, psso, yfwd, K1, yfwd, sl 1, K1, psso, K1, K2 tog, rep from * to end. 170 sts.

34th round *K3, (yfwd, K1, yfwd, sl 1, K1, psso, K1, K2 tog) 4 times, yfwd, K1, yfwd, K3, yfwd, sl 1, K2 tog, psso, yfwd, rep from * to end. 180 sts.

Change to set of No.11 needles.

35th round *Sl 1, K2 tog, psso, yfwd, K3, yfwd, rep from * to end.

36th round *Yfwd, K1, yfwd, sl 1, K1, psso, K1, K2 tog, rep from * to end.

37th round *Yfwd, K3, yfwd, sl 1, K2 tog, psso, rep from * to end.

38th round *Sl 1, K1, psso, K1, K2 tog, yfwd, K1, yfwd, rep from * to end.

39th round As 35th.

40th round As 36th.

41st round As 37th. 180 sts.

42nd round *(K1 and P1 into each of next 2 sts, K1) twice, K1 and P1 into each of next 2 sts, K2, rep from * inc in last st. 289 sts.

Change to circular needle and place coloured marker loop before first st to mark round beginning.

43rd round *Yfwd, K15, K2 tog, rep from * to end.

44th round K.

Rep last 2 rounds 9 times more.

63rd round *Yfwd, K1, yfwd, sl 1, K1, psso, K12, K2 tog, rep from * to end.

64th round *Yfwd, K3, yfwd, sl 1, K1, psso, K10, K2 tog, rep from * to end.

65th round *Yfwd, sl 1, K1, psso, K1, K2 tog, yfwd, sl 1, K1, psso, K10, rep from * to end. 272 sts.

66th round *Yfwd, K1, yfwd, sl 1, K2 tog, psso, yfwd, K1, yfwd, sl 1, K1, psso, K7, K2 tog, rep from * to end.

67th round *Yfwd, K3, yfwd, K1, yfwd, K3, yfwd, sl 1, K1, psso, K7, rep from * to end. 323 sts.

68th round *Yfwd, sl 1, K1, psso, K1, K2 tog, yfwd, K1, yfwd, sl 1, K1, psso, K1, K2 tog, yfwd, sl 1, K1, psso, K4, K2 tog, rep from * to end. 289 sts.

69th round *Yfwd, K1, yfwd, sl 1, K2 tog, psso, yfwd, K3, yfwd, sl 1, K2 tog, psso, yfwd, K1, yfwd, sl 1, K1, psso, K4, rep from * to end. 306 sts.

70th round *Yfwd, K3, yfwd, K1, yfwd, sl 1, K1, psso, K1, K2 tog, yfwd, K1, yfwd, K3, yfwd, sl 1, K1, psso, K1, K2 tog, rep from * to end. 340 sts.

71st round * (Sl 1, K1, psso, K1, K2 tog, yfwd, K1, yfwd) twice, sl 1, K1, psso, K1, K2 tog, yfwd, sl 1, K2 tog, psso, yfwd, rep from * to end. 306 sts.

72nd round *Sl 1, K2 tog, psso, yfwd, K3, yfwd, rep from * to end. 306 sts.

73rd round As 36th.

74th round As 37th.

75th round As 38th.

76th round As 35th.

77th-79th rounds As 36th to 38th. 306 sts.

80th round *K1, K1 and P1 into each of next 2 sts, rep from * to end. 510 sts.

81st round K inc 3 sts evenly in round. 513 sts.

82nd and 83rd rounds K.

84th round *Yfwd, sl 1, K1, psso, rep from * to last st, K1.

85th round K.

86th round *Yfwd, K7, K2 tog, rep from * to end.

87th round K.

88th round As 86th.

89th round K.

90th round As 86th.

91st round *Yfwd, K1, yfwd, sl 1, K1, psso, K4, K2 tog, rep from * to end.

92nd round *Yfwd, K3, yfwd, K6, rep from * to end. 627 sts.

93rd round *Yfwd, sl 1, K1, psso, K1, K2 tog, yfwd, sl 1, K1, psso, K2 tog, rep from * to end. 513 sts.

94th round *Yfwd, K1, yfwd, sl 1, K2 tog, psso, yfwd, K1, yfwd, K4, rep from * to end. 627 sts.

95th round *Yfwd, K3, yfwd, K1, yfwd, K3, yfwd, sl 1, K1, psso, K2, rep from * to end. 798 sts.

96th round *Sl 1, K1, psso, K1, K2 tog, yfwd, K1, yfwd, sl 1, K1, psso, K1, K2 tog, yfwd, K3, yfwd, rep from * to end. 798 sts.

97th round *Sl 1, K2 tog, psso, yfwd, K3, yfwd, rep from * to end. 306 sts.

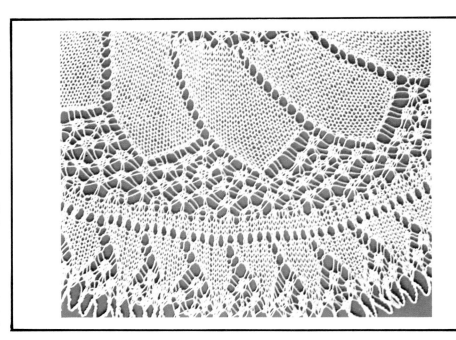

Above: Detail of the stitches

yfwd, K3, yfwd, sl 1, K2 tog, psso, yfwd, sl 1, K1, psso, K1, K2 tog, yfwd, rep from * to end. 684 sts.

98th round *Yfwd, K1, yfwd, sl 1, K1, psso, K1, K2 tog, rep from * to end. 684 sts.

Edging

Using No. 1.25 hook, *work 1dc into next 3 sts and slip off, 10ch, rep from * ending with 1ss into first dc. Fasten off.

To finish Finish off ends. Damp evenly and pin out to size. Leave to dry.

U.S. technique

This beautiful circular lace coffee table mat is achieved by graduating from a set of four needles to a slightly larger size and so on to a circular needle. In this way it is possible to cope with the ever increasing circumference.

Size

58cm *(23in)* diameter

Tension

8 sts and 9 rows to 2.5cm *(1in)* over st st worked on No.2 needles

Materials

#20 mercerized crochet cotton No.1 steel crochet hook

One No.2 circular needle 61cm *(24in)* long

One set of 4 No.1 double pointed needles

One set of 4 No.2 double pointed needles

Using set of No.1 needles, cast on 10 sts, 3 sts on each of first and second needles and 4 sts on third needle.

1st round K.

2nd round *Yo, K1, rep from * to end. 20 sts.

3rd, 4th and 5th rounds K.

6th round *Yo, K2, rep from * to end. 30 sts.

7th round K.

8th round *Yo, K3, rep from * to end. 40 sts.

9th and following 5 alt rounds K.

10th round *Yo, K4, rep from * to end. 50 sts.

12th round *Yo, K5, rep from * to end. 60 sts.

14th round *Yo, K6, rep from * to end. 70 sts.

16th round *Yo, K7, rep from * to end. 80 sts.

18th round *Yo, K8, rep from * to end. 90 sts.

20th round *Yo, K9, rep from * to end. 100 sts.

21st round *Yo, K1, yo, K8, K2 tog, K9, rep from * to end. 105 sts.

22nd round *Yo, K3, yo, sl 1, K1, psso, K16, rep from * to end. 110 sts.

23rd round *Yo, K1, yo, sl 1, K2 tog, psso, yo, K1, yo, K15, K2 tog, rep from * to end. 115 sts.

24th round *Yo, K3, yo, K1, yo, K3, yo, sl 1, K1, psso, K14, rep from * to end. 130 sts.

25th round *Yo, sl 1, K1, psso, K1, K2 tog, yo, K1, yo, sl 1, K1, psso, K1, K2 tog, yo, K15, rep from * to end. 130 sts.

26th round *Yo, K1, yo, sl 1, K2 tog, psso, yo, K3, yo, sl 1, K2 tog, psso, yo, K1, yo, sl 1, K1, psso, K11, K2 tog, rep from * to end. 130 sts.

27th round *Yo, K3, yo, K1, yo, sl 1, K1, psso, K1, K2 tog, yo, K1, yo, K3, yo, K13, rep from * to end. 150 sts.

28th round *Yo, (sl 1, K1, psso, K1, K2 tog, yo, K1, yo) twice, sl 1, K1, psso, K1, K2 tog, yo, sl 1, K1, psso, K9, K2 tog, rep from * to end. 140 sts.

29th round *Yo, K1, (yo, sl 1, K2 tog, psso, yo, K3) twice, yo, sl 1, K2 tog, psso, yo, K1, yo, K11, rep from * to end. 150 sts.

30th round *Yo, K3, (yo, K1, yo, sl 1, K1, psso, K1, K2 tog) twice, yo, K1, yo, K3, yo, sl 1, K1, psso, K7, K2 tog, rep from * to end. 160 sts.

31st round *Yo, K1, (yo, sl 1, K2 tog, psso, yo, K3) 3 times, yo, sl 1, K2 tog, psso, yo, K1, yo, sl 1, K1, psso, K5, K2 tog, rep from * to end. 160 sts.

32nd round *Yo, K3, (yo, K1, yo, sl 1, K1, psso, K1, K2 tog) 3 times, yo, K1, yo, K3, yo, sl 1, K1, psso, K3, K2 tog, rep from * to end. 170 sts.

33rd round *Yo K1, (yo, sl 1, K2 tog, psso, yo, K3) 4 times, yo, sl 1, K2 tog, psso, yo, K1, yo, sl 1, K1, psso, K1, K2 tog, rep from * to end. 170 sts.

34th round *K3, (yo, K1, yo, sl 1, K1, psso, K1, K2 tog) 4 times, yo, K1, yo, K3, yo, sl 1, K2 tog, psso, yo, rep from * to end. 180 sts.

Change to set of No. 2 needles.

35th round *Sl 1, K2 tog, psso, yo, K3, yo, rep from * to end.

36th round *Yo, K1, yo, sl 1, K1, psso, K1, K2 tog, rep from * to end.

37th round *Yo, K3, yo, sl 1, K2 tog, psso, rep from * to end.

38th round *Sl 1, K1, psso, K1, K2 tog, yo, K1, yo, rep from * to end.

39th round As 35th.

40th round As 36th.

41st round As 37th. 180 sts.

42nd round *(K1 and P1 into each of next 2 sts, K1) twice, K1 and P1 into each of next 2 sts, K2, rep from * inc in last st. 289 sts.

Change to circular needle and place coloured marker loop before first st to mark round beginning.

43rd round *Yo, K15, K2 tog, rep from * to end.

44th round K.

Rep last 2 round 9 times more.

63rd round *Yo, K1, yo, sl 1, K1, psso, K12, K2 tog, rep from * to end.

64th round *Yo, K3, yo, sl 1, K1, psso, K10, K2 tog, rep from * to end.

65th round *Yo, sl 1, K1, psso, K1, K2 tog, yo, K1, yo, sl 1, K1, psso, K10, rep from * to end. 272 sts.

66th round *Yo, K1, yo, sl 1, K2 tog, psso, yo, K1, yo, sl 1, K1, psso, K7, K2 tog, rep from * to end.

67th round *Yo, K3, yo, K1, yo, K3, yo, sl 1, K1, psso, K7, rep from * to end. 323 sts.

68th round *Yo, sl 1, K1, psso, K1, K2 tog, yo, K1, yo, sl 1, K1, psso, K1, K2 tog, yo, sl 1, K1, psso, K4, K2 tog, yo, sl 1, K1, psso, K4, K2 tog, rep from * to end. 289 sts.

69th round *Yo, K1, yo, sl 1, K2 tog, psso, yo, K3, yo, sl 1, K2 tog, psso, yo, K1, yo, sl 1, K1, psso, K4, rep from * to end. 306 sts.

70th round *Yo, K3, yo, K1, yo, sl 1, K1, psso, K1, K2 tog, yo, K1, yo, K3, yo, sl 1, K1, psso, K1, K2 tog, rep from * to end. 340 sts.

71st round * (Sl 1, K1, psso, K1, K2 tog, yo, K1, yo) twice, sl 1, K1, psso, K1, K2 tog, yo, sl 1, K2 tog, psso, yo, rep from * to end. 306 sts.

72nd round *Sl 1, K2 tog, psso, yo, K3, yo, rep from * to end. 306 sts.

73rd round As 36th.

74th round As 37th.

75th round As 38th.

76th round As 35th.

77th-79th rounds As 36th to 38th. 306 sts.

80th round *K1, K1 and P1 into each of next 2 sts, rep from * to end. 510 sts.

81st round K inc 3 sts evenly in round. 513 sts.

82nd and 83rd rounds K.

84th round *Yo, sl 1, K1, psso, rep from * to last st, K1.

85th round K.

86th round *Yo, K7, K2 tog, rep from * to end.

87th round K.

88th round As 86th.

89th round K.

90th round As 86th.

91st round *Yo, K1, yo, sl 1, K1, psso, K4, K2 tog, rep from * to end.

92nd round *Yo, K3, yo, K6, rep from * to end. 627 sts.

93rd round *Yo, sl 1, K1, psso, K1, K2 tog, yo, sl 1, K1, psso, K2 tog, rep from * to end. 513 sts.

94th round *Yo, K1, yo, sl 1, K2 tog, psso, yo, K1, yo, K4, rep from * to end. 627 sts.

95th round *Yo, K3, yo, K1, yo, K3, yo, sl 1, K1, psso, K2, rep from * to end. 798 sts.

96th round *Sl 1, K1, psso, K1, K2 tog, yo, K1, yo, sl 1, K1, psso, K1, K2 tog, yo, K3, yo, rep from * to end. 798 sts.

97th round *Sl 1, K2 tog, psso, yo, K3, yo, sl 1, K2 tog, psso, yo, sl 1, K1, psso, K1, K2 tog, yo, rep from * to end. 684 sts.

98th round *Yo, K1, yo, sl 1, K1, psso, K1, K2 tog, rep from * to end. 684 sts.

Edging

Using steel crochet hook # 1, *work 1dc into next 3 sts and slip off, 10ch, rep from * ending with 1ss into first dc. Fasten off.

To finish Finish off ends. Damp evenly and pin out to size. Leave to dry.

Lace tray cloth

A simple open-work pattern gives elegant charm to a tray-cloth.

U.K. technique

Size

35cm by 53.5cm *(14in by 21in)*

Tension

2 patts (36 sts) to 9.5cm *(3¾in)* unstretched

Materials

Coats Mercer Crochet No. 20, 2 x 20g *(1oz)* balls

One pair No. 13 needles

One No. 12 circular needle, 75cm *(30in)* long

One No. 1.25 crochet hook

Main section

Using No. 13 needles, cast on 98 sts.

1st row P.

1st patt row (RS) K1, *K6, (K2 tog, yrn twice, sl 1, K1, psso) 3 times, rep from * to last 7 sts, K7.

2nd patt row P, working P1 and K1 into each 'yrn twice' on previous row.

Rep last 2 rows 6 times more.

15th patt row K2, (yrn twice, K2) twice, yrn twice, K1, *(K2 tog, sl 1,

44

K1, psso) 3 times, K1, (yrn twice, K2) twice, yrn twice, K1, rep from * to last st, K1.104 sts.

16th patt row As 2nd.

17th patt row K1, (K2 tog, yrn twice, sl 1, K1, psso) 3 times, *K6, (K2 tog, yrn twice, sl 1, K1, psso) 3 times, rep from * to last st, K1.

18th patt row As 2nd.

Rep last 2 rows 6 times more.

31st patt row K1, (K2 tog, sl 1, K1, psso) 3 times, *K1, (yrn twice, K2) twice, yrn twice, K1, (K2 tog, sl 1, K1, psso) 3 times, rep from * to last st, K1. 98 sts.

32nd row As 2nd.

These 32 rows form patt.

Rep patt 5 times, then first 12 rows once more.

Border

Change to No. 12 circular needle.

K across all sts, pick up and K156 sts down left side edge, K98 sts along cast-on edge and 156 sts up right side edge. 508 sts.

1st round *Inc 1 in next st, K96, inc 1 in next st, K156, rep from * once more. 512 sts.

2nd round *K1 tbl, yrn twice, K1 tbl, (K2 tog, yrn twice, sl 1, K1, psso) 24 times, K1 tbl, yrn twice, K1 tbl, (K2 tog, yrn twice, sl 1, K1, psso) 39 times, rep from * once more. 520 sts.

3rd and alt rounds K, working K1 and P1 into each 'yrn twice, on previous round.

4th round *K2 tog, yrn twice, sl 1, K1, psso, rep from * to end.

6th, 8th, 10th and 12th rounds As 4th.

14th round *K2 tog, yfwd, sl 1, K1, psso, rep from * to end. 390 sts.

15th and 16th rounds K.

Edging

Using No. 1.25 hook, insert into next 3 sts tog as one, draw yarn through, *10ch, 1dc into next 3 sts taken tog as one, rep from * omitting 1dc at end of last rep, ss into first dc.

Fasten off.

To finish

Damp and pin out to measurements.

U.S. technique
Size
35.5cm by 53.5cm *(14in by 21in)*
Tension
2 Patts (36 sts) to 9.5cm *(3¾in)* unstretched

Materials

#20 mercerized crochet cotton 2 20g balls
One pair No.0 needles
One No. 1 circular needle, 76cm *(30in) long*
Steel crochet hook # E

Main section

Using No. 0 needles, cast on 98 sts.

1st row P.

1st patt row (RS) K1, *K6, (K2 tog, yo twice, sl 1, K1, psso) 3 times, rep from * to last 7 sts, K7.

2nd patt row P, working P1 and K1 into each 'yo twice' on previous row.

Rep last 2 rows 6 times more.

15th patt row K2, (yo twice, K2) twice, yo twice, K1, *(K2 tog, sl 1, K1, psso) 3 times, K1, (yo twice, K2) twice, yo twice, K1, rep from * to last st, K1.104 sts.

16th patt row As 2nd.

17th patt row K1, (K2 tog, yo twice, sl 1, K1, psso) 3 times, *K6, (K2 tog, yo, twice, sl 1, K1, psso) 3 times, rep from * to last st, K1.

18th patt row As 2nd.

Rep last 2 rows 6 times more.

31st patt row K1, (K2 tog, sl 1, K1, psso) 3 times, *K1, (yo twice, K2) twice, yo twice, K1, (K2 tog, sl 1, K1, psso) 3 times, rep from * to last st, K1. 98 sts.

32nd row As 2nd.

These 32 rows form patt.

Rep patt 5 times, then first 12 rows once more.

Border

Change to No. 1 circular needle.

K across all sts, pick up and K156 sts down left side edge, K98 sts along cast-on edge and 156 sts up right side edge. 508 sts.

1st round *Inc 1 in next st, K96, inc 1 in next st, K156, rep from * once more. 512 sts.

2nd round *K1 through back lp, yo twice, K1 through back lp, (K2 tog, yo twice, sl 1, K1, psso) 24 times, K1 through back lp, yo twice, K1 through back lp, (K2 tog, yo twice, sl 1, K1, psso) 39 times, rep from * once more. 520 sts.

3rd and alt rounds K, working K1 and P1 into each yo twice, on previous round.

4th round *K2 tog, yo twice, sl 1, K1, psso, rep from * to end.

6th, 8th, 10th and 12th rounds As 4th.

14th round *K2 tog, yo, sl 1, K1, psso, rep from * to end. 390 sts.

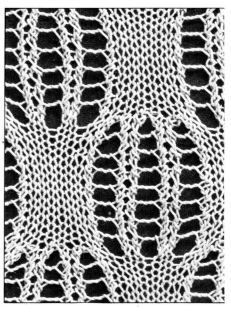

15th and 16th rounds K.

Edging

Using steel crochet hook # 1, insert into next 3 sts tog as one, draw yarn through, *10ch, 1sc into next 3 sts taken tog as one, rep from * omitting 1sc at end of last rep, ss into first sc.

Fasten off.

To finish

Damp and pin out to measurements.

Top: Detail of the lace stitch shows how the open areas contrast with the solid parts of the knitting, giving an airy effect.

Opposite: The stylish elegance of knitted lace giving a luxury touch to a breakfast tray. This pattern is one of the simpler projects, and would be ideal to try as a first attempt to make knitted lace.

Luxury lace teacloth

The cobweb-fine intricacy of this beautiful knitted lace teacloth makes it the ideal project for those who like the working of their knitting to be interesting and a challenge. The finished article is an exquisite example of lacy knitting.

U.K. technique

Size
114.5cm *(45in)* diameter

Tension
8 sts and 10 rows to 2.5cm *(1in)* over st st worked on No. 12 needles

Materials
Coats Mercer Crochet No. 20 9 x 20g *(1oz)* balls
Set of four No. 12 needles pointed at both ends
One 75cm *(30in)* circular knitting needle No. 12
One No. 1.00 crochet hook
Note Number of sts given in brackets () after rounds 71 to 142 refer to the number of sts after corresponding rounds 143 to 204.

Main section
Using set of four No. 12 needles, cast on 3 sts onto each of 2 needles and 4 sts onto third needle. 10 sts.
1st and 2nd rounds K.
3rd round *Yrn twice, K1, rep from * to end. 30 sts.
4th round *K1 into first yrn of previous row, P1 into second yrn of previous row, K1, rep from * to end.
5th and 6th rounds K.
7th round *K1, yfwd, K1 tbl, yfwd, K1, rep from * to end. 50 sts.
8th and following alt rounds K, but K tbl into all sts worked tbl in previous round.
9th round *Sl 1, K1, psso, yfwd, K1 tbl, yfwd, K2 tog, rep from * to end.
11th round *K2, yfwd, K1 tbl, yfwd, K2, rep from * to end. 70 sts.
13th round *Sl 1, K1, psso, K1, yfwd, K1 tbl, yfwd, K1, K2 tog, rep from * to end.
15th round *K3, yfwd, K1 tbl, yfwd, K3, rep from * to end. 90 sts.
17th round *Sl 1, K1, psso, K2, yfwd, K1 tbl, yfwd, K2, K2 tog, rep

from * to end.
19th round *K4, yfwd, K1 tbl, yfwd, K4, rep from * to end. 110 sts.
21st round *Sl 1, K1, psso, K3, yfwd, K1 tbl, yfwd, K3, K2 tog, rep from * to end.
23rd round *K5, yfwd, K1 tbl, yfwd, K5, rep from * to end. 130 sts.
25th round *Sl 1, K1, psso, K4, yfwd, K1 tbl, yfwd, K4, K2 tog, rep from * to end.
27th round *K6, yfwd, K1 tbl, yfwd, K6, rep from * to end. 150 sts.
29th round *Sl 1, K1, psso, K5, yfwd, K1 tbl, yfwd, K5, K2 tog, rep from * to end.
31st round *Yfwd, K6, sl 1, K2 tog, psso, K6, rep from * to end. 140 sts.
33rd round *Yfwd, K1 tbl, yfwd, K5, sl 1, K2 tog, psso, K5, rep from * to end.
35th round *Yfwd, K3, yfwd, K4, sl 1, K2 tog, psso, K4, rep from * to end.
37th round *Yfwd, K2 tog, yfwd, K1 tbl, yfwd, sl 1, K1, psso, yfwd, K3, sl 1, K2 tog, psso, K3, rep from * to end.
39th round *Yfwd, K2 tog, yfwd, sl 1, K2 tog, psso, yfwd, sl 1, K1, psso, yfwd, K2, sl 1, K2 tog, psso, K2, rep from * to end. 120 sts.
41st round *Yfwd, K2 tog, yfwd, K3, yfwd, sl 1, K1, psso, yfwd, K1, sl 1, K2 tog, psso, K1, rep from * to end.
43rd round *Yfwd, K2 tog, yfwd, K5, yfwd, sl 1, K1, psso, yfwd, sl 1, K2 tog, psso, rep from * to end.
45th round *K 2 tog, yfwd, K1 tbl, yfwd, sl 1, K1, psso, K1, K2 tog, yfwd, K1 tbl, yfwd, sl 1, K2 tog, psso, yfwd, rep from * to end.
47th round K first st onto end of last needle, *yfwd, K3, yfwd, sl 1, K2 tog, psso, rep from * to end.
49th round *Yfwd, K5, yfwd, K1 tbl, rep from * to end. 160 sts.
51st round *Yfwd, K1 tbl, yfwd, sl 1, K1, psso, K1, K2 tog, yfwd, sl 1, K2 tog, psso, yfwd, sl 1, K1, psso, K1, K2 tog, (yfwd, K1 tbl) twice, rep from * to end.
53rd round *Yfwd, K3, yfwd, (sl 1, K2 tog, psso, yfwd, K3, yfwd) twice, K1 tbl, rep from * to end. 180 sts.
55th round *K5, yfwd, K1 tbl, yfwd, rep from * to end. 240 sts.

57th round *Sl 1, K1, psso, K1, K2 tog, yfwd, sl 1, K2 tog, psso, yfwd, rep from * to end. 180 sts.

59th round *Sl 1, K2 tog, psso, yfwd, K3, yfwd, rep from * to end.

61st round *Yfwd, K1 tbl, yfwd, K5, rep from * to end. 240 sts.

63rd round *Yfwd, K3, yfwd, sl 1, K1, psso, K1, K2 tog, rep from * to end.

65th round *Yfwd, K5, yfwd, sl 1, K2 tog, psso, rep from * to end.

67th and 69th rounds P.

71st round *Yrn twice, sl 1, K1, psso, K2 tog, rep from * to end. 240 (480) sts.

72nd, 74th and 76th rounds K, but P1 into each first yrn and K1 into each second yrn of previous round.

73rd round K first st onto end of last needle, *K2 tog, yrn twice, sl 1, K1, psso, rep from * to end.

75th round As 71st.

77th and 79th rounds P.

78th and 80th rounds K.

81st round *Yfwd, K1 tbl, yfwd, sl 1, K1, psso, K3, rep from * to end. 280 (560) sts.

82nd and following alt rounds K, but K tbl into all sts worked tbl in previous round.

83rd round *K1, yfwd, K1 tbl, yfwd, sl 1, K1, psso, K3, rep from * to end. 320 (640) sts.

85th round *K2, yfwd, K1 tbl, yfwd, sl 1, K1, psso, K3, rep from * to end. 360 (720) sts.

87th round *K3, yfwd, K1 tbl, yfwd, sl 1, K1, psso, K3, rep from * to end. 400 (800) sts.

89th round *K4, yfwd, K1 tbl, yfwd, sl 1, K1, psso, K3, rep from * to end. 440 (880) sts.

91st round *K5, yfwd, K1 tbl, yfwd, sl 1, K1, psso, K3, rep from * to end. 480 (960) sts.

Change to circular needle.

93rd round K1, mark this point with coloured thread for beg of round, *yfwd, K5, yfwd, K1 tbl, yfwd, sl 1, K1, psso, K4, rep from * to end. 560 (1120) sts.

95th round *Yfwd, K1 tbl, yfwd, K5, sl 1, K2 tog, psso, K5, rep from * to end.

97th round *Yfwd, K3, yfwd, K4, sl 1, K2 tog, psso, K4, rep from * to end.

Left: Although this is a major knitting project, the results are fantastic. Once you have made up this beautiful cloth, you can keep it as a family heirloom.

99th round *Yfwd, K2 tog, yfwd, K1 tbl, yfwd, sl 1, K1, psso, yfwd, K3, sl 1, K2 tog, psso, K3, rep from * to end.

101st round *Yfwd, K2 tog, yfwd, sl 1, K2 tog, psso, yfwd, sl 1, K1, psso, yfwd, K2, sl 1, K2 tog, psso, K2, rep from * to end. 480 (960) sts.

103rd round *Yfwd, K2 tog, yfwd, K3, yfwd, sl 1, K1, psso, yfwd, K1, sl 1, K2 tog, psso, K1, rep from * to end.

105th round *Yfwd, K2 tog, yfwd, K5, yfwd, sl 1, K1, psso, yfwd, sl 1, K2 tog, psso, rep from * to end.

107th round *K2 tog, yfwd, K1 tbl, yfwd, sl 1, K1, psso, K1, K2 tog, yfwd, K1 tbl, yfwd, sl 1, K2 tog, psso, yfwd, rep from * to end.

109th round K1, mark this point with a coloured thread for beg of round, *yfwd, K3, yfwd, sl 1, K2 tog, psso, rep from * to end.

111th round *K5, yfwd, K1 tbl, yfwd, rep from * to end. 640 (1280) sts.

113th round *Sl 1, K1, psso, K1, K2 tog, yfwd , sl 1, K2 tog, psso, yfwd, rep from * to end. 480 (960) sts.

115th round *Sl 1, K2 tog, psso, yfwd, K3, yfwd, rep from * to end.

117th round *Yfwd, K1 tbl, yfwd, K5, rep from * to end. 640 (1280) sts.

119th round *Yfwd, sl 1, K2 tog, psso, yfwd, sl 1, K1, psso, K1, K2 tog, rep from * to end. 480 (960) sts.

121st round *Yfwd, K3, yfwd, sl 1, K2 tog, psso, rep from * to end.

123rd round As 111th. 640 (1280) sts.

125th round As 113th. 480 (960) sts.

127th round As 115th.

129th and 131st rounds P.

133rd round As 71st. 480 (960) sts.

134th, 136th and 138th rounds As 72nd.

135th round As 73rd.

137th round As 75th.

139th and 141st rounds P.

142nd round K. 480 (960) sts.

143rd to 204th round As 81st to 142nd.

205th round *Yfwd, K1 tbl, yfwd, (sl 1, K1, psso, yfwd) 5 times, sl 1, K2 tog, psso, (yfwd, K2 tog) 5 times, rep from * to end.

207th round *Yfwd, sl 1, K2 tog, psso, yfwd, (sl 1, K1, psso, yfwd) 4 times, sl 1, K2 tog, psso, (yfwd, K2 tog) 5 times, rep from * to end. 880 sts.

209th round *Yfwd, K3, yfwd, (sl 1, K1, psso, yfwd) 4 times, sl 1, K2 tog, psso, (yfwd, K2 tog) 4 times, rep from * to end.

211th round *Yfwd, K2, yfwd, K1

tbl, yfwd, K2, yfwd, (sl 1, K1, psso, yfwd) 3 times, sl 1, K2 tog, psso, (yfwd, K2 tog) 4 times, rep from * to end. 960 sts.

213th round *(Yfwd, K3) 3 times, yfwd, (sl 1, K1, psso, yfwd) 3 times, sl 1, K2 tog, psso, (yfwd, K2 tog) 3 times, rep from * to end. 1040 sts.

215th round *Yfwd, K4, yfwd, K2 tog, yfwd, K1 tbl, yfwd, sl 1, K1, psso, yfwd, K4, yfwd, (sl 1, K1, psso, yfwd) twice, sl 1, K2 tog, psso, (yfwd, K2 tog) 3 times, rep from * to end. 1120 sts.

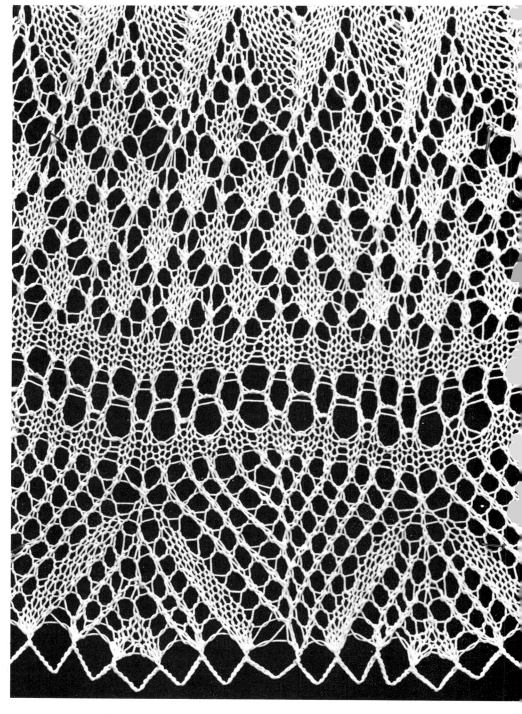

Above: A close-up detail of the table cloth photographed on the previous page. It is an excellent view of the intricate border pattern of the cloth.

217th round *Yfwd, K3, (K2 tog, yfwd) twice, K3, (yfwd, sl 1, K1, psso) twice, K3, yfwd, (sl 1, K1, psso, yfwd) twice, sl 1, K2 tog, psso, (yfwd, K2 tog) twice, rep from * to end.

219th round *Yfwd, K3, (K2 tog, yfwd) 3 times, K1 tbl, (yfwd, sl 1, K1,

psso) 3 times, K3, yfwd, sl 1, K1, psso, yfwd, sl 1, K2 tog, psso, (yfwd, K2 tog) twice, rep from * to end.
221st round *Yfwd, K3, (K2 tog, yfwd) 3 times, K3, (yfwd, sl 1, K1, psso) 3 times, K3, yfwd, sl 1, K1, psso, yfwd, sl 1, K2 tog, psso, yfwd, K2 tog, rep from * to end.
223rd round *Yfwd, K3, (K2 tog, yfwd) 3 times, K2, K into front and back of next st, K2, (yfwd, sl 1, K1, psso) 3 times, K3, yfwd, sl 1, K2 tog, psso, yfwd, K2 tog, rep from * to end. 1160 sts.
224th round K.

Edging
Using No. 1.00 hook, insert hook into next 5 sts tog and pull yarn through. *10ch, (1dc into next 4 sts tog, 10ch) 4 times, 1dc into next 5 sts tog, 10ch, 1dc into next 3 sts tog, 10ch, 1dc into next 5 sts tog, rep from * omitting 1dc at end of last rep, ss to first dc. Fasten off.

To finish
Dampen work and pin out to size on a clean, flat surface.

U.S. technique
Size
114.5cm *(45in)* diameter

Tension
8 sts and 10 rows to 2.5cm *(1in)* over st st worked on No. 1 needles

Materials
#20 mercerized crochet cotton 9 20g balls
Set of four No. 1 needles pointed at both ends
One 76cm *(30in)* circular knitting needle No. 1
Steel crochet hook # 2
Note Number of sts given in brackets () after rounds 71 to 142 refer to the number of sts after corresponding rounds 143 to 204.

Main section
Using set of four No. 1 needles, cast on 3 sts onto each of 2 needles and 4 sts onto third needle. 10 sts.
1st and 2nd rounds K.
3rd round *Yo twice, K1, rep from * to end. 30 sts.
4th round *K1 into first yo of previous row, P1 into second yo of previous row, K1, rep from * to end.
5th and 6th rounds K.
7th round *K1, yo, K1 through back lp, yo, K1, rep from * to end. 50 sts.

8th and following alt rounds K. but K through back lp into all sts worked through back lp in previous round.
9th round *Sl 1, K1, psso, yo, K1 through back lp, yo, K2 tog, rep from * to end.
11th round *K2, yo, K1 through back lp, yo, K2, rep from * to end. 70 sts.
13th round *Sl 1, K1, psso, K1, yo, K1 through back lp, yo, K1, K2 tog, rep from * to end.
15th round *K3, yo, K1 through back lp, yo, K3, rep from * to end. 90 sts.
17th round *Sl 1, K1, psso, K2, yo, K1 through back lp, yo, K2, K2 tog, rep from * to end.
19th round *K4, yo, K1 through back lp, yo, K4, rep from * to end. 110 sts.
21st round *Sl 1, K1, psso, K3, yo, K1 through back lp, yo, K3, K2 tog, rep from * to end.
23rd round *K5, yo, K1 through back lp, yo, K5, rep from * to end. 130 sts.
25th round *Sl 1, K1, psso, K4, yo, K1 through back lp, K4, K2 tog, rep from * to end.
27th round *K6, yo, K1 through back lp, yo, K6, rep from * to end. 150 sts.
29th round *Sl 1, K1, psso, K5, yo, K1 through back lp, K5, K2 tog, rep from * to end.
31st round *Yo, K6, sl 1, K2 tog, psso, K6, rep from * to end. 140 sts.
33rd round *Yo, K1 through back lp, yo, K5, sl 1, K2 tog, psso, K5, rep from * to end.
35th round *Yo, K3, yo, K4, sl 1, K2 tog, psso, K4, rep from * to end.
37th round *Yo, K2 tog, yo, K1 through back lp, sl 1, K1, psso, yo, K3, sl 1, K2 tog, psso, K3, rep from * to end.
39th round *Yo, K2 tog, yo, sl 1, K2 tog, psso, yo, sl 1, K1, psso, yo, K2, sl 1, K2 tog, psso, K2, rep from * to end. 120 sts.
41st round *Yo, K2 tog, yo, K3, yo, sl 1, K1, psso, yo, K1, sl 1, K2 tog, psso, K1, rep from * to end.
43rd round *Yo, K2 tog, yo, K5, yo, sl 1, K1, psso, yo, sl 1, K2 tog, psso, rep from * to end.
45th round *K 2 tog, yo, K1 through back lp yo, sl 1, K1, psso, K1, K2 tog, yo, K1 through back lp, yo, sl 1, K2 tog, psso, yo, rep from * to end.
47th round K first st onto end of last needle, *yo, K3, yo, sl 1, K2 tog,

psso, rep from * to end.
49th round *Yo, K5, yo, K1 through back lp, rep from * to end. 160 sts.
51st round *Yo, K1 through back lp, yo, sl 1, K1, psso, K1, K2 tog, yo sl 1, K2 tog, psso, yo, sl 1, K1, psso, K1, K2 tog, (yo, K1 through back lp) twice, rep from * to end.
53rd round *Yo, K3, yo, (sl 1, K2 tog, psso, yo, K3, yo) twice, K1 through back lp, rep from * to end. 180 sts.
55th round *K5, yo, K1 through back lp, yo, rep from * to end. 240 sts.
57th round *Sl 1, K1, psso, K1, K2 tog, yo, sl 1, K2 tog, psso, yo, rep from * to end. 180 sts.
59th round *Sl 1, K2 tog, psso, yo, K3, yo, rep from * to end.
61st round *Yo, K1 through back lp, yo, K5, rep from * to end. 240 sts.
63rd round *Yo, K3, yo, sl 1, K1, psso. K1, K2 tog, rep from * to end.
65th round *Yo, K5, yo, sl 1, K2 tog, psso, rep from * to end.
67th and 69th rounds P.
71st round *Yo twice, sl 1, K1, psso, K2 tog, rep from * to end. 240 (480) sts.
72nd, 74th and 76th rounds K. but P1 into each first yo and K1 into each second yo of previous round.
73rd round K first st onto end of last needle, *K2 tog, yo, twice, sl 1, K1, psso, rep from * to end.
75th round As 71st.
77th and 79th rounds P.
78th and 80th rounds K.
81st round *Yo, K1 through back lp, yo, sl 1, K1, psso, K3, rep from * to end. 280 (560) sts.
82nd and following alt rounds K. but K through back lp into all sts worked through back lp in previous round.
83rd round *K1, yo, K1 through back lp, yo, sl 1, K1, psso, K3 from * to end. 320 (640) sts.
85th round *K2, yo, K1 through back lp, yo, sl 1, K1, psso, K3, rep from * to end. 360 (720) sts.
87th round *K3, yo, K1 through back lp, yo, sl 1, K1, psso, K3, rep from * to end. 400 (800) sts.
89th round *K4, yo, K1 through back lp, yo, sl 1, K1, psso, K3, rep from * to end. 440 (880) sts.
91st round *K5, yo, K1 through back lp, yo, sl 1, K1, psso, K3, rep from * to end. 480 (960) sts.
Change to circular needle.
93rd round K1, mark this point with coloured thread for beg of round, *yo, K5, yo, K1 through back

49

lp, yo, sl 1, K1, psso, K4, rep from * to end. 560 (1120) sts.

95th round *Yo, K1 through back lp, yo, K5, sl 1, K2 tog, psso, K5, rep from * to end.

97th round *Yo, K3, yo, K4, sl 1, K2 tog, psso, K4, rep from * to end.

99th round *Yo, K2 tog, yo, K1 through back lp, yo, sl 1, K1, psso, yo, K3, sl 1, K2 tog, psso, K3, rep from * to end.

101st round *Yo, K2 tog, yo, sl 1, K2 tog, psso, yo, sl 1, K1, psso, yo, K2, sl 1, K2 tog, psso, K2, rep from * to end. 480 (960) sts.

103rd round *Yo, K2 tog, yo, K3, yo, sl 1, K1, psso, yo, K1, sl 1, K2 tog, psso, K1, rep from * to end.

105th round *Yo, K2 tog, yo, K5, yo, sl 1, K1, psso, yo, sl 1, K2 tog, psso, rep from * to end.

107th round *K2 tog, yo, K1 through back lp, yo, sl 1, K1, psso, K1, K2 tog, yo, K1 through back lp, yo, sl 1, K2 tog, psso, yo, rep from * to end.

109th round K1, mark this point with a coloured thread for beg of round *yo, K3, yo, sl 1, K2 tog, psso, rep from * to end.

111th round *K5, yo, K1 through back lp, yo, rep from * to end. 640 (1280) sts.

113th round *Sl 1, K1, psso, K1, K2, tog, yo, sl 1, K2 tog, psso, yo, rep from * to end. 480 (960) sts.

115th round *Sl 1, K2 tog, psso, yo, K3, yo, rep from * to end.

117th round *Yo, K1 through back lp, yo, K5, rep from * to end. 640 (1280) sts.

119th round *Yo, sl 1, K2 tog, psso, yo, sl 1, K1, psso, K1, K2 tog, rep from * to end. 480 (960) sts.

121st round *Yo, K3, yo, sl 1, K2 tog, psso, rep from * to end.

123rd round As 111th. 640 (1280) sts.

125th round As 113th. 480 (960) sts.

127th round As 115th.

129th and 131st rounds P.

133rd round As 71st. 480 (960) sts.

134th, 136th and 138th rounds As 72nd.

135th round As 73rd.

137th round As 75th.

139th and 141st rounds P.

142nd round K. 480 (960) sts.

143rd to 204th round As 81st to 142nd.

205th round *Yo, K1 through back lp, yo, (sl 1, K1, psso, yo) 5 times, sl 1, K2 tog, psso, (yo, K2 tog) 5 times, rep from * to end.

207th round *Yo, sl 1, K2 tog, psso, yo, (sl 1, K1, psso, yo) 4 times, sl 1,

K2 tog, psso, (yo, K2 tog) 5 times, rep from * to end. 880 sts.

209th round *Yo, K3, yo, (sl 1, K1, psso, yo) 4 times, sl 1, K2 tog, psso, (yo, K2 tog) 4 times, rep from * to end.

211th round *Yo, K2, yo, K1 through back lp, yo, K2, yo, (sl 1, K1, psso, yo) 3 times, sl 1, K2 tog, psso, (yo, K2 tog) 4 times, rep from * to end. 960 sts.

213th round *(Yo, K3) 3 times, yo, (sl 1, K1, psso, yo) 3 times, sl 1, K2 tog, psso, (yo, K2 tog) 3 times, rep from * to end. 1040 sts.

215th round *Yo, K4, yo, K2 tog, yo, K1 through back lp, yo, sl 1, K1, psso, yo, K4, yo, (sl 1, K1, psso, yo) twice, sl 1, K2 tog, psso, K2 tog) 3 times, rep from * to end. 1120 sts.

217th round *Yo, K3, (K2 tog, yo) twice, K3, (yo, sl 1, K1, psso) twice, K3, yo, (sl 1, K1, psso, yo) twice, sl 1, K2 tog, psso, (yo, K2 tog) twice, rep from * to end.

219th round *Yo, K3, (K2 tog, yo) 3 times, K1 through back lp, (yo, sl 1, K1, psso) 3 times, K3, yo, sl 1, K1, psso, yo, sl 1, K2 tog, psso, (yo, K2 tog) twice, rep from * to end

221st round *Yo, K3, (K2 tog, yo) 3 times, K3, (yo, sl 1, K1 psso) 3 times, K3, yo, sl 1, K1, psso, yo, sl 1, K2 tog, psso, yo, K2 tog, rep from* to end.

223rd round *Yo, K3, (K2 tog, yo) 3 times, K2, K into front and back of next st, K2, (yo, sl 1, K1, psso) 3 times, K3, yo, sl 1, K2 tog, psso, yo, K2 tog, rep from * to end. 1160 sts.

224th round K.

Edging

Using steel crochet hook #2 insert hook into next 5 sts tog and pull yarn through. *10ch, (1sc into next 4 sts tog, 10ch) 4 times, 1sc into next 5 sts tog, 10ch, 1sc into next 3 sts tog, 10ch, 1sc into next 5 sts tog, rep from * omitting 1sc at end of last rep, ss to first sc. Fasten off.

To finish

Dampen work and pin out to size on a clean, flat surface.

Irish crochet

Irish crochet, also known as Honiton crochet, is a form of lace which originated as an imitation of the Guipure laces of Spain. The lace background and various motifs, such as the rose, leaf, shamrock plus other flowers and curves, are both major characteristics of this work.

This introduction to the craft will cover some of the techniques for working the background and also a selection of some of the more simple motifs. The motifs may be applied directly onto the background or the lace mesh may be worked around the motif.

The samples shown here were worked in a No.5 cotton yarn with a No. 2.00 crochet hook. When you understand the basic techniques, try experimenting.

U.K. technique
Rose motif
To work the net background Make 50ch loosely.
1st row Into 10th ch from hook work 1dc, *6ch, miss 3ch, 1dc into next ch, rep from * to end of row. Turn.
2nd row 9ch, 1dc into first ch sp, *6ch, 1dc into next ch sp, rep from * to end of row. Turn.
The 2nd row is repeated throughout.
To work the rose motif Wrap the yarn 20 times round a pencil.
1st round Remove yarn carefully from the pencil, work 18dc into the ring. Join with a ss into first dc.
2nd round 6ch, miss 2dc, 1htr into next dc, *4ch, miss 2dc, 1htr into next dc, rep from * 3 times more, 4ch. Join with a ss into 2nd of 6ch.
3rd round Into each 4ch sp work 1dc, 1htr, 3tr, 1htr and 1dc to form a petal. Join with a ss into first dc.
4th round Ss into back of nearest htr of 2nd round, *5ch, passing chain behind petal of previous round, ss into next htr of 2nd round, rep from * times more.
5th round Into each 5ch sp work 1dc, 1htr, 5tr, 1 htr and 1dc. Join with a ss into first dc.
6th round Ss into back of ss of 4th round, *6ch, passing chain behind petal of previous round, ss into next ss of 4th round, rep from * 5 times more.
7th round Into each 6ch sp work 1dc, 1htr, 6tr, 1htr and 1dc. Join with a ss into first dc. Fasten off.

Motif 2
To work the net background Make 58ch loosely.
1st row Into 16th ch from hook work 1dc, 3ch, 1dc into same ch as last dc, *9ch, miss 5ch, 1dc into next ch, 3ch, 1dc into same ch as last dc, rep from * to end of row. Turn.
2nd row 13ch, 1dc into first ch sp, 3ch, 1dc into same sp, *9ch, 1dc into next ch sp, 3ch, 1dc into same sp, rep from * to end of row. Turn.
The 2nd row is repeated throughout.
To work the motif Wrap yarn 12 times round a pencil.

Below: A rose and shamrock, two typical Irish crochet motifs, together with two net background patterns, provide the perfect introduction to this lovely kind of crochet lace.

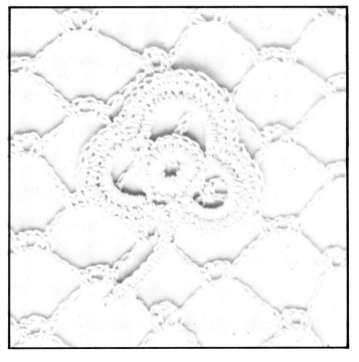

1st round Remove yarn carefully from the pencil, work 18dc into the ring. Join with a ss into first dc.

2nd round 8ch, miss 4dc, ss into next dc, 10ch, miss 4dc, ss into next dc, 8ch, miss 4dc, ss into next dc, work 12ch for stem, into 3rd ch from hook work 1dc, 1dc into each of next 9ch, turn.

3rd row Into first ch sp work 16dc, 20dc into next ch sp and 16dc into next ch sp. Turn.

4th row 3ch to count as first tr, miss first dc, 1tr into each dc to end of row. Fasten off.

Motif 3

To work the net background This background incorporates an attractive picot design. Make 47ch loosely.

1st row Work 4ch, ss into 4th ch from hook – called a picot –, 2ch, into 12th ch from picot work 1dc, *4ch, work a picot, 2ch, miss 4ch 1dc into next ch, rep from * to end of row. Turn.

2nd row 6ch, work a picot, 2ch, 1dc into first ch sp, *4ch, work a picot, 2ch, 1dc into next ch sp, rep from * to end of row. Turn.

The 2nd row is repeated throughout

To work the motif Wrap yarn 14 times round little finger of left hand.

1st round Remove yarn carefully from finger, work 38dc into the ring. Join with a ss into first dc.

2nd round *9ch, miss 6dc, ss into next dc, rep from * 4 times more, ss into each of next 3dc.

3rd round Into each 9ch sp work 12dc, work 14ch for stem, into 3rd ch

from hook work 1dc, 1dc into each of next 11ch. Join with a ss into first dc.

4th round 3ch to count as first tr, miss first dc, 1tr into each dc on all 5 loops. Fasten off.

Raffia motif

This has the same net background as motif 2, but it is worked in an ordinary parcel string and the raffia motif is made in the same way as the motif 3. Use different coloured motifs to decorate a string hold-all.

Motif 5

Use the rose motif described for Motif 1 to decorate a wedding veil. This rose is worked in an extremely fine yarn and has beads sewn onto the motif over the background. The net here is a commercial one, but you could, with time and

The pretty floral motifs made in Irish crochet can be used in many ways. Individual motifs can be sewn onto filmy curtains, lampshades or clothes. Wedding dresses and veils look particularly lovely trimmed in this way.

patience, make a valuable family heirloom if you worked your veil in a crochet net. Here is a more complicated background net and several different motifs.

The crochet lace background could be used for a scarf or evening shawl, made either into a stole shape or a large triangle trimmed with a fringe. By working the motifs illustrated here you will learn the two techniques which are most common in this type of work. They both give a raised look to the work but by different means. One is working over several thicknesses of yarn and the other way is to insert the hook into the horizontal loop under the two loops where the hook is usually placed. All the following motifs were worked in a very fine cotton yarn, No.25, and a fine crochet hook, but the size of the hook will vary depending on the sort of yarn you use.

Motif 6

To work the net background Make 57ch loosely.

1st row Into 4th ch from hook work a ss – one picot formed –, 8ch, ss into 4th ch from hook, 2ch, 1dc into 8th ch from first picot worked, *6ch, ss into 4th ch from hook, 8ch, ss into 4th ch from hook, 2ch, miss 4ch, 1dc into next ch, rep from * to end. Turn.

2nd row 9ch, ss into 4th ch from hook, 8ch, ss into 4th ch from hook, 2ch, 1dc into first ch sp (i.e. between the 2 picots), *6ch, ss into 4th ch from hook, 8ch, ss into 4th ch from hook, 2ch, 1dc into next ch sp, rep from * to end. Turn.

The 2nd row is repeated throughout.

To work the rose motif Repeat the instructions given for the rose in motif 1, do not fasten off but continue as follows:

Next round *7ch, passing chain behind petal of previous round ss between the 2dc of next adjoining petals, rep from * 5 times more.

Next round Into each 7ch sp work 1dc, 1htr, 8tr, 1htr, 1dc. Join with a ss into first dc. Turn work.

Next round 1ch to count as first dc, miss first st, work 1dc into each st all round placing the hook into the horizontal loop of the st in the previous row – this st gives a raised effect on the right side of the work. Fasten off.

To work the leaf motif All the double crochet stitches from a given point in the pattern are worked over four thicknesses of yarn to give a ridged effect. Cut four lengths of yarn, each 40.5cm *(16in)* long, and when the first dc to be worked in this way is indicated, place the yarn behind the work on a level with the stitch into which the hook is to be placed.

Make 16ch. Into 3rd ch from hook work 1dc, 1dc into each ch to last ch, 5dc into last ch to form tip of leaf, then work 1dc into each st on other side of chain. Work 3dc over the 4 thicknesses of yarn, still working over the yarn and continuing towards tip of leaf, work 1dc into each of next 12dc, working into

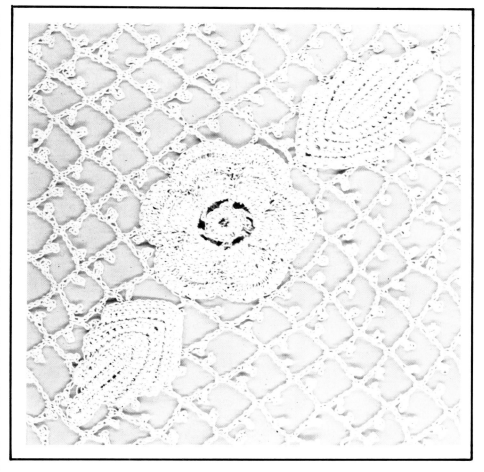

back loop only of each st. Turn work, 1ch, miss first dc, working down one side of leaf and up the other side, work 1dc into each dc to within 4dc of tip of leaf. Turn work, *1ch, miss first st, 1dc into each dc of previous row to last 4dc of row and working 3dc into dc at base of leaf. Turn work. *. Repeat from * to * until the leaf is the required size.

Motif 7
Wrap yarn 14 times round a pencil.
1st round Remove yarn carefully from pencil, work 21dc into ring. Join with a ss into first dc.
2nd round 1ch to count as first dc,

miss first st, 1dc into each dc all round. Join with a ss into first ch.

3rd round 1ch to count as first dc, miss first dc, 1dc into each of next 6 sts, (12ch, 1dc into each of next 7 sts) twice, 14ch. Join with a ss into first ch.

4th round 1ch to count as first dc, miss first dc, 1dc into each of next 4 sts, (22dc into next 12ch sp, 1dc

Top: A delicate rose and leaf motif on a crisp background net incorporating picots.

Below: Making the outline of the rose motif.

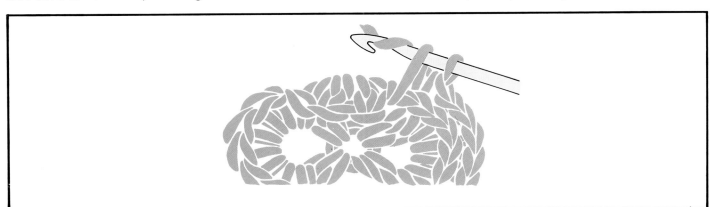

into each of next 5 sts) twice, 24dc into next 14ch sp. Join with a ss into first ch.

5th round Ss into each of next 4 sts, *4ch, miss 2 sts, ss into next st, *, rep from * to * 6 times more, miss next 3 sts, ss into each of next 3 sts, rep from * to * 7 times, miss next 3 sts, ss into each of next 3 sts, rep from * to * 8 times. Join with a ss into first ss.

6th round 1ch to count as first dc, miss first st, 1dc into each of next 2 sts, (6dc into next 4ch sp) 7 times, ss into next st, work 18ch for stem, into 3rd ch from hook work 1dc, 1dc into each of next 15ch, ss into next st on main motif, (6dc into next 4ch sp) 7 times, 1dc into each of next 3 sts, (6dc into next 4ch sp) 8 times. Join with a ss into first ch. Fasten off.

Motif 8
Make 40ch.

1st row Into 3rd ch from hook work 1dc, 1dc into each ch to last ch, 5dc into last ch. Do not turn.

2nd row 1dc into each ch on opposite side of 1st row. Turn.

3rd row The petals are worked individually down each side of the stem beginning from the tip where the last dc was worked as follows: *12ch, ss into st at base of ch, 3ch, miss 2dc, ss into next dc, turn, work 25tr into 12ch sp, ss into first dc on row 1, turn, 1ch to count as first dc, miss first tr, 1dc into each tr round petal, ss into same ss as last ss – one petal has been completed –, rep

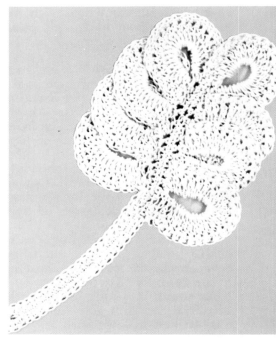

from * to give the required number of petals noting that when the 25tr have been worked, the ss is placed in front of the previous petal by inserting the hook into the 3rd dc up from the base of the petal being worked.
Fasten off.

To complete the other side, rejoin yarn at the tip and work the petals in the same way, but join the last of the 25tr behind the previous petal.

So far, instructions have been given for working the background and motifs separately. Now you can learn the alternative techniques of producing the background and

motifs together.

Motif 9
This is a six-sided figure where the net background has been worked around the central motif. The shapes may eventually be joined together to form a whole fabric which would

Above: A shamrock and flower

Below: Two rather unusual motifs. The six-sided rose is perfect for working up into a bedspread or lace curtain, while the paisley-like motif gives a new technique for joining.

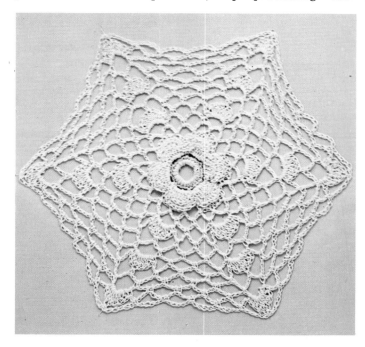
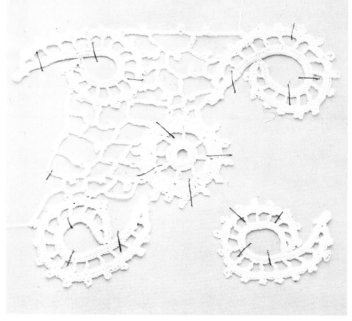

make an attractive bedcover or lampshade covering.

To work the motif Using a No.2.00 crochet hook and a No.25 cotton yarn, make a rose motif in the same way as that explained in Motif 7.

Next round Ss into each of next 3 sts of first petal, *(5ch, miss 2 sts, ss into next st) twice, 5ch, miss 3 sts, ss into next st, rep from * 5 times more.

Next round Ss into each of next 2 sts, 6ch, *1dc into next 5ch sp, 5ch, rep from * 16 times more. Join with a ss into 2nd of 6ch.

Next round * Into next 5ch sp work 1dc, 1htr, 5tr, 1htr and 1dc, (5ch, 1dc into next 5ch sp) twice, 5ch, rep from * 5 times more. Join with a ss into first dc.

Next round Ss into each of next 5 sts, 6ch, (1dc into next 5ch sp, 5ch) 3 times, *1dc into centre tr of next petal gr, (5ch, 1dc into next 5ch sp) 3 times, 5ch, rep from * 4 times more. Join with a ss into 2nd of 6ch.

Next round Ss into each of next 2 sts, 6ch, *1dc into next 5ch sp, 5ch, rep from * 22 times more. Join with a ss into 2nd of 6ch.

Next round Ss into each of next 2 sts, 6ch, (1dc into next 5ch sp, 5ch) twice, into next 5ch sp work 1dc, 1htr, 5tr, 1htr and 1dc, *(5ch, 1dc into next 5ch sp) 3 times, 5ch, into next 5ch sp work 1dc, 1htr, 5tr, 1htr and 1dc, rep from * 4 times more, 5ch. Join with a ss into 2nd of 4ch.

Next round Ss into each of next 2 sts, 6ch, 1dc into next ch sp, 5ch, 1dc into next ch sp, 5ch, 1dc, into centre tr of next petal gr, *(5ch, 1dc into next ch sp) 4 times, 5ch, 1dc into centre tr of next petal gr, rep from * 4 times more, 5ch, 1dc into next ch sp, 5ch. Join with a ss into 2nd of 6ch.

Next round Ss into each of next 2 sts, 6ch, *1dc into next ch sp, 5ch, rep from * 28 times more. Join with a ss into 2nd of 6ch.

Next round Ss into each of next 2 sts, 6ch, 1dc into next ch sp, 5ch, into next ch sp work 1dc, 1htr, 5tr, 1htr, and 1dc, *(5ch, 1dc into next ch sp) 4 times, 5ch, into next ch sp work 1dc, 1htr, 5tr, 1htr and 1dc, rep from * 4 times more, (5ch, 1dc into next ch sp) twice, 5ch. Join with a ss into 2nd of 6ch.

Next round Ss into each of next 2 sts, 6ch, 1dc into next ch sp, 5ch, 1dc into centre tr of next petal gr, *(5ch, 1dc into next 5ch sp) 5 times, 5ch, 1dc into centre tr of next petal

gr, rep from * 4 times more, (5ch, 1dc into next ch sp) 3 times, 5ch. Join with a ss into 2nd of 6ch. Fasten off.

Motif 10

The technique shown here is the method of working motifs and placing them on to paper so that a chain stitch may be worked to join the motifs together to form a fabric.

To work the circle Wrap yarn 20 times round a pencil.

1st round Remove yarn carefully from pencil, work 24dc into circle. Join with a ss into first dc.

2nd round 8ch, miss 2dc, *1tr into next dc, 5ch, miss 2dc, rep from * 6 times more. Join with a ss into 3rd of 8 ch.

3rd round 3ch to count as first tr, 3tr into first ch sp, 4ch, ss into 4th ch from hook – called 1 picot –, 4tr into same ch sp, 1 picot, *(4tr, 1 picot) twice into next ch sp, rep from * 6 times more. Join with a ss into 3rd of 3ch. Fasten off.

To work the curve Cut ten lengths of yarn, each 18cm (7in) long. Work 60dc over yarn. Turn work and leave extra yarn to hang freely.

Next row 1ch, ss into 2nd dc, 3ch, miss 3dc, 1htr into next dc, (3ch, miss 3dc, 1tr into next dc) 5 times, (3ch, miss 2dc, 1tr into next dc) 8 times, (3ch, miss 2dc, 1htr into next dc) 3 times, 3ch, ss into last dc. Join with a ss into dc below 3rd tr worked at beg of row to give a circle plus a small length of work. Turn.

Next row Into first ch sp work 5dc, (4dc into next ch, sp, 1 picot) 16 times, 4dc into next ch sp, double back the extra ten yarn lengths and work 4dc very tightly over the double length, 1 dc into end loop, 1ch. Fasten off working yarn. Pull ten lengths of yarn tight to neaten, then cut away.

To join the motifs Make the desired number of motifs and baste onto a firm paper background. The green basting stitches may be seen in the illustration and more stitches rather than pins which tend to fall out, should be used as the filling-in progresses.

The sample shows a circle and four curves, but any of the previous motifs which you have learnt could be incorporated in this method of working. Only half the filling-in has been completed so that the working method may be clearly seen.

A dress pattern of an evening

bodice could be used as the paper backing and then the various motifs would be joined together to give the appearance of lace. It would then be necessary to make a lining for this lace.

Chain stitches are used for the filling-in which was started at the top right-hand corner of the work. At random intervals a picot is worked by making four chain and slip stitching into the first of these. It is easiest to work in lines to and fro, so joining the motifs together and slip stitching back across some chain stitches where necessary or even breaking off the yarn and re-joining it at a new position on the work. When all the motifs are joined, the tacks may be removed and all the cut ends of yarn should be neatened on the wrong side of the work.

U.S. technique
Rose motif
To work the net background Make 50ch loosely.

1st row Into 10th ch from hook work 1sc, *6ch, miss 3ch, 1sc into next ch, rep from * to end of row. Turn.

2nd row 9ch, 1sc into first ch sp, *6ch, 1sc into next ch sp, rep from * to end of row. Turn.

The 2nd row is repeated throughout.

To work the rose motif Wrap the yarn 20 times round a pencil.

1st round Remove yarn carefully from the pencil, work 18sc into the ring. Join with a ss into first sc.

2nd round 6ch, miss 2sc, 1hdc into next sc, *4ch, miss 2sc, 1hdc into next sc, rep from * 3 times more, 4ch, Join with a ss into 2nd of 6ch.

3rd round Into each 4ch sp work 1sc, 1hdc, 3dc, 1hdc and 1sc to form a petal. Join with a ss into first dc.

4th round Ss into back of nearest hdc of 2nd round, *5ch, passing chain behind petal of previous round, ss into next hdc of 2nd round, rep from * times more.

5th round Into each 5ch sp work 1sc, 1hdc, 5dc, 1 hdc and 1sc. Join with a ss into first sc.

6th round Ss into back of ss of 4th round, *6ch, passing chain behind petal of previous round, ss into next ss of 4th round, rep from * 5 times more.

7th round Into each 6ch sp work 1sc, 1hdc, 6dc, 1hdc and 1sc. Join with a ss into first sc. Fasten off.

Motif 2

To work the net background
Make 58ch loosely.

1st row Into 16th ch from hook work 1sc, 3ch, 1sc into same ch as last sc, *9ch, miss 5ch, 1sc into next ch, 3ch, 1sc into same ch as last sc, rep from * to end of row. Turn.

2nd row 13ch, 1sc into first ch sp, 3ch, 1sc into same sp, *9ch, 1sc into next ch sp, 3ch, 1sc into same sp, rep from * to end of row. Turn.

The 2nd row is repeated throughout.

To work the motif Wrap yarn 12 times round a pencil.

1st round Remove yarn carefully from the pencil, work 18sc into the ring. Join with a ss into first sc.

2nd round 8ch, miss 4sc, ss into next sc, 10ch, miss 4sc, ss into next sc, 8ch, miss 4sc, ss into next sc, work 12ch for stem into 3rd ch from hook work 1sc, 1sc into each of next 9ch, turn.

3rd row Into first ch sp work 16sc, 20sc into next ch sp and 16sc into next ch sp. Turn.

4th row 3ch to count as first dc, miss first sc, 1dc into each sc to end of row. Fasten off.

Motif 3

To work the net background This background incorporates an attractive picot design. Make 47ch loosely.

1st row Work 4ch, ss into 4th ch from hook – called a picot –, 2ch, into 12th ch from picot work 1sc, *4ch, work a picot, 2ch, miss 4ch 1sc into next ch, rep from * to end of row. Turn.

2nd row 6ch, work a picot, 2ch, 1sc into first ch sp, *4ch, work a picot, 2ch, 1sc into next ch sp, rep from * to end of row. Turn.

The 2nd row is repeated throughout

To work the motif Wrap yarn 14 times round little finger of left hand.

1st round Remove yarn carefully from finger, work 38sc into the ring. Join with a ss into first sc.

2nd round *9ch, miss 6sc, ss into next sc, rep from * 4 times more, ss into each of next 3sc.

3rd round Into each 9ch sp work 12sc, work 14ch for stem, into 3rd ch from hook work 1sc, 1sc into each of next 11ch. Join with a ss into first sc.

4th round 3ch to count as first dc, miss first sc, 1dc into each sc on all 5 loops. Fasten off.

Raffia motif

This has the same net background as motif 2, but it is worked in an ordinary parcel string and the raffia motif is made in the same way as the motif 3. Use different coloured motifs to decorate a string hold-all.

Motif 5

Use the rose motif described for motif 1 to decorate a wedding veil. This rose is worked in an extremely fine yarn and has beads sewn on to the motif over the background. The net here is a commercial one, but you could, with time and patience, make a valuable family heirloom if you worked your veil in a crochet net. Here is a more complicated background net and several different motifs.

The crochet lace background could be used for a scarf or evening shawl, made either into a stole shape or a large triangle trimmed with a fringe. By working the motifs illustrated here you will learn the two techniques which are most common in this type of work. They both give a raised look to the work but by different means. One is working over several thicknesses of yarn and the other way is to insert the hook into the horizontal loop under the two loops where the hook is usually placed. All the following motifs were worked in a very fine cotton yarn, No.25, and a fine crochet hook, but the size of the hook will vary depending on the sort of yarn you use.

Motif 6

To work the net background
Make 57ch loosely.

1st row Into 4th ch from hook work a ss – one picot formed –, 8ch, ss into 4th ch from hook, 2ch, 1sc into 8th ch from first picot worked, *6ch, ss into 4th ch from hook, 8ch, ss into 4th ch from hook, 2ch, miss 4ch, 1sc into next ch, rep from * to end. Turn.

2nd row 9ch, ss into 4th ch from hook, 8ch, ss into 4th ch from hook, 2ch, 1sc into first ch sp (i.e. between the 2 picots), *6ch, ss into 4th ch from hook, 8ch, ss into 4th ch from hook, 2ch, 1sc into next ch sp, rep from * to end. Turn.

The 2nd row is repeated throughout.

To work the rose motif Repeat the instructions given for the rose in motif 1, do not fasten off but continue as follows:

Next round *7ch, passing chain behind petal of previous round ss between the 2sc of next adjoining petals, rep from * 5 times more.

Next round Into each 7ch sp work 1sc, 1hdc, 8dc, 1hdc, 1sc. Join with a ss into first sc. Turn work.

Next round 1ch to count as first sc, miss first st, work 1sc into each st all round placing the hook into the horizontal loop of the st in the previous row – this st gives a raised effect on the right side of the work. Fasten off.

To work the leaf motif All the single crochet stitches from a given point in the pattern are worked over four thicknesses of yarn to give a ridged effect. Cut four lengths of yarn, each 40.5cm *(16in)* long, and when the first sc to be worked in this way is indicated, place the yarn behind the work on a level with the stitch into which the hook is to be placed.

Make 16ch. Into 3rd ch from hook work 1sc, 1sc into each ch to last ch, 5sc into last ch to form tip of leaf, then work 1sc into each st on other side of chain. Work 3sc over the 4 thicknesses of yarn, still working over the yarn and continuing towards tip of leaf, work 1sc into each of next 12sc, working into back loop only of each st. Turn work, 1ch, miss first sc, working down one side of leaf and up the other side, work 1sc into each sc to within 4sc of tip of leaf. Turn work, *1ch, miss first st, 1sc into each sc of previous row to last 4sc of row and working 3sc into sc at base of leaf. Turn work. * Repeat from * to * until the leaf is the required size.

Motif 7

Wrap yarn 14 times round a pencil.

1st round Remove yarn carefully from pencil, work 21sc into ring. Join with a ss into first sc.

2nd round 1ch to count as first sc, miss first st, 1sc into each sc all round. Join with a ss into first ch.

3rd round 1ch to count as first sc, miss first sc, 1sc into each of next 6 sts, (12ch, 1sc into each of next 7 sts) twice, 14ch. Join with a ss into first ch.

4th round 1ch to count as first sc, miss first sc, 1sc into each of next 4 sts, (22sc into next 12ch sp, 1sc into each of next 5 sts) twice, 24sc into next 14ch sp. Join with a ss into first ch.

5th round Ss into each of next 4 sts, *4ch, miss 2 sts, ss into next st, *, rep from * to * 6 times more, miss next 3 sts, ss into each of next 3 sts, rep from * to * 7 times, miss next 3 sts, ss into each of next 3 sts, rep from * to * 8 times. Join with a ss into first ss.

6th round 1ch to count as first sc, miss first st, 1sc into each of next 2 sts, (6sc into next 4ch sp) 7 times, ss into next st, work 18ch for stem, into 3rd ch from hook work 1sc, 1sc into each of next 15ch, ss into next st on main motif, (6sc into next 4ch sp) 7 times, 1sc into each of next 3 sts, (6sc into next 4ch sp) 8 times. Join with a ss into first ch. Fasten off.

Motif 8

Make 40ch.

1st row Into 3rd ch from hook work 1sc, 1sc into each ch to last ch, 5sc into last ch. Do not turn.

2nd row 1sc into each ch on opposite side of 1st row. Turn.

3rd row The petals are worked individually down each side of the stem beginning from the tip where the last sc was worked as follows: *12ch, ss into st at base of ch, 3ch, miss 2sc, ss into next sc, turn, work 25dc into 12ch sp, ss into first sc on row 1, turn, 1ch to count as first sc, miss first dc, 1sc into each dc round petal, ss into same ss as last ss – one petal has been completed –, rep from * to give the required number of petals noting that when the 25dc have been worked, the ss is placed in front of the previous petal by inserting the hook into the 3rd sc up from the base of the petal being worked. Fasten off.

To complete the other side, rejoin yarn at the tip and work the petals in the same way, but join the last of the 25dc behind the previous petal.

So far, instructions have been given for working the background and motifs separately. Now you can learn the alternative techniques of producing the background and motifs together.

Motif 9

This is a six-sided figure where the net background has been worked around the central motif. The shapes may eventually be joined together to form a whole fabric which would make an attractive bedcover or lampshade covering.

To work the motif Using a steel crochet hook #00 and a No. 25 cotton yarn, make a rose motif in the same way as motif 7.

Next round Ss into each of next 3 sts of first petal, *(5ch, miss 2 sts, ss into next st) twice, 5ch, miss 3 sts, ss into next st, rep from * 5 times more.

Next round Ss into each of next 2 sts, 6ch, *1sc into next 5ch sp, 5ch, rep from * 16 times more. Join with a ss into 2nd of 6ch.

Next round *Into next 5ch sp work 1sc, 1hdc, 5dc, 1hdc and 1sc, (5ch, 1sc into next 5ch sp) twice, 5ch, rep from * 5 times more. Join with a ss into first dc.

Next round Ss into each of next 5 sts, 6ch, (1sc into next 5ch sp, 5ch) 3 times, *1sc into centre dc of next petal gr, (5ch, 1sc into next 5ch sp) 3 times, 5ch, rep from * 4 times more. Join with a ss into 2nd of 6ch.

Next round Ss into each of next 2 sts, 6ch, *1sc into next 5ch sp, 5ch, rep from * 22 times more. Join with a ss into 2nd of 6ch.

Next round Ss into each of next 2 sts, 6ch, (1sc into next 5ch sp, 5ch) twice, into next 5ch sp work 1sc 1hdc, 5dc, 1hdc and 1sc, *(5ch, 1sc into next 5ch ps) 3 times, 5ch, into next 5ch sp work 1sc, 1hdc, 5dc, 1hdc and 1sc, rep from * 4 times more, 5ch. Join with a ss into 2nd of 4ch.

Next round Ss into each of next 2 sts, 6ch 1sc into next ch sp, 5ch, 1sc into next ch sp, 5ch, 1sc into centre dc of next petal gr, *(5ch, 1sc into next ch sp) 4 times, 5ch, 1sc into centre dc of next petal gr. rep from * 4 times more, 5ch, 1sc into next ch sp, 5ch. Join with a ss into 2nd of 6ch.

Next round Ss into each of next 2 sts, 6ch, *1sc into next ch sp, 5ch, rep from * 28 times more. Join with a ss into 2nd of 6ch.

Next round Ss into each of next 2 sts, 6ch, 1sc into next ch sp, 5ch, into next ch sp work 1sc, 1hdc, 5dc, 1hdc, and 1sc, *(5ch, 1sc into next ch sp) 4 times, 5ch, into next ch sp work 1sc, 1hdc, 5dc, 1hdc and 1sc, rep from * 4 times more, (5ch, 1sc into next ch sp) twice, 5ch. Join with a ss into 2nd of 6ch.

Next round Ss into each of next 2 sts, 6ch, 1sc into next ch sp, 5ch, 1sc into centre dc of next petal gr, *(5ch, 1sc into next 5ch sp) 5 times, 5ch, 1sc into centre dc of next petal gr, rep from * 4 times more, (5ch, 1sc into next ch sp) 3 times, 5ch. Join with a ss into 2nd of 6ch. Fasten off.

Motif 10

The technique shown here is the method of working motifs and placing them onto paper so that a chain stitch may be worked to join the motifs together to form a fabric.

To work the circle Wrap yarn 20 times round a pencil.

1st round Remove yarn carefully from pencil, work 24sc into circle. Join with a ss into first sc.

2nd round 8ch, miss 2sc, *1dc into next sc, 5ch, miss 2sc, rep from * 6 times more. Join with a ss into 3rd of 8 ch.

3rd round 3ch to count as first dc, 3dc into first ch sp, 4ch, ss into 4th ch from hook – called 1 picot –, 4dc into same ch sp, 1 picot, *(4dc, 1 picot) twice into next ch sp, rep from * 6 times more. Join with a ss into 3rd of 3ch. Fasten off.

To work the curve Cut ten lengths of yarn, each 18cm *(7in)* long. Work 60sc over yarn. Turn work and leave extra yarn to hang freely.

Next row 1ch, ss into 2nd sc, 3ch, miss 3sc, 1hdc into next sc, (3ch, miss 3sc, 1dc into next sc) 5 times, (3ch, miss 2sc, 1dc into next sc) 8 times, (3ch, miss 2sc, 1hdc into next sc) 3 times, 3ch, ss into last sc. Join with a ss into sc below 3rd dc worked at beg of row to give a circle plus a small length of work. Turn.

Next row Into first ch sp work 5sc, (4sc into next ch, sp, 1 picot) 16 times, 4sc into next ch sp, double back the extra 10 lengths of yarn and work 4sc very tightly over the double length, 1 sc into end loop, 1ch. Fasten off working yarn. Pull ten lengths of yarn tight to neaten, then cut away.

To join the motifs Make the desired number of motifs and baste onto a firm paper background. The green basting stitches may be seen in the illustration and further stitches rather than pins which tend to fall out, should be used as the filling-in progresses.

The sample shows a circle and four curves, but any of the previous motifs which you have learnt could be incorporated in this method of working. Only half the filling-in has been completed so that the working method may be clearly seen.

Irish crochet bedspread

Irish crochet is usually very fine and similar to lace, but the techniques have been updated for this bedspread, using chunky yarn and modern colours. The result is both attractive and quick and easy.

U.K. technique

Size
About 229cm by 178cm *(90in by 70in)*, excluding fringe
Fringe About 18cm *(7in)*

Tension
Motif measures 25.5cm *(10in)* square

Materials
Mahony's Blarney Bainin 34 x 50g *(2oz)* balls main shade, A, Dried Grass
9 x 50g *(2oz)* balls B, Dark Brown
4 x 50g *(2oz)* balls C, Yellow
Fringe 5 x 50g *(2oz)* balls A
One No. 5.50 crochet hook

Motif
Using No. 5.50 hook and leaving a 10cm *(4in)* end of yarn, make 8ch,
join with ss to first ch to form a ring.
1st round Wind 10cm *(4in)* length round into ring with ch and work 18dc into ring over ch and yarn, join with ss to first dc.
2nd round 1dc into same place as ss, *5ch, miss 2dc, 1dc into next dc, rep from * 4 times more, 5ch, miss 2dc, ss to first dc. 6 loops.
3rd round Into each loop work 1dc, 1htr, 3tr, 1htr and 1dc, ending with ss into first dc.
4th round *5ch, inserting hook from behind work 1dc into next dc on 2nd round, rep from * 4 times more, 5ch, ss into first dc.
5th round Into each loop work 1dc, 1htr, 5tr, 1htr, 1dc.
6th round 1dc into first dc of next petal, *4ch, 1dc into 3rd ch from hook – called 1 picot – 5ch, 1 picot, 2ch, 1dc into centre tr of same petal, 4ch, 1 picot, 5ch, 1 picot, 2ch, 1dc into first dc of next petal, rep from * all round, omitting 1dc at end of last rep, ss into first dc.
7th round Ss to centre ch between
first 2 picots, 1dc into this ch, *8ch, 1dc into centre ch between next 2 picots, turn, 3ch, 9tr into 8ch loop, 1tr into dc, turn, 4ch, miss first 2tr, 1tr into next tr, **1ch, miss 1tr, 1tr into next tr, rep from ** twice more, 1ch, miss 1tr, 1tr into 3rd of 3ch, 4ch, 1 picot, 2ch, 1dc into same place as next dc, (4ch, 1 picot, 5ch, 1 picot, 2ch, 1dc into centre ch between next 2 picots) twice, rep from * 3 times more, omitting 1dc at end of last rep, ss into first dc.
8th round Ss up side of gr and along to 3rd of 4ch, 1dc into ch sp, *4ch, 1 picot, 5ch, 1 picot, 2ch, miss 1sp, 1dc into next sp, 4ch, 1 picot, 5ch, 1 picot, 2ch, miss 1sp, 1dc into next sp, (4ch, 1 picot, 5ch, 1 picot, 2ch, 1dc into centre ch between next 2 picots) twice, 4ch, 1 picot, 5ch, 1 picot, 2ch, 1dc into first ch sp of next gr, rep from * 3 times more, omitting 1dc at end of last rep, ss into first dc.
Fasten off.

To finish
Make 44 squares in A, 14 squares in B and 5 squares in C. Darn in all ends. Press each square under a damp cloth using a warm iron and omitting centre flower. Sew squares together by joining at picots, using A. Join in colour sequence as shown in chart.
Fringe Cut yarn into 45.5cm *(18in)* lengths. Taking six strands together, knot into the centre of a picot loop. Work all round three sides of the bedspread in this way.

U.S. technique

Size
About 229cm by 178cm *(90in by 70in)*, excluding fringe
Fringe About 18cm *(7in)*

Tension
Motif measures 25.5cm *(10in)* square

Materials
4 ply knitting worsted
15 x 100g *(4oz)* skeins A Green
4 x 100g *(4oz)* skeins B Dark Brown
2 x 100g *(4oz)* skeins C Yellow
Fringe 2 x 100g *(4oz)* skeins A
Aluminium crochet hook

Motif
Using crochet hook and leaving a

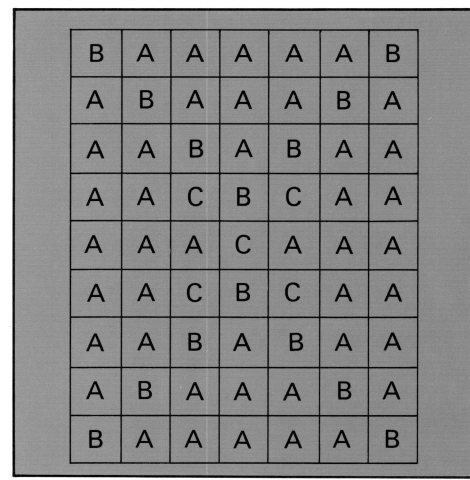

B	A	A	A	A	A	B
A	B	A	A	A	B	A
A	A	B	A	B	A	A
A	A	C	B	C	A	A
A	A	A	C	A	A	A
A	A	C	B	C	A	A
A	A	B	A	B	A	A
A	B	A	A	A	B	A
B	A	A	A	A	A	B

10cm *(4in)* end of yarn, make 8ch, join with ss to first ch to form a ring.

1st round Wind 10cm *(4in)* length round into ring with ch and work 18sc into ring over ch and yarn, join with ss to first sc.

2nd round 1sc into same place as ss, *5ch, miss 2sc, 1sc into next sc, rep from * 4 times more, 5ch, miss 2sc, ss to first sc, 6 loops.

3rd round Into each loop work 1sc, 1hdc, 3dc, 1hdc and 1sc, ending with ss into first sc.

4th round *5ch, inserting hook from behind work 1sc into next sc on 2nd round, rep from * 4 times more, 5ch, ss into first sc.

5th round Into each loop work 1sc, 1hdc, 5dc, 1hdc, 1sc.

6th round 1sc into first sc of next petal, *4ch, 1sc into 3rd ch from hook – called 1 picot – 5ch, 1 picot, 2ch, 1sc into centre dc of same petal, 4ch, 1 picot, 5ch, 1 picot, 2ch, 1sc into first sc of next petal, rep from * all round, omitting 1sc at end of last rep, ss into first sc.

7th round Ss to centre ch between first 2 picots, 1sc into this ch, *8ch, 1sc into centre ch between next 2 picots, turn, 3ch, 9dc into 8ch loop, 1dc into sc, turn, 4ch, miss first 2dc, 1dc into next dc, **1ch, miss 1dc, 1dc into next dc, rep from ** twice more, 1ch, miss 1dc, 1dc into 3rd of 3ch, 4ch, 1 picot, 2ch, 1sc into same place as next sc, (4 ch, 1 picot, 5ch, 4 picot, 2ch, 1sc into centre ch between next 2 picots) twice, rep from * 3 times more, omitting 1sc at end of last rep, ss into first sc.

8th round Ss up side of gr and along to 3rd of 4ch, 1sc into ch sp, *4ch, 1 picot, 5ch, 1 picot, 2ch, miss 1sp, 1sc into next sp, 4ch, 1 picot, 5ch, 1 picot, 2ch, miss 1sp, 1sc into next sp, (4ch, 1 picot, 5ch, 1 picot, 2ch, 1sc into centre ch between next 2 picots) twice, 4ch, 1 picot, 5ch, 1 picot, 2ch, 1sc into first ch sp of next gr, rep from * 3 times more, omitting 1sc at end of last rep, ss into first sc.

Fasten off.

Crochet lace

This delicate dressing table set looks pretty in both traditional and modern settings.

U.K. technique
Sizes
Side mats About 16cm *(6¼in)* diameter
Centre mat About 26.5cm *(10½in)* diameter

Tension
First 3 rounds measure about 5cm *(2in)* diameter worked on No. 1.25 crochet hook

Materials
Coats Mercer Crochet No. 20 2 balls
One No. 1.25 crochet hook

Side mat
Using No. 1.25 hook, make 7ch, join with ss to form a ring.
1st round 2ch, leaving last loop of each on hook work 2tr into ring, yrh and draw through all loops on hook – called 2tr cl –, *5ch, leaving last loop of each on hook work 3tr into ring, yrh and draw through all loops on hook – called 3tr cl –, rep from * 5 times more, 2ch, 1tr into first cl.
2nd round 6ch, 1tr into last st on previous round, *6ch, (1tr, 3ch, 1tr) into centre ch of next loop, rep from * ending with 6ch, ss into 3rd of first 6ch.
3rd round Ss into first loop, 3ch, leaving last loop of each on hook work 2dtr into same loop – called 2dtr cl –, 5ch, leaving last loop of each on hook work 3dtr into same loop – called 3dtr cl –, *3ch, 1dc into next loop, 3ch, (3dtr cl, 5ch, 3dtr cl) into next loop, rep from * ending with 3ch, 1dc into next loop, 3ch, ss into first cl.
4th round Ss into each of next 3ch, 1dc into same loop, *12ch, 1dc into next 5ch loop, rep from * ending with 12ch, ss into first dc.
5th round *14dc into next 12ch loop, rep from * all round, ss into first dc.
6th round Ss into each of next 2dc, 1dc into next dc, *9ch, miss 6dc, 1dc into next dc, rep from * ending with 4ch, 1tr tr into first dc.
7th round As 2nd.
8th round Ss into first loop, 3ch, (2dtr cl, 5ch, 3dtr cl) into same loop, *3ch, 1dc into next loop, 3ch, 3dtr cl into next loop, 4ch, leaving last loop of each on hook work 1 quad tr into same loop and 2dtr into centre of quad tr, yrh and draw through all loops on hook – called 1 stem and leaf –, 4ch, 1 stem and leaf into centre of previous quad tr, 7ch, 3dtr cl into same place as last leaf, 4ch, 3dtr cl into base of previous quad tr, 4ch, 3dtr cl into same loop – called 1 large point –, 3ch, 1dc into next loop, 3ch, (3dtr cl, 5ch, 3dtr cl) into next loop – called 4 small point –, rep from * omitting small point at end of last rep, ss into first cl.
9th round 1dc into same place as ss, 3ch, ss into last dc – called 1 picot –, *(4dc, 1 picot, 3dc) into next loop, 1dc into next cl, 1 picot, 2dc into next loop, insert hook into same loop and draw yarn through, insert hook into next loop and draw yarn through, yrh and draw through all loops on hook – called 1 joint dc –, 2dc into same loop, (1dc into next cl, 1 picot, 4dc into next loop) twice, 1dc into next cl, 1 picot, (5dc, 1 picot, 4dc) into next loop, (1dc into next cl, 1 picot, 4dc into next loop) twice, 1dc into next cl, 1 picot, 2dc into next loop, 1 joint dc over same loop and next loop, 2dc into same loop, 1dc into next cl, 1 picot, rep from * omitting 1dc and 1 picot at end of last rep, ss into first dc. Fasten off.
Make a second mat the same.

Centre mat
Centre section
Work as given for Side Mat to end.

First motif
Using No. 1.25 hook, make 6ch, join with ss to form a ring.
1st round 2ch, 2tr cl into ring, *5ch, 3tr cl into ring, rep from * 4 times more, 2ch, 1tr into first cl.

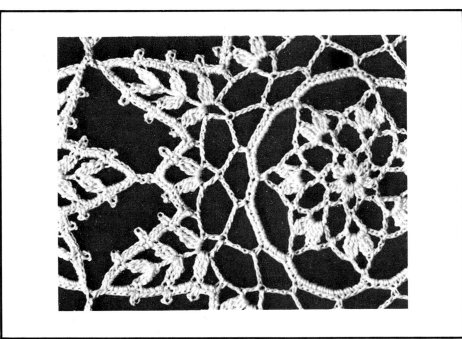

Above: As light and lacy as real snowflakes, this pretty dressing table set is ultra-feminine, and an ideal background to delicate porcelain or china.

Opposite: A detail of the pattern, giving a close-up view of the snowflake motif.

2nd round As 2nd round of Side Mat.

3rd round Ss into first loop, 3ch, (2dtr cl, 4ch, 1 stem and leaf) into same loop, *7ch, 3dtr cl into centre of previous quad tr, 4ch, 3dtr cl into same loop, 3ch, 1dc into next loop, 3ch, (3dtr cl, 4ch, 1 stem and leaf) into next loop, rep from * omitting 3dtr cl, 4ch and stem and leaf at end of last rep, ss into first cl.

4th round 1dc into same place as ss, 1 picot, 4dc into next loop, 1dc into next cl, 1 picot, 5dc into next loop, 1ch, ss into centre picot on any large point on centre section, 1ch, ss into last dc on first motif – called 1 joining picot –, *4dc into same loop, 1dc into next cl, 1 picot, 4dc into next loop, 1dc into next cl, 1 picot, 2dc into next loop, 1 joint dc over same loop and next loop, 2dc into same loop, 1dc into next cl, 1 picot, 4dc into next loop, 1dc into next cl, 1 picot, 5dc into next loop, * 1 joining picot into centre picot on next small point on centre section, rep from * to * once more, 1 joining picot into centre picot on next large point on centre section, (rep from * to * once more, 1 picot) 3 times, 4dc into same loop, 1dc into next cl, 1 picot, 4dc into next loop, 1dc into next cl, 1 picot, 2dc into next loop, 1 joint dc over same loop and next loop, 2dc into same loop, ss into first dc. Fasten off.

Second motif
Work as given for first motif to within first joining picot on last row, 1 joining picot into last joining picot between first motif and centre section, complete as given for first motif.
Work 5 motifs more, joining each to the previous motif and the centre section as given, and joining the last motif to the first to correspond.

To finish
Dampen and pin out to measurements. Remove pins when dry.

U.S. technique

Sizes

Side mats About 16cm *(6¼in)* diameter

Centre mat About 26.5cm *(102in)* diameter

Tension

First 3 rounds measure about 5cm *(2in)* diameter worked on No. 1.25 crochet hook

Materials

Mercerized crochet cotton #20 2 balls

One steel crochet hook #1

Side mat

Using crochet hook, make 7ch, join with ss to form a ring.

1st round 2ch, leaving last loop of each on hook work 2dc into ring, yo and draw through all loops on hook – called 2dc cl –, *5ch, leaving last loop of each on hook work 3dc into ring, yo and draw through all loops on hook – called 3dc cl –, rep from * 5 times more, 2ch, 1dc into first cl.

2nd round 6ch, 1dc into last st on previous round, *6ch, (1dc, 3ch, 1dc) into centre ch of next loop, rep from * ending with 6ch, ss into 3rd of first 6ch.

3rd round Ss into first loop, 3ch, leaving last loop of each on hook work 2tr into same loop – called 2tr cl –, 5ch, leaving last loop of each on hook work 3tr into same loop – called 3tr cl –, *3ch, 1dc into next loop, 3ch, (3tr cl, 5ch, 3tr cl) into next loop, rep from * ending with 3ch, 1sc into next loop, 3ch, ss into first cl.

4th round Ss into each of next 3ch, 1sc into same loop, *12ch, 1sc into next 5ch loop, rep from * ending with 12ch, ss into first dc.

5th round *14sc into next 12ch loop, rep from * all round, ss into first sc.

6th round Ss into each of next 2sc, 1sc into next sc, *9ch, miss 6sc, 1sc into next sc, rep from * ending with 4ch, 1dtr into first sc,

7th round As 2nd,

8th round Ss into first loop, 3ch, (2tr cl, 5ch, 3tr cl) into same loop, *3ch, 1sc into next loop, 3ch, 3tr cl into next loop, 4ch, leaving last loop of each on hook work 1 quad dc into same loop and 2tr into centre of quad dc, yo and draw through all loops on hook – called

1 stem and leaf –, 4ch, 1 stem and leaf into centre of previous quad dc, 7ch, 3tr cl into same place as last leaf, 4ch, 3tr cl into base of previous quad dc, 4ch, 3tr cl into same loop – called 1 large point –, 3ch, 1sc into next loop, 3ch, (3tr cl, 5ch, 3tr cl) into next loop – called 4 small point –, rep from * omitting small point at end of last rep, ss into first cl.

9th round 1sc into same place as ss, 3ch, ss into last sc – called 1 picot –, *(4sc, 1 picot, 3sc) into next loop, 1sc into next cl, 1 picot, 2sc into next loop, insert hook into same loop and draw yarn through, insert hook into next loop and draw yarn through, yo and draw through all loops on hook – called 1 joint sc –, 2sc into same loop, (1sc into next cl, 1 picot, 4sc into next loop) twice, 1sc into next cl, 1 picot, (5sc, 1 picot, 4sc) into next loop, (1sc into next cl, 1 picot, 4sc into next loop) twice, 1sc into next cl, 1 picot, 2sc into next loop, 1 joint sc over same loop and next loop, 2sc into same loop, 1sc into next cl, 1 picot, rep from * omitting 1sc and 1 picot at end of last rep, ss into first sc. Fasten off.

Make a second mat the same.

Centre mat

Centre section

Work as given for Side Mat to end.

First motif

Using steel crochet hook # 1, make 6ch, join with ss to form a ring.

1st round 2ch, 2dc cl into ring, *5ch, 3dc cl into ring, rep from * 4 times more, 2ch, 1dc into first cl.

2nd round As 2nd round of Side Mat.

3rd round Ss into first loop, 3ch, (2tr cl, 4ch, 1 stem and leaf) into same loop, *7ch, 3tr cl into centre of previous quad dc, 4ch, 3tr cl into same loop, 3ch, 1sc into next loop, 3ch, (3tr cl, 4ch, 1 stem and leaf) into next loop, rep from * omitting 3tr cl, 4ch and stem and leaf at end of last rep, ss into first cl.

4th round 1sc into same place as ss, 1 picot, 4sc into next loop, 1sc into next cl, 1 picot, 5sc into next loop, 1ch, ss into centre picot on any large point on centre section, 1ch, ss into last sc on first motif – called 1 joining picot –, *4sc into same loop, 1sc into next cl, 1 picot, 4sc into next loop, 1sc into next cl, 1 picot,

2sc into next loop, 1 joint sc over same loop and next loop, 2sc into same loop, 1sc into next cl, 1 picot, 4sc into next loop, 1sc into next cl, 1 picot, 5sc into next. loop, * 1 joining picot into centre picot on next small point on centre section, rep from * to * once more, 1 joining picot into centre picot on next large point on centre section, (rep from * to * once more, 1 picot) 3 times, 4sc into same loop, 1sc into next cl, 1 picot, 4sc into next loop, 1sc into next cl, 1 picot, 2sc into next loop, 1 joint sc over same loop and next loop, 2sc into same loop, ss into first sc. Fasten off.

Second motif

Work as given for first motif to within first joining picot on last row, 1 joining picot into last joining picot between first motif and centre section, complete as given for first motif.

Work 5 motifs more, joining each to the previous motif and the centre section as given, and joining the last motif to the first to correspond.

To finish

Dampen and pin out to measurements. Remove pins when dry.

Lace curtain

This finely crocheted curtain creates a pretty filigree against a window. Worked here to fairly small dimensions, the curtain could easily be made much larger. It could also be extended for use as a bedspread, possibly in a slightly thicker yarn.

U.K. technique
Size
75cm by 100cm *(30in by 40in)* excluding top casing.

Tension
Each motif measures 6cm *(2½in)* square.

Materials
Coats Mercer Crochet No. 20, 10 x 20g balls
One No. 1.25 crochet hook

First motif
Using No. 1.25 hook, make 23ch.
1st row 1tr into 8th ch from hook, *2ch, miss 2ch, 1tr into next ch, rep from * to end, 5ch, turn.
2nd row Miss first tr, *1tr into next tr, 2ch, rep from * 4 times more, miss 2ch, 1tr into next ch, 5ch, turn.
Rep last row 4 times more, omitting turning ch at end of last row.
7th row Working along side, 2dc over last tr worked, (1dc into base of same tr, 2dc over next row end, 1dc into top of next tr, 2dc over same tr) twice, 1dc into base of same tr, 5dc into corner sp, (1dc into base of next tr, 2dc into next sp) 4 times, 1dc into base of next tr, 5dc into corner sp, complete rem 2 sides to correspond, ending with 3dc into last corner sp, ss into first dc.
8th row 1dc into same place as ss, 1dc into each of next 2dc, *(5ch, 1dc into 4th ch from hook – called 1 picot –) 5 times, 1ch, miss 11dc, 1 dc into each of next 7dc, rep from *, ending last rep with 4dc, ss into first dc.
9th row 1dc into same place as ss, *(6ch, 1 picot) twice, 2ch, miss next picot, 1dc into next picot, rep from * twice more, omitting 1dc at end of last rep, miss 2dc, 1dc into each of next 3dc, rep from *, ending last rep with 2dc, ss into first dc.
Fasten off.

Second motif
Work as first motif for 8 rows.
9th row 1dc into same place as ss, (6ch, 1 picot) twice, 2ch, miss next picot, 1dc into next picot, 6ch, 1 picot, 4ch, ss into corresponding picot on first motif, 1ch, 1dc into 3rd of previous 4ch – called 1 joining picot –, 2ch, miss next picot on second motif, 1dc into next picot, (4ch, 1 joining picot into next picot on first motif) twice, 2ch, miss 2dc on second motif, 1dc into each of next 3dc, (4ch, 1 joining picot into next picot on first motif) twice, 2ch, miss next picot on second motif, 1dc into next picot, 4ch, 1 joining picot into next picot on first motif, 6ch, 1 picot, 2ch, miss next picot on second motif, 1dc into next picot, complete as for first motif.
Make 16 rows of 12 motifs each, or required number, joining adjacent sides in the same way as given.

Casing
1st row With RS facing, rejoin yarn at top right-hand corner to 7th picot before the joining of the corner motif to the next motif along, 9ch, *1tr into next picot, 4ch, 1dc into next picot, 4ch, 1dc into next picot, 5ch, (1dc into next picot, 4ch) twice, 1tr into next picot, 5ch, rep from *, ending last rep with 4ch, 1dtr into next picot, 1ch, turn.
2nd row 1dc into first dtr, 4dc into next sp, *1dc into next tr, (4dc into next sp, 1dc into next dc) twice, 5dc into next sp, (1dc into next dc, 4dc into next sp) twice, 1dc into next tr,

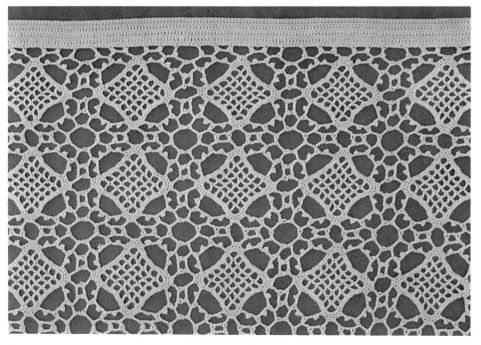

Top: A detail of the lace curtain pattern shows the casing at the top to which rings are attached.

5dc into next sp, rep from *, ending last rep with 4dc, 1dc into 4th of 7ch, 3ch, turn.
3rd row Miss first dc, 1tr into each dc to end, 3ch, turn.
4th row Miss first tr, 1tr into each tr to end, 1tr into 3rd of 3ch, 3ch, turn.
5th and 6th rows As 4th.
7th row Miss first tr, 1tr into back loop of each tr to end, 1tr into 3rd of 3ch, 3ch, turn.
8th-10th rows As 4th, omitting turning ch at end of last row.
Fasten off.

To finish
Pin out to measurements on a clean, flat surface.
Cover with a damp cloth and leave until completely dry. Remove pins, fold last 4 rows of casing to WS and slip stitch in place to row of dc to form casing.

U.S. technique

Size

76cm by 102cm (*30in by 40in*) excluding top casing.

Tension for this design

Each motif measures 6cm (*22in*) square.

Materials

Mercerized crochet cotton # 20
10 x 20g balls
Steel crochet hook # 1

First motif

Using crochet hook, make 23ch.

1st row 1dc into 8th ch from hook, *2ch, miss 2ch, 1dc into next ch, rep from * to end, 5ch, turn.

2nd row Miss first dc, *1dc into next dc, 2ch, rep from * 4 times more, miss 2ch, 1dc into next ch, 5ch, turn.
Rep last row 4 times more, omitting turning ch at end of last row.

7th row Working along side, 2sc over last dc worked, (1sc into base of same dc, 2sc over next row end, 1sc into top of next dc, 2sc over same dc) twice, 1sc into base of same dc, 5sc into corner sp, (1sc into base of next dc, 2sc into next sp) 4 times, 1sc into base of next dc, 5sc into corner sp, complete rem 2 sides to correspond, ending with 3sc into last corner sp, ss into first sc.

8th row 1sc into same place as ss, 1sc into each of next 2sc, *(5ch, 1sc into 4th ch from hook – called 1 picot–) 5 times, 1ch, miss 11sc, 1 sc into each of next 7sc, rep from *, ending last rep with 4sc, ss into first sc.

9th row 1sc into same place as ss, *(6ch, 1 picot) twice, 2ch, miss next picot, 1sc into next picot, rep from * twice more, omitting 1sc at end of last rep, miss 2sc, 1sc into each of next 3sc, rep from *, ending last rep with 2sc, ss into first sc.
Fasten off.

Second motif

9th row 1sc into same place as ss, (6ch, 1 picot) twice, 2ch, miss next picot, 1sc into next picot, 6ch, 1 picot, 4ch, ss into corresponding picot on first motif, 1ch, 1sc into 3rd of previous 4ch – called 1 joining picot –, 2ch, miss next picot on second motif, 1sc into next picot, (4ch, 1 joining picot into next picot on first motif) twice, 2ch, miss 2sc on second motif, 1sc into each of next 3sc, (4ch, 1 joining picot into next picot on first motif) twice, 2ch,

miss next picot on second motif, 1sc into next picot, 4ch, 1 joining picot into next picot on first motif, 6ch, 1 picot, 2ch, miss next picot on second motif, 1sc into next picot, complete as for first motif.
Make 16 rows of 12 motifs each, or required number, joining adjacent sides in the same way as given.

Casing

1st row With RS facing, rejoin yarn at top right-hand corner to 7th picot before the joining of the corner motif to the next motif along, 9ch, *1dc into next picot, 4ch, 1sc into next picot, 4ch, 1sc into next picot, 5ch, (1sc into next picot, 4ch) twice, 1dc into next picot, 5ch, rep from *, ending last rep with 4ch, 1tr into next picot, 1ch, turn.

2nd row 1sc into first tr, 4sc into next sp, *1sc into next dc, (4sc into next sp, 1sc into next sc) twice, 5sc into next sp, (1sc into next sc, 4sc into next sp) twice, 1sc into next dc 5sc into next sp, rep from *, ending last rep with 4sc, 1sc into 4th of 7ch, 3ch, turn.

3rd row Miss first sc, 1dc into each sc to end, 3ch, turn.

4th row Miss first dc, 1dc into each dc to end, 1dc into 3rd of 3ch, 3ch, turn.

5th and 6th rows As 4th.

7th row Miss first dc, 1dc into back loop of each dc to end, 1dc into 3rd of 3ch, 3ch, turn.

8th-10th rows As 4th, omitting turning ch at end of last row.
Fasten off.

To finish

Pin out to measurements on a clean, flat surface.
Cover with a damp cloth and leave until completely dry. Remove pins, fold last 4 rows of casing to WS and slip stitch in place to row of sc to form casing.

Right: A magnificent yet dainty curtain in crochet lace, in a lovely filigree pattern. Versatile as well as delicate, the curtain can be made up to fit any size of window. Worked in a thicker yarn, the pattern would make a really beautiful bedspread.

Crochet shelf edging

Crochet this crisp, cotton edging to brighten up a shelf.

U.K. technique
Size
Depth of edging approx 10cm *(4in)*

Tension
20 sps and 2 patt rows to 10cm *(4in)* over patt worked on No. 1.25 crochet hook

Materials
Coats Mercer Crochet Cotton No. 20 Approx 10½ scallops can be worked from 20g *(1oz)* ball
One No. 1.25 crochet hook

Edging
Using No. 1.25 hook make 42ch.

1st row Into 4th ch from hook work 1tr, 1tr into each of next 2ch, (1 block made), 3ch, miss 2ch, 1dc into next ch, 3ch, miss 2ch, 1tr into next ch, (1 lacet made), 1tr into each of next 3ch, (1 block made), (2ch, miss 2ch, 1tr into next ch) 7 times, (7 spaces made), 1tr into each of last 6ch, (2 blocks made). Turn.

2nd row 5ch, into 4th ch from hook work 1tr, 1tr into next ch, 1tr into next tr, (1 block inc), 1tr into each of next 6tr, (2 blocks over 2 blocks), 2tr into next sp, 1tr into next tr, (1 block over sp), (2ch, tr into next tr) 6 times, (6 sps over 6 sps), 1tr into each of next 3tr, (1 block over 1 block), 5ch, 1tr into next tr, (1 bar made over 1 lacet), 1tr into each of next 2tr, 1tr into 3rd of first 3ch, (1 block over 1 block). Turn

3rd row 3ch to count as first tr, miss first tr, 1tr into each of next 3tr, (1 block over 1 block), 3ch, miss 2ch, 1dc into next ch, 3ch, miss 2ch, 1tr into next tr, (1 lacet made over 1 bar), work 1 block, 6 sps, 1 block, 3ch, miss 2tr, 1dc into next tr, 3ch, miss 2tr, 1tr into next tr, (1 lacet made over 2 blocks), work 1 block. Turn.

4th row 8ch, into 4th ch from hook work 1tr, 1tr into each of next 4ch, 1tr into next tr, (2 blocks inc), work as given in diagram to end of row. Turn.

5th and 6th rows Work as given in diagram.

7th row Work 1 block, 1 lacet, 1 block, 1 sp, 2 blocks, 5 lacets, 1tr into each of next 2tr, yrh, insert hook into next ch and draw loop through, yrh and draw through one loop on hook, (1 foundation ch made), (yrh and draw through 2 loops on hook) twice, *yrh, insert hook into foundation ch and draw loop through, yrh and draw through one loop on hook, (1 foundation ch made), complete as for tr, *, rep from * to * twice more, (1 block inc at end of row). Turn.

8th row Work as given in diagram.

9th row Work 1 block, 1 lacet, 1 block, 1 sp, 2ch, miss 2tr, 1tr into next tr, (1 sp made over 1 block), work 1 block, 5tr over next 5ch sp, 1tr into next tr, (2 blocks made over 1 bar), work 3 lacets, 3 blocks. Turn.

10th row Ss into each of first 7tr, (2 blocks dec), 3ch to count as first tr, work 1 block, 3 bars, 1 block, 4 sps, 1 block, 1 bar, 1 block. Turn.

11th to 14th rows Work as given in diagram.

These 14 rows form patt and are rep throughout. Cont in patt until edging is required length. Fasten off.

To finish
Press under a damp cloth with a warm iron.

U.S. technique
Size
Depth of edging approx 10cm *(4in)*
Tension
20 sps and 2p rows to 10cm *(3.9in)* over patt worked on steel crochet hook # 1

Materials
Mercerized crochet cotton # 20 Approx 10½ scallops can be worked from 1 by 20g ball
Steel crochet hook # 1

Edging
Using steel crochet hook # 1 make 42ch.

1st row Into 4ch ch from hook work 1dc, 1dc into each of next 2ch, (1 block made), 3ch, miss 2ch, 1sc into next ch, 3ch, miss 2ch, 1dc into next ch, (1 lacet made), 1dc into each of next 3ch, (1 block made), (2ch, miss 2ch, 1dc into next ch) 7 times, (7 spaces made), 1dc into each of last 6ch, (2 blocks made). Turn.

2nd row 5ch, into 4th ch from hook work 1dc, 1dc into next ch, 1dc into next dc, (1 block inc), 1dc into each of next 6dc, (2 blocks over 2 blocks), 2dc into next sp, 1dc into next dc, (1 block over sp), (2ch, into next dc) 6 times, (6 sps over 6 sps), 1dc into each of next 3dc, (1 block over 1 block), 5ch, 1dc into next dc, (1 bar made over 1 lacet), 1dc into each of next 2dc, 1dc into 3rd of first 3ch, (1 block over 1 block). Turn.

3rd row 3ch to count as first dc, miss first dc, 1dc into each of next 3dc, (1 block over 1 block), 3ch, miss 2ch, 1sc into next ch, 3ch, miss 2ch, 1dc into next dc, (1 lacet made over 1 bar), work 1 block, 6 sps, 1 block, 3ch, miss 2dc, 1sc into next dc, 3ch, miss 2dc, 1dc into next dc, (1 lacet made over 2 blocks), work 1 block. Turn.

4th row 8ch, into 4th ch from hook work 1 dc, 1dc into each of next 4ch, 1dc into next dc, (2 blocks inc), work as given in diagram to end of row. Turn.

5th and 6th rows Work as given in diagram.

7th row Work 1 block, 1 lacet, 1 block, 1 sp, 2 blocks, 5 lacets, 1dc into each of next 2dc, yo, insert hook into next ch, and draw loop through, yo and draw through one loop on hook, (1 foundation ch made), (yo and draw through 2 loops on hook) twice, *yo, insert hook into foundation ch and draw loop through yo and draw through one loop on hook, (1 foundation ch made), complete as for dc, *, rep from * to * twice more, (1 block inc

Right: A crisp shelf edging adds a country cottage effect to shelves and dressers, and really shows off pretty china. The same edging could be used as a lacy trim on a peasant skirt, and on various household linens.

at end of row). Turn.

8th row Work as given in diagram.

9th row Work 1 block, 1 lacet, 1 block, 1 sp, 2ch, miss 2dc, 1dc into next dc, (1 sp made over 1 block), work 1 block, 5dc over next 5ch sp, 1dc into next dc, (2 blocks made over 1 bar), work 3 lacets, 3 blocks. Turn.

10th row Ss into each of first 7dc, (2 blocks ec), 3ch to count as first dc, work 1 block, 3 bars, 1 block, 4 sps, 1 block, 1 bar, a block. Turn.

11th – 14th rows Work as given in diagram.

These 14 rows form patt and are rep throughout. Cont in patt until edging is required length. Fasten off.

To finish

Press under a damp cloth with a warm iron.

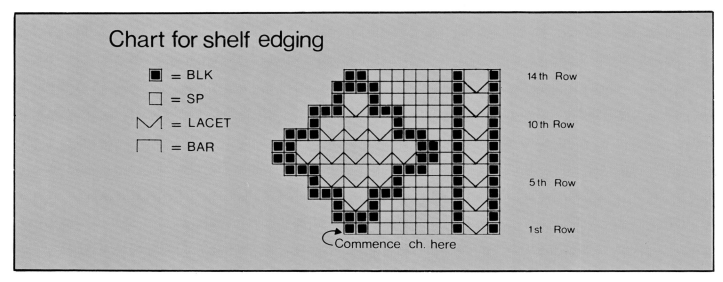

Chart for shelf edging

- ■ = BLK
- □ = SP
- ⋁ = LACET
- ⊓ = BAR

14 th Row

10th Row

5th Row

1st Row

Commence ch. here

Edwardian mat

The hexagonal coffee table mat is formed by linking delicate snowflake motifs. The design of the motif is adapted from Edwardian lace.

U.K. technique

Size
Width at widest points, about 56cm (22in).

Tension
Each motif is about 6cm (2½in).

Materials
Coats Mercer Crochet No. 20 x 5 balls
One No. 1.50 crochet hook

First motif
Using No. 1.50 hook, make 10ch. Join with ss to form a ring.
1st round 4ch, (1tr into ring, 1ch) 11 times, ss into 3rd of 4ch.
1st row 13ch, 1tr into 4th ch from hook, placing hook round length of ch for each st work 12tr over ch, *1tr into next 1ch sp on first round, 7ch, turn.
2nd row 1tr into 7th tr of previous row, (1ch, miss 1tr, 1tr into next tr) 3 times, 4ch, turn.
3rd row (1tr into next 1ch sp, 1ch) 3 times, 13tr into 7ch loop.
Rep from * 10 times more
Ss into 3rd of first 13ch, turn, ss across each of first 7tr of previous row, 3ch, ss into base of turning ch at outer edge of first row, (1ch, miss 1tr, 1tr into next tr) 3 times, 4ch, turn, (1tr into next 1ch sp, 1ch) 3 times, ss into top of turning ch at outer edge of first row. Fasten off.

Second motif
Work as given for first motif to end of first row.
2nd row 1tr into 7th tr of previous row, (1ch, miss 1tr, 1tr into next tr) 3 times, 3ch, ss into corresponding 4ch at outer edge of any row of first motif, 1ch, complete row on second motif as before.
Join the following row of the second motif to the corresponding row of the first motif in the same way, then complete the second motif as given for the first motif.
Make a row of five motifs in all.
Make a second row of six motifs, joining each one to the previous motif and also to two points on each

motif of the first row.
Continue in this way until there are 61 motifs in all, joined to form a hexagon as shown in the illustration.

Edging
With RS facing, rejoin yarn at 4ch loop on outer edge of the first free row on any motif, 5dc into 4ch loop, *7ch, 5dc into next free 4ch loop, rep from * all round, ending with 7ch, ss into first dc.
2nd round 3ch, *13tr into next 7ch loop, rep from * all round, ending with 12tr into last 7ch loop, ss into 3rd of 3ch.
3rd round 4ch, *miss first tr of next 13tr gr, (1tr into next tr, 1ch, miss 1tr) 6 times, rep from * into each 13tr gr all round except when the 13tr gr links two motifs work instead miss 2tr, (1tr into next tr, 1ch, miss 1tr) 5 times, and ending with ss into 3rd of first 4ch. Fasten off.

To finish
Press under a damp cloth, using a warm iron.

U.S. technique

Size
Width at widest point, about 56cm (22in)

Tension
Each motif measures about 6cm (2¼in)

Materials
Mercerized crochet cotton # 20 5 balls
Steel crochet hook # 0

First motif
Using crochet hook, make 10ch. Join with ss to form a ring.
1st round 4ch, (1dc into ring, 1ch) 11 times, ss into 3rd of 4ch.
1st row 13ch, 1dc into 4th ch from hook, placing hook round length of ch for each st work 12dc over ch, *1dc into next 1ch sp on first round, 7ch, turn.
2nd row 1dc into 7th dc of previous row, (1ch, miss 1dc, 1dc into next dc) 3 times, 4ch, turn.
3rd row (1dc into next 1ch sp, 1ch) 3 times, 13dc into 7ch loop.

Rep from * 10 times more.
Ss into 3rd of first 13ch.
Ss into 3rd of first 13ch, turn, ss across each of first 7dc of previous row, 3ch, ss into base of turning ch at outer edge of first row, (1ch, miss 1dc, 1dc into next dc) 3 times, 4ch, turn, (1dc into next 1ch sp, 1ch) 3 times, ss into top of turning ch at outer edge of first row. Fasten off.

Second motif
Work as given for First Motif to end of first row.
2nd row 1dc into 7th dc of previous row, (1ch, miss 1dc, 1dc into next dc) 3 times, 3ch, ss into corresponding 4ch at outer edge of any row of first motif, 1ch, complete row on second motif as before.
Join the following row of the second motif to the corresponding row of the First Motif in the same way, then complete the second motif as given for the First Motif.
Make a row of five motifs in all.
Make a second row of six motifs, joining each one to the previous motif and also to two points on each motif of the first row.
Continue in this way until there are 61 motifs in all, joined to form a hexagon as shown in the illustration.

Edging
With RS facing, rejoin yarn at 4ch loop on outer edge of the first free row on any motif, 5sc into 4ch loop, *7ch, 5sc into next free 4ch loop, rep from * all round, ending with 7ch, ss into first dc.
2nd round 3ch, *13dc into next 7ch loop, rep from * all round, ending with 12sc into last 7ch loop, ss into 3rd of 3ch.
3rd round 4ch, *miss first dc of next 13dc gr, (1dc into next dc, 1ch, miss 1dc) 6 times, rep from * into each 13dc gr all round except when the 13dc gr links two motifs work instead miss 2dc, (1dc into next dc, 1ch, miss 1dc) 5 times, and ending with ss into 3rd of first 4ch. Fasten off.

To finish
Press under a damp cloth, using a warm iron.

Left: An elegant table mat in a delicate snowflake pattern adapted from a piece of old Edwardian lace. Use the motifs to make larger items too.

Crochet lace shawl

For romantic evenings, an unusually patterned cobweb of a shawl. For extra sparkle, use lurex yarn.

U.K. technique

Size
Length 101cm *(40in)* at centre point, excluding fringe
Fringe about 18cm *(7in)*

Tension
23dtr to 10cm *(4in)* worked on No. 3.50 hook

Materials
Sirdar Prelude
10 x 25g balls
One No. 3.50 crochet hook

Main section
Using No. 3.50 hook, make 13ch.
1st row 1dtr into 4th ch from hook, * 1dtr into next ch, rep from * to end.
2nd row 4ch, 2dtr into first dtr, 6ch, 1dc into 6th dtr, 6ch, 3dtr into 4th of 4ch.
3rd row 4ch, 2dtr into base of ch, 6ch, 1dc into 6ch loop, 6ch, 1dc into next ch loop, 6ch, 3dtr into 4th of 4ch.
4th row 4ch, 2dtr into base of ch, 6ch, 1dc into next ch loop, 6ch, 3dtr into next ch loop, 6ch, 1dc into next ch loop, 6ch, 3dtr into 4th of 4ch.

5th row 4ch, 2dtr into base of 4ch, 6ch, 1dc into next ch loop, 6ch, 3dtr into next ch loop, 3ch, 3dtr into next ch loop, 6ch, 1dc into next ch loop, 6ch, 3dtr into 4th of 4ch
6th row 4ch, 2dtr into base of 4ch, (6ch, 1dc into next loop) twice, 6ch, 3dtr into 3ch loop, (6ch, 1dc into next ch loop) twice, 6ch, 3dtr into 4th of 4ch.
7th row 4ch, 2dtr into base of 4ch, 6ch, 1dc into next ch loop, 6ch, 3dtr into next ch loop, (6ch, 1dc into next ch loop) twice, 6ch, 3dtr into next ch loop, 6ch, 1dc into next ch loop, 6ch, 3dtr into 4th of 4ch.
8th row 4ch, 2dtr into base of 4ch, 6ch, 1dc into next ch loop, 6ch, 3dtr into next ch loop, 3ch, 3dtr into next ch loop, 6ch, 1dc into next ch loop, 6ch, 3dtr into next ch loop, 3ch, 3dtr into next ch loop, 6ch, 1dc into next ch loop, 6ch, 3dtr into 4th of 4ch.
9th row 4ch, 2dtr into base of ch, (6ch, 1dc into next ch loop) twice, 6ch, 3dtr into 3ch loop, (6ch, 1dc into next ch loop) twice, 6ch, 3dtr into 3ch loop, (6ch, 1dc into next ch loop) twice, 6ch, 3dtr into 4th of 4ch.
10th row 4ch, 2dtr into base of 4ch, 6ch, 1dc into next ch loop, 6ch, 3dtr into next ch loop, * ((6ch, 1dc into next ch loop) twice, 6ch, 3dtr into next ch loop, rep from * once more,

6ch, 1dc into next ch loop, 6ch, 3dtr into 4th of 4ch
11th row 4ch, 2dtr into base of 4ch, *6ch, 1dc into next ch loop, 6ch, 3dtr into next ch loop, 3ch, 3dtr into next ch loop, rep from * twice more, 6ch, 1dc into next ch loop, 6ch, 3dtr into 4th of 4ch.
12th row 4ch, 2dtr into base of 4ch, *6ch, (1dc into next ch loop) twice, 6ch, 3dtr into 3ch loop, rep from * twice more, (6ch, 1dc into next ch loop) twice, 6ch, 3dtr into 4th of 4ch. Continue in this way making an extra diamond motif on every third row by positioning the lower 3dtr gr of each motif over the centre 6ch loop of each gr of three 6ch loops on previous row, until 61 rows have been worked in all. Fasten off.

Edging
With RS facing, rejoin yarn to top left-hand corner of shawl at edge dtr.
1st round 6ch, 1dc into base of same dtr, 3ch, 1dc into first of 3ch – called 1 picot –, 1dc into same place, *6ch, (1dc, 1 picot, 1dc) into base of edge dtr on the row below, rep from * down side edge of shawl to point, 6ch, (1dc, 1 picot, 1dc) into base of 6th dtr of first row, 6ch, (1dc, 1 picot, 1dc) into opposite edge dtr of first row, continue up second side of

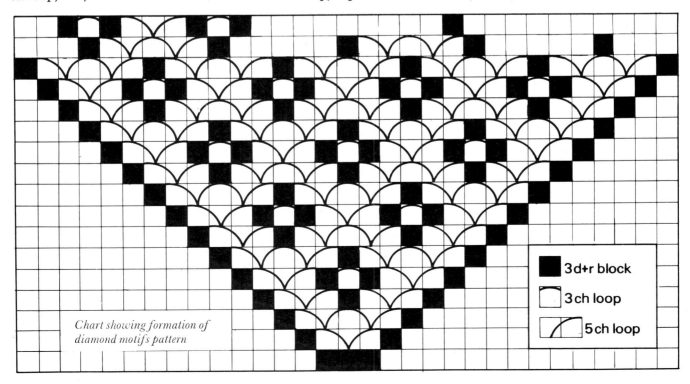

Chart showing formation of diamond motifs pattern

3d+r block

3ch loop

5ch loop

rows

15 14 13 12 11 10 9 8 7 6 5 4 3 2 1

shawl to correspond with first side to right-hand corner, ending with (1dc, 1 picot, 1dc) into top of edge dtr on 61st row, *6ch, (1dc, 1 picot, 1dc) into next 6ch loop, rep from * to beg of round, ending with (1dc, 1 picot, 1dc) into base of first 6ch.

2nd round Ss to 3rd of 6ch, (1dc, 1 picot, 1dc) into 6ch loop, *5ch, (1dc, 1 picot, a dc) into next 6ch loop, rep from * all round, and working an extra (1dc, 1 picot, 1dc) into corner picot at each end of top edge.

Fringing

Cut lengths of yarn each 51cm *(20in)* and knot ten strands together into first and every alt ch loop down side edges and every ch loop across the base.

Work 2 rows of alternated overhand knots by knotting five strands of the first fringe together with five strands of the next fringe and with each row 4cm *(1½in)* down the strands. Trim fringes evenly.

Size

Length 102cm *(40in)* at centre point, excluding fringe

Fringe about 18cm *(7in)*

Tension

23tr to 10cm *(4in)* worked on Aluminium crochet hook # E

Materials

Medium weight lurex yarn
5 x 50g (2oz) balls
Aluminium crochet hook # E

Main section

Using crochet hook, make 13ch.

1st row 1tr into 4th ch from hook, * 1tr into next chs rep from * to end.

2nd row 4ch, 2tr into first tr, 6ch, 1sc into 6th tr, 6ch 3tr into 4th of 4ch.

3rd row 4ch, 2tr into base of ch, 6ch, 1sc into 6ch loop, 6ch, 1sc into next ch loop, 6ch, 3tr into 4th of 4ch.

4th row 4ch, 2tr into base of ch, 6ch, 1 sc into next ch loop, 6ch, 3tr into next ch loop, 6ch, 1sc into next ch loop, 6ch, 3tr into 4th of 4ch.

5th row 4ch, 2tr into base of 4ch, 6ch, 1sc into next ch loop, 6ch, 3tr into next ch loop, 3ch, 3tr into next ch loop, 6ch, 1sc into next ch loop, 6ch, 3tr into 4th of 4ch.

6th row 4ch, 2tr into base of 4ch, (6ch, 1sc into next loop) twice, 6ch, 3tr into 3ch loop, (6ch, 1sc into next ch loop) twice, 6ch, 3tr into 4th of 4ch.

7th row 4ch, 2tr into base of 4ch, 6ch, 1sc into next ch loop, 6ch, 3tr into next ch loop, (6ch, 1sc into next ch loop) twice, 6ch, 3tr into next ch loop, 6ch, 1sc into next ch loop, 6ch, 3tr into 4th of 4ch.

8th row 4ch, 2tr into base of 4ch, 6ch, 1sc into next ch loop, 6ch, 3tr into next ch loop, 3ch, 3tr into next ch loop, 6ch, 1sc into next ch loop, 6ch, 3tr into next ch loop, 3ch, 3tr into next ch loop, 6ch, 1sc into next ch loop, 6ch, 3tr into 4th of 4ch.

9th row 4ch, 2tr into base of ch, (6ch, 1sc into next ch loop) twice, 6ch, 3tr into 3ch loop, (6ch, 1sc into next ch loop) twice, 6ch, 3tr into 3ch loop, (6ch, 1sc into next ch loop) twice, 6ch, 3tr into 4th of 4ch.

10th row 4ch, 2tr into base of 4ch, 6ch, 1sc into next ch loop, 6ch, 3tr into next ch loop, * (6ch, 1sc into next ch loop) twice, 6ch, 3tr into next ch loop, rep from * once more, 6ch, 1sc into next ch loop, 6ch, 3tr into 4th of 4ch.

11th row 4ch, 2tr into base of 4ch, *6ch, 1sc into next ch loop, 6ch, 3tr into next ch loop, 3ch, 3tr into next ch loop, rep from * twice more, 6ch, 1sc into next ch loop, 6ch, 3tr into 4th of 4ch.

12th row 4ch, 2tr into base of 4ch, *6ch, (1sc into next ch loop) twice, 6ch, 3tr into 3ch loop, rep from * twice more, (6ch, 1sc into next ch loop) twice, 6ch, 3tr into 4th of 4ch. Continue in this way making an extra diamond motif on every third row by positioning the lower 3tr gr of each motif over the centre 6ch loop of each gr of three 6ch loops on previous row, until 61 rows have been worked in all. Fasten off.

Edging

With RS facing, rejoin yarn to top left-hand corner of shawl at edge tr. **1st round** 6ch, 1sc into base of same tr, 3ch, 1sc into first of 3ch – called 1 picot –, 1sc into same place, *6ch, (1sc, 1 picot, 1sc) into base of edge tr on the row below, rep from * down side edge of shawl to point, 6ch, (1sc, 1 picot, 1sc) into base of 6th tr of first row, 6ch, (1sc, 1 picot, 1sc) into opposite edge tr of first row, continue up second side of shawl to correspond with first side to right-hand corner, ending with (1sc, 1 picot, 1sc) into top of edge tr on 61st row, *6ch, (1sc, 1 picot, 1sc) into next 6ch loop, rep from * to beg of round, ending with (1sc, 1 picot, 1sc) into base of first 6ch.

2nd round Ss to 3rd of 6ch, (1sc, 1 picot, 1sc) into 6ch loop, *5ch, (1sc, 1 picot, 1sc) into next 6ch loop, rep from * all round, and working an extra (1sc, 1 picot, 1sc) into corner picot at each end of top edge.

Fringe

Cut lengths of yarn each 51cm *(20in)* and knot ten strands together into first and every alt ch loop down side edges and every ch loop across the base.

Work 2 rows of alternated overhand knots by knotting five strands of the first fringe together with five strands of the next fringe and with each row 4cm *(1½in)* down the strands. Trim fringes evenly.

Right: Gossamer light shawls are made by a few skilled Shetland Islanders. Known as 'ring shawls', they are among the finest examples of knitted lace ever known.

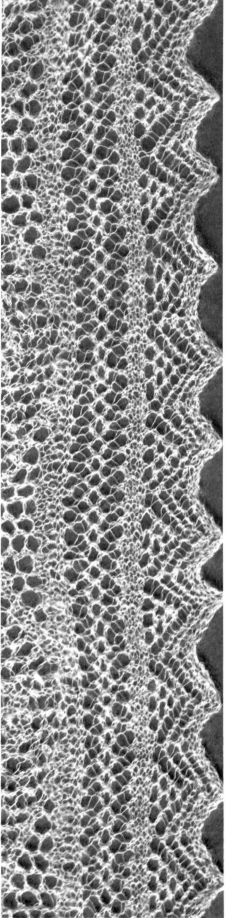

Tatting

Tatting is a simple form of lace making which is worked with one basic stitch throughout. It involves the use only of your fingers and – on large or fine pieces of work – a simple shuttle to hold the thread and a fine crochet hook to join the motifs. At its simplest, tatting can be worked as a length of loops to form an edging or as individual circles to be mounted onto fabric. At its most elaborate, it can be worked as beautiful gossamer-fine borders for fabric or as a piece of fabric itself.

Like macramé, tatting derives from the art of knotting which was popular throughout Europe in the 17th and 18th centuries. Rows of knots were worked with a shuttle and thread and the resultant cord was couched in various patterns on to fabric.

In the eighteenth century, when it was discovered how to form a fabric with this method, it evolved into what became known as tatting. Tatting became widespread as a pastime in the nineteenth century when caps, collars, cuffs, doilies and edgings for all kinds of things were made with it.

The yarn
Because it was intended to resemble other types of lace made by a more intricate method, tatting has traditionally been worked in fine threads such as linen or cotton. For delicate work these are still the best to use.

Linen lace threads are less readily available and are more expensive than cotton which is made in a variety of weights, colours and textures – both crochet cotton and pearl embroidery cotton may be used. Wool and other knitting yarns are not normally suitable for tatting, particularly for beginners, because they tend to stretch. String and cord such as used for macramé, however, are suitable for more chunky textures

Amount of yarn It is not usually easy to estimate the amount of yarn required for any particular project because this varies with the tension of the individual worker. When working a pattern in individual motifs, however, it is possible to calculate how much yarn will be required from the amount used for the first motif. To measure this, unravel several metres (yards) of yarn and make a note of the exact

measurement. Work the motif and measure the amount of yarn left. This, subtracted from the total amount, gives the length used in the motif.

Double stitch——
The stitch used throughout tatting, and the one from which all the intricate patterns evolve, is in fact a simple knot of the kind which many people use regularly about the house when tying on baggage or parcel labels without necessarily knowing the correct name: the double reverse half hitch or lark's head. When worked in tatting it is called double stitch.

This double stitch may be worked either to form a length, known as a chain, or to form rings, and most tatting patterns combine the two methods. Although the basic principle in working the chains and rings is the same, it is easier to start with a chain and progress to rings when you have learnt the knack of forming the stitch. It is advisable to start in string rather than cotton so that you can see the formation of the stitch.

To make a practice length of about 7.5cm *(3in)*, you will need:
One 60cm *(24in)* length of string and one 15cm *(6in)* length. You will find it easier to start with two different colours.

The basic knot Double the shorter piece of string, loop it round the longer piece as shown in fig.1a and pull the ends of the shorter piece through the loop. Tighten the resulting knot round the longer piece. Pick up the ends of the shorter piece and pull them straight out to the sides in opposite directions (fig.1b). Pull tightly allowing the ends of the longer piece to rise. As the length you are pulling straightens the other length will form an identical knot, known as the double stitch, around it (fig.1c).

This process shows what the basic knot looks like and how the loops are transferred. The next process shows how the knot is tied in two stages in tatting so that several stitches can be worked to form a chain.

Tying the knot in two stages
Undo the first knot and re-tie it by wrapping the shorter length over the longer one, thus forming the

Below: The simple knot shown here is the basis of all tatting
1a. Tying the basic knot
1b. Pulling ends of knot
1c. Double stitch is formed

Opposite: Tatting can make up into some really exquisite and unusual designs such as this hexagonal table mat.

1a

1b

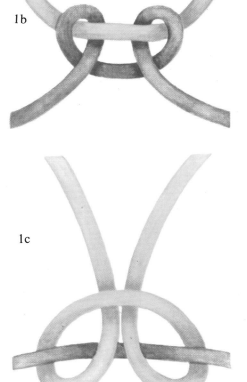

1c

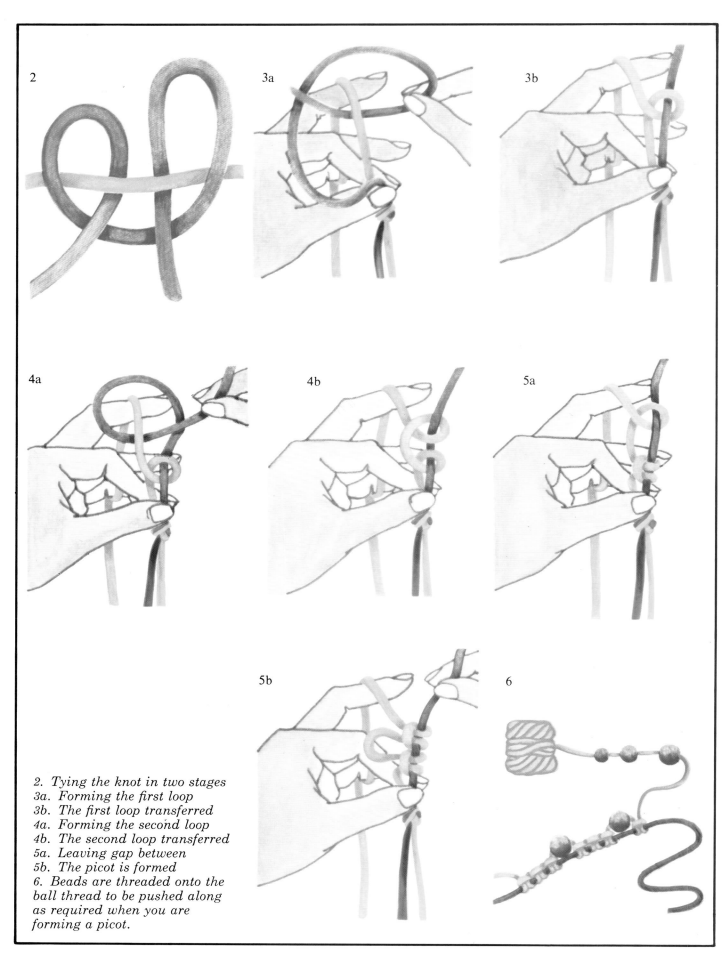

2. *Tying the knot in two stages*
3a. *Forming the first loop*
3b. *The first loop transferred*
4a. *Forming the second loop*
4b. *The second loop transferred*
5a. *Leaving gap between*
5b. *The picot is formed*
6. *Beads are threaded onto the ball thread to be pushed along as required when you are forming a picot.*

knot in two motions (fig.2).

Working over the hand Undo this second knot and tie the lengths together at one end with a simple overhand knot. Hold the knot between the fingers and thumb of your left hand and wrap the two lengths over the back of the fingers with the shorter length on the right.

Work the first half of the double stitch with the shorter length (fig.3a).

Pull the shorter length, or push the loop with your fingers, to transfer the loop so it is formed by the longer length (fig.3b). Keeping the shorter length on the right, work the second half of the stitch with it (fig.4a) and transfer the loop to the longer length (fig.4b). Push the complete stitch along to the overhand knot. Work another stitch in the same way and push along each loop when transferred to the first stitch. Continue like this for the whole chain.

Combining threads When you are working a chain to form an edging it is usually better to use threads of the same colour because a different-coloured core would show through between the stitches. However, you could use a thicker thread for the core which would prevent confusion and would also give a thicker edge for stitching the chain to fabric.

Spirals If you work chain using one half of the double stitch only, it will form an attractive spiral effect, as shown in part of the necklace in the photograph. It does not matter which half of the stitch you work as long as you are consistent.

Picots

These make a very attractive addition to double stitches by forming loops between them. Make one double stitch in the normal way, then form the first half of a second stitch, pushing this one along to first stitch to leave a gap of 12mm ($\frac{1}{2}in$) between the two (fig.5a). Complete the second half of the stitch and then push the whole stitch along to the first one (fig.5b).

You will then see that the gap left between the two stitches forms a small loop. The size of the loop can be varied by leaving a smaller or larger gap between the stitches. Any number of stitches may be worked between picots.

Adding beads An unusual variation is to hang beads from the picots. To do this, thread the beads onto the longer piece of yarn or ball thread (knot the end to prevent the beads from sliding off). Start tatting in the normal way and, when you form a picot, slide a bead along to the part of the yarn which forms the gap between the double stitches. Work the following stitch and push it along (fig.6).

Shuttles

When you develop the technique of tatting it is easier to wind the thread onto a shuttle and use this to pass the yarn which forms the loops initially (that is, before transferring them) over the other thread which can be taken direct from the ball. These are known respectively as the shuttle thread and the ball thread.

Most shuttles today are made from plastic and are about 5cm (2in) long. It is worth looking out for old shuttles in antique shops because many of these were made from ivory or even silver, with interesting designs.

Preparing the shuttle Place the end of the yarn into the notch at the centre of the shuttle and start winding the yarn round until the shuttle is full but not projecting beyond the edge. Cut the thread leaving a working length of about 40cm (16in).

Heavier yarns These are not suitable for winding onto standard-size shuttles because they may damage the opening. Instead, simply wind the yarn in a figure of eight round your fingers and secure with a rubber band. It is then easy to let out more yarn as you need it.

Below: An original chunky and bright necklace is worked in macrame twine. It is made with a chain of double stitches and spirals, and the beads are all hung from the picots.

Decorative trimming

Typical tatting designs resemble clusters of snowflakes and are formed by groups of rings arranged individually or joined by picots. The rings are worked with the same basic double stitch as used for chain although they are formed with one length of yarn instead of two (figs. 1-5). For joining rings you will also need a fine crochet hook.

Using a shuttle When working several rings which are linked, it is advisable to wind the yarn on to a shuttle. For individual rings, however, you can wind the yarn in a figure of eight to form a 'butterfly' and secure it with a rubber band.

Hold the end of the yarn between the thumb and index finger of your left hand. Pass it over the other three fingers and back underneath to form a large ring.

To make the first half of the stitch hold the shuttle or butterfly of yarn in your right hand and make a large loop over the top of the left hand. Pass the shuttle or butterfly from underneath up and through both the ring and the loop from right to left.

Transfer the loop thus formed to the ring round your hand by pulling the shuttle firmly to the right, and lowering the middle finger of the left hand. Tighten the stitch by raising the middle finger of the left hand again so that the stitch slides along the shuttle thread into position as shown. Then hold it between the thumb and index finger of the left hand.

Work the second half of the stitch by passing the shuttle downwards from left to right through the ring round the left hand, and through the loop thus formed with the shuttle thread.

Pull the shuttle thread to the right as before to transfer the loop and draw up the stitch to the first half.

By forming more double stitches in this way you will form a ring. To complete the ring, release the thread from your left hand and gently pull up the shuttle thread to close it.

Picots may be added between the double stitches as described in the introductory chapter.

To complete the ring If you are making individual rings knot the ends of the yarn together to secure the ring and cut off close to the knot.

Lampshade trimming
The lampshade in the photograph was trimmed with individually made tatted rings of varying sizes, some of which include picots to form daisy shapes. The lampshade can be of any size, and the rings made of any cotton crochet yarn of medium thickness. The rings and daisies are arranged to form a random pattern and stuck onto the lampshade.

Materials
Plain lampshade.
Cotton crochet yarn [mercerized crochet cotton 30].
Tatting shuttle (optional).
Latex adhesive [Rubber cement].

Wind several metres (yards) of the

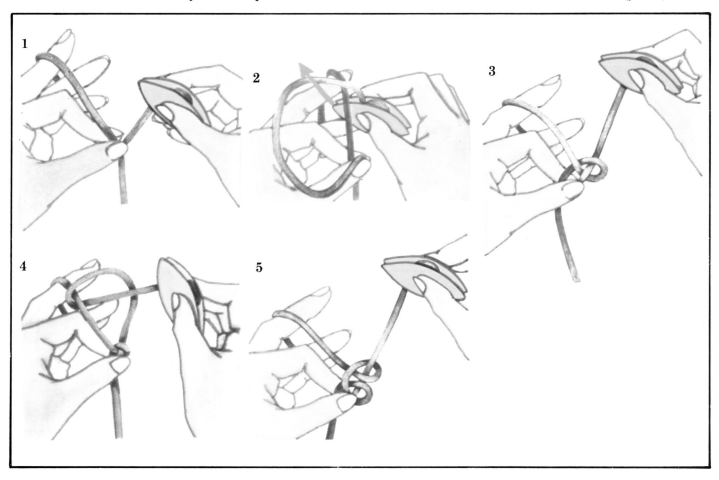

How to use the tatting shuttle
1. *Holding yarn and shuttle*
2. *First half of the stitch*
3. *Tightening the stitch*
4. *Second half of the stitch*
5. *Completing the stitch by drawing up the thread.*

Above: An elegant, classically shaped lampshade looks lovely with a trim of single rings and daisies. This is just one of the many ways in which a tatted motif can be used successfully.

yarn onto the shuttle (or tie in a butterfly) and form the rings and daisies as described below.
Large rings about 18mm (¾in) diameter. Make a ring of 20 double stitches and close it. Knot the ends of the yarn together to secure the ring and cut off close to the knot.
Medium rings about 12mm (½in) diameter. Make a ring of 14 double stitches, finish as for the large rings.
Small rings about 1cm (⅜in) diameter. Make a ring of 8 double stitches, finish as for the large rings.
Large daisies about 2.5cm (1in) diameter. Make a ring as follows: 1 double stitch, (large picot, 2 double stitches) 6 times, large picot, 1 double stitch, close ring. Tie the ends and cut close to the knot.
Small daisies about 18mm (¾in) diameter. Make a ring as following: 1 double stitch, (large picot, 2 double stitches) four times, large picot, 1 double stitch, close ring. Tie the ends and cut close to the knot.
Arrange the rings and daisies at random round the lampshade. Affix each one with a dab of adhesive,

making sure that the ends of yarn are tucked underneath.

Decorated net
Fine nets look most attractive when decorated with tatted daisies. On the net in the photograph the daisies were made in a fairly fine crochet cotton and measure 12mm (½in) in diameter. They were attached to the net with adhesive.

Materials
Net of required size.
Fine crochet cotton.
Tatting shuttle (optional).
Latex adhesive [Rubber cement].

Make each daisy as follows: 1 double stitch, (picot, 2 double stitches) 6 times, picot, 1 double stitch, close ring. Tie the ends and cut close to

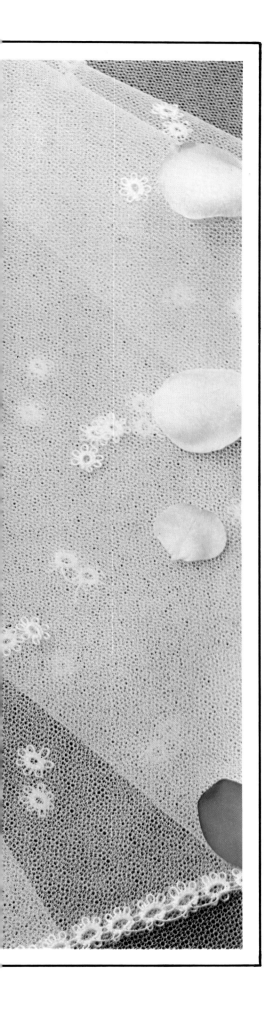

the knot. Arrange the daisies in an attractive random pattern over the net and stick on with a dab of adhesive, making sure that the ends of yarn are tucked underneath. For the edging make a continuous length of daisies to the required length, joining them as described below. Fix in place with adhesive.

Joining rings
A row of rings can be formed without a break by joining them where they touch at corresponding picots. The best way of judging which picots to use for this is, when you have worked one ring, to draw a diagram of an identical ring and place the worked ring to the left-hand side of the drawing with the ends of the yarn at the bottom. In this way one picot on the first ring will naturally touch a picot on the second ring, thus indicating which picots should be used for joining. You will also see how much yarn should be left to form the loop at the bottom between the rings (fig.6).

For example, if you are joining the daisy motifs previously described for decorating the net, the most suitable picots for joining would be the sixth one worked in the first daisy and the second picot worked in the second daisy.

Work one daisy as described for the net, do not cut off the yarn but start the second daisy with the same thread, working one double stitch. Draw up the stitch, leaving the required amount to form the loop at the bottom. Work a picot and two double stitches (fig.7).

Insert the crochet hook through the sixth picot of the first ring, draw through the loop round your hand and hold in place. Thread the shuttle thread through the loop and draw up the thread (fig.8). This join stands for a picot and forms the first half of a double stitch. The second half of the stitch is then worked in the normal way.

To complete the second daisy so that it is like the first, work one double stitch, (picot, two double) four times, picot, a double stitch, close ring. It is at this point that you will see how essential it is that the loops are transferred from the shuttle thread onto the loop round your hand when you work each stitch – if you have not done this correctly the stitches will lock and you will not be able to close the rings.

6

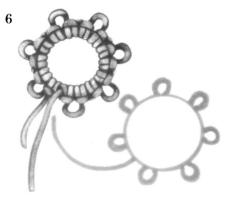

7

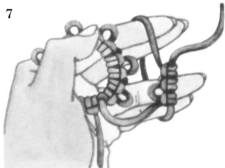

8

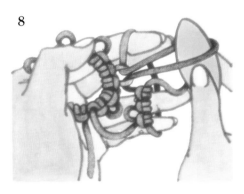

6. Placing the ring to the side of the drawing so that the picots all match up.
7. Starting the second ring
8. Joining the rings by threading the shuttle through the loop which has been pulled through the picot of the first ring.

Left: A filmy wedding veil for a memorable day, with a trim of rings and picots. The rings were worked singly and in pairs for the main area of the veil, and were joined to make a continuous strip for the edging.

Combination edgings

Some of the most attractive tatting patterns are formed by combining chains with rings. Although the chains are worked with two threads and the rings with one, it is not difficult to switch from one technique to another in a pattern, provided you remember which is the working thread and which will be forming the transferred stitches.

The easiest way of remembering this is to work with yarns of different colours, winding one colour onto the shuttle and working with the other colour direct from the ball. This produces an attractive effect, with the rings formed in the shuttle thread and the chains in the ball thread.

In many tatting patterns rings and chains are worked alternately, in which case the chain takes the place of the loop linking the rings (fig.1). The rings are also usually linked at corresponding picots.

Making a practice piece The simplest way to begin is to make a practice piece using fine string or thick crochet cotton of different colours. Wind the yarn of one colour onto a shuttle (or into a butterfly round your fingers) and use the other colour direct from the ball.

Using the shuttle alone, make a ring of three double stitches, one picot, two double stitches, one picot, three double stitches. Close the ring. Turn the ring upside down so that the shuttle is on the right. Hold the thread from the ball alongside and above the shuttle thread. Then place both the ring and the ball thread between your left thumb and forefinger and loop the ball thread

over the back of your left hand and round the little finger.

Using your shuttle, make a double stitch over the ball thread. Transfer the loops so that they are formed by the ball thread and push them up close to the ring (fig.2). Work two more double stitches, one picot and three double stitches to complete the chain. Reverse the work again so that the ring is above the chain and the shuttle is still to the right.

Leaving the ball thread hanging, use the shuttle alone to make a second ring. Start the ring with a double stitch, pushing it close to the chain. Work two more double stitches in the same way, join the ring to the second picot of the first ring and complete the ring with one double stitch, one picot and three double stitches. You will now see how the chain forms the link between the rings. Reverse the work and make a second chain like the first one.

Reading patterns

As with knitting and crochet, printed tatting patterns are always abbreviated. Examples are: r (ring); ds (double stitch); p (picot); ps (picots); smp (small picot); lp (long picot); cl (close ring); rw (reverse work); ch (chain); tog (together); sep (separated); rep (repeat).

In a pattern you might come across: r of 4 ds, 2 ps sep by 4 ds, 4 ds, cl.

This means: a ring of 4 double stitches, 1 picot, 4 double stitches, 1 picot, 4 double stitches, close ring.

Mounting tatting

Motifs If you are applying tatting to fabric, the simplest way is to stick it

lightly with a fabric adhesive. Alternatively you can sew it with a couple of small oversewing stitches placed between double tatting stitches on each side of the motif.

Edgings Prepare the fabric by forming a narrow hem all round the edge. Sew the edging to the hem at suitable points with neat oversewing stitches.

Two-tone edging

The instructions are for a trimming 18mm (¾in) deep with each individual motif 12mm (½in) wide. You can easily work the required number to fit cuffs, a handkerchief or even a tray cloth and napkins.

In a medium-fine crochet cotton you will use about 1.80m (2yd) of each colour to make 7.5cm (3in) of the edging.

Materials

Crochet cotton No.20 [mercerized crochet cotton 20], one ball 20g each for main colour and contrasting colour.

Tatting shuttle.

Sewing thread to match foundation.

Wind the contrasting yarn onto the shuttle and use the main colour straight from the ball. Work all the rings with the shuttle thread only and the chains with the shuttle thread over the ball thread.

1st row Tie thread from the ball of main colour and shuttle threads together at one end with an overhand knot.

Basic motif * R of 5 ds, 3 ps sep by 3 ds, 5 ds, cl, rw. Ch of 3 ds, 2 ps sep

1. The chains form a linking loop between the rings
2. Pushing up the first stitch of the chain close to the ring.

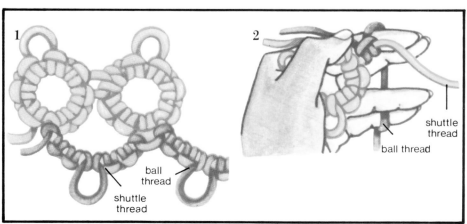

1

ball thread

shuttle thread

2

shuttle thread

ball thread

by 4 ds, 3 ds, rw. Repeat from * for required length or to within 6mm (¼in) of corner.

Corner motif R as before, rw. Ch of 5 ds, smp, 5 ds, rw. R as before, rw. Ch of 5 ds, join to smp on previous ch, 5 ds, rw.
Continue working the basic motif for the required length with the corner motif as necessary. To finish, join the last stitch of the last chain to the base of the first ring. Tie the ends of the yarn together, cut and oversew neatly on the wrong side.

2nd row Tie the ball and shuttle threads together. Attach ball thread to third p of any ring. * Ch of 3 ds, join by shuttle thread to first p on next r. Ch of 2 ds, 5 ps sep by 2 ds, 2 ds miss next p, join by shuttle thread to next p. Rep from * to end including corner motifs (below) where necessary.

Corner motif Ch of 3 ds, join by shuttle thread to first p on corner r. Ch of 2 ds, 8 ps sep by 2 ds, 2 ds, miss next p, join by shuttle thread to next p.

Above: A delightful combination edging is worked in contrast yarn to trim a plain blouse. The same edging can be used to decorate a variety of clothes and household linens.

Bookmark

A gentle reminder to keep you place – a tatted bookmark. It can be made wider or longer and would make a beautiful gift.

Size
15cm by 4.5cm *(6in by 1¾in)* excluding fringes

Materials
Coats Mercer Crochet [medium weight crochet cotton]
1 ball No. 160
(2) tatting shuttle(s)
Note This design can be worked with one shuttle and a ball thread.

1st row R of 7ds, 1p, 7ds, close. Reverse work.
Ch of 7ds, 1p, 7ds. Reverse work.
R of 7ds, join to p or first r, 7ds, close. Reverse work.
*R of 7ds, 1p, 7ds, close. Reverse work.
Ch of 7ds, 1p, 7ds. Reverse work.
R of 7ds, join to p of last r, 7ds, close. Reverse work.
Repeat from * 13 times more, or for length required and making the total number of ch worked an uneven number.
Turn the row with r of 7ds, 1p, 7ds, close. Reverse work. Ch of 7ds, 1p, 11ds. Reverse work.
R of 7ds, join to p of last r, 7ds, close. Reverse work.
Ch of 11ds, 1p, 7ds. Reverse work.
R of 7ds, join to previous pair of rs, 7ds, close. Reverse work.
2nd row *R of 7ds, 1p, 7ds, close. Reverse work.
Ch of 7ds, join to p of opposite ch of previous row, 7ds. Reverse work.
R of 7ds, join to p of last r, 7ds, close. Reverse work.
R of 7ds, join to opposite pair of rs of previous row, 7ds, close. Reverse work.
Ch of 7ds, 1p, 7ds. Reverse work.
R of 7ds, join to group of 3rs, 7ds, close. Reverse work.
Repeat from * all along, turning the end of the row as before and joining the first turning ch to the opposite ch on previous row.
3rd and 4th rows As 2nd, finishing the end of the 4th row to match the beginning of the first row.

Fringe
Cut 6 lengths of thread, each 15cm

Above: An unusual and dainty gift idea, this tatted bookmark makes a perfect trial project for the beginner. Quickly and simply made, it will encourage you to attempt more ambitious patterns.

(6in) long for each tassel and knot four tassels at each end of the bookmark as illustrated.

Tatted placemats

These delicate tatted placemats are worked in an interesting lace design. Make them up using contrasting colours as shown here, or in a single colour for a genuine lace effect.

Size
About 30cm (12in) by 43cm (17in)

Tension
One motif measures 4cm (1⅝in) square

Materials
Coats Mercer Crochet No. 20 [mercerized crochet cotton 20]
4 x 20g balls main shade, A
2 x 20g (1oz) balls, contrast colour, B
Tatting shuttle(s)
Note This design can be worked with either two shuttles or one shuttle and a ball thread
One No. 1.25 crochet hook [steel crochet hook 1]

First motif
1st row Using A, large r of 6ds, 2p separated by 6ds, 8ds, 2p separated by 8ds, 6ds, 1p, 6ds, close.
*Sp of 2mm (⅛in), small r of 6ds, join to last p of previous r, 3ds, 1p, 6ds, close.
Sp of 2mm (⅛in), r of 6ds, join to last p of previous r, 6ds, 2p separated by 6ds, 6ds, close.
Sp of 2mm (⅛in), small r as before, sp of 2mm (⅛in), large r of 6ds, join to last p of previous r, 6ds, 3p separated by 8ds, 6ds, 1p, 6ds, close.
Repeat from * 3 times more, omitting one r at end of last repeat and joining last p of small r to first p of first large r.
Join last small r to first large r at base.
Tie ends, cut and oversew to wrong side.
2nd row Using the crochet hook and B, join to sp before any large r, 1dc into same place as join. * miss next large r, (1dc into next sp, 1dc into next r) 3 times, 1dc into next sp, repeat from * 3 times more, omitting 1dc at end of last repeat, ss to first dc. Fasten off.

Second motif
1st row Using A, make one large r of 6ds, 2p separated by 6ds, 8ds, join to corresponding p on first motif, 8ds, 2p separated by 6ds, 6ds, close.
Sp, small r and sp as before, r of 6ds, join to last of previous r, 6ds, join to corresponding p on first motif, 6ds, 1p, 6ds, close.
Sp, small r and sp as before, large r of 6ds, join to last p of previous r, 6ds, 1p, 8ds, join to corresponding p on first motif, 8ds, 2p separated by 6ds, 6ds, close.
Complete as given for first motif.
Make 6 rows of 9 motifs each, joining the motifs in the same way to the previous motif in the same row and at the corresponding positions to the motifs of the previous row.

Edging
1st row Using C together with a second thread of C, tie the two threads together.
R of 6ds, 3p separated by 6ds, 6ds, close and reverse work.
Ch of 6ds, 1p, 7ds, join to centre free p on side of first motif, 7ds, 1p, 6ds, reverse work.
*R as previous r, reverse work.
Ch of 6ds, 1p, 7ds, miss next free p, join to next p between motifs, 7ds, 1p, 6ds, reverse work.
R as previous r, reverse work.
Ch of 6ds, 1p, 7ds, miss next free p, join to next free p, 7ds, 1p, 6ds, reverse work.
Repeat from * along side to within

Below: A close-up detail of the corner of the placemat shows the formation of the lace.

next corner, r as previous r, ch of 6ds, 1p, 7ds, reverse work.

R as previous r, reverse work.

Miss next free p, join to next p, ch of 7ds, 1p, 6ds, reverse work.

R as previous r, reverse work.

Ch of 6ds, 1p, 7ds, miss next free p, join to next free p, 7d, 1p, 6ds, reverse work.

Repeat from * all round, omitting last r and ch at end of last rep and join to base of first r.

Tie ends, cut and oversew to wrong side.

2nd row Using 2 threads of B tied together, r of 6ds, 1p, 6ds, join to centre p of r at any corner of previous row, 6ds, 1p, 6ds, close, reverse work.

**Ch of 6ds, 3p separated by 7ds, 6ds, reverse work.

R of 6ds, join to last p of previous r, 6ds, 1p, 6ds, join to next p of next r, 6ds, close, reverse work.

*Ch as previous ch, reverse work.

R of 6ds, miss next p, join to next p, 6ds, 1p, 6ds, join to next p of next r, 6ds, close, reverse work.

Repeat from * to within next corner, ch as previous ch, reverse work.

R of 6ds, miss next p, join to next p, 6ds, 2p separated by 6ds, 6ds, close, reverse work.

Ch as previous ch, reverse work.

R of 6ds, join to last p of previous r, 6ds, join to centre p of next corner r, 6ds, 1p, 6ds, close, reverse work.

Repeat from ** all round, omitting last r at end of last repeat and joining last r and ch to correspond. Tie ends, cut and oversew to wrong side. Make a second place mat in the same way.

To finish
Damp and pin out to size.

Left: Tatted placemats make any mealtime a gracious occasion, and look really beautiful.

Thirties chairback

With the revival of Twenties and Thirties fashions in furnishing, comes the return of the chairback cover. Here a tatted edging in toning colours has been worked on a plain cover for maximum effect.

Size
Depth of tatting 11.5cm *(4½in)*
Chairback, including edging, 59cm by 42cm *(23½in x 16½in)*

Tension
One motif measures 5cm *(2in)* wide by 6cm *(2¼in)* deep

Materials
Coats Mercer Crochet No. 10 [mercerized crochet cotton 10] 1 ball each of A and B, pink and black
2 tatting shuttles
50cm *(½yd)* 90cm *(36in)* wide fabric

First row Edging
First motif Fill one shuttle with A, the other with B and tie the ends of the threads together.

Using A shuttle, make a r of 5ds, 1p, 3ds, 3p separated by 2ds, 3ds, 1p, 5ds, close and reverse work.

Using B shuttle, r as before, reverse work.

With A shuttle in the left hand and working with B shuttle, make a ch of 4ds. Using A shuttle, r of 5ds, join to last p on previous A r, 3ds, 3p separated by 2ds, 3ds, 1p, 5ds, close and reverse work.

Using B shuttle, r as r just worked, joining to last p of previous B r, reverse work. Working as before, ch of 4ds.

Using A shuttle, r as before. Working as before, ch of 9ds, reverse work.

Using B shuttle, small r of 8ds, join to second last p on previous B r, 3ds, 1p, 8ds, close, reverse work.

Using A shuttle, r of 5ds, join to last p of previous A r, 3ds, 3p separated by 2ds, 3ds, 1p, 5ds, close.

Using A shuttle, r of 5ds, join to last p of previous A r, 3ds, 4p separated by 2ds, 3ds, 1p, 5ds, close.

Using A shuttle, r of 5ds, join to last p or previous A r, 3ds, 3p separated by 2ds, 3ds, 1p, 5ds, close.

Working as before, ch of 9ds.

Using A shuttle, r as previous r.

Working as before, ch of 4ds.

Using A shuttle, r as previous r, reverse work. Using B shuttle, r of 5ds, 1p, 3ds, join to last p of small B r, 2ds, join to next p on previous large B r, 2ds, join to next p on same r, 3ds, 1p, 5ds, close and reverse work.

Working as before, ch of 4ds.

Using A shuttle, r of 5ds, join to last p on previous A r, 3ds, 3p separated by 2ds, 3ds, 1p, 5ds, close and reverse work.

Using B shuttle, r of 5ds, join to next p on previous B r, 3ds, join to first free p on first B r, 2ds, join to next p on same r, 2ds, 2p separated by 3ds, 5ds, close. Tie ends, cut and oversew to wrong side.

Second motif Tie the shuttle threads together.

Using A shuttle, r of 5ds, 2p separated by 3ds, 2ds, join to corresponding p on first motif, 2ds, join to next p on same r, 3ds, 1p, 5ds, close and reverse work.

Using B shuttle, r of 5ds, 1p, 3ds, 3p separated by 2ds, 3ds, 1p, 5ds, close and reverse work.

Working as before, ch of 4ds.

Using A shuttle, r of 5ds, join to last p on previous A r, 3ds, join to next p on next r of first motif, 2ds, join to next p on same r, 2ds, 2p separated by 3ds, 5ds, close and reverse work. Complete as given for first motif.

Make 6 motifs more, joining each to the previous motif as before.

2nd row
Tie the end of a ball thread of A together with the end of shuttle thread A.

Working along the straight edge of the first row, join working thread to fourth free p on first A r.

*Ch of 7ds, 2p separated by 4ds, 7ds, join by shuttle thread to first free p on next (B) ring, ch of 5ds, 2p separated by 2ds, 5ds, join by shuttle thread to second free p on next (B) ring, rep from * omitting ch at end of last rep. Tie ends, cut and oversew to wrong side.

3rd row
Work as given for first row.

4th row
Work as given for 2nd row of just before first p, join to corresponding p on 2nd row, 4ds, join to next p on 2nd row, 7ds, join by shuttle thread to first free p on next r, *ch of 5ds, 2p separated by 2ds, 5ds, join with the shuttle thread to the second free p on the next r, ch of 7ds, miss next ch on 2nd row, join to next p on next p on 2nd row, 7ds, join with shuttle thread to first free p on next r, rep from * to end. Tie ends, cut and oversew neatly to wrong side.

To finish
Damp and pin out to measurements. Cut the fabric to 59cm by 46cm *(23½in x 18in)*.

Turn back hems at top and side edges of 18mm *(¾in)* each, and at lower edge of 4cm *(1½in)*. Mitre corners and double under 6mm *(¼in)* of hem allowance. Slip in place.

Sew edging to lower edge of cover.

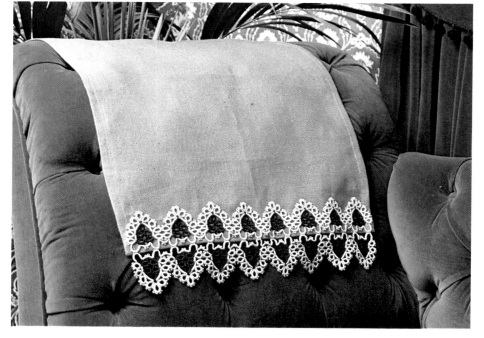

Embroidery on tulle

Despite its light and gauzy appearance, tulle is very hard-wearing. It consists of threads woven into hexagonal holes and the fabric makes an ideal background for embroidery for wedding veils, christening robes and lingerie. There are two types of embroidery on tulle – each with its own working technique. The simplest is worked free style, without pattern, on a coarse meshed tulle. The other looks rather like lace, the embroidery stitches being worked within a stitched outline, on a tulle of finer mesh. Simple geometric shapes and straightforward patterns are usually worked on the coarser meshes. For complicated designs on finer meshes, it is better to use a pattern.

Materials
Tulle is sold in varying widths and is made of either nylon or of silk. Both are suitable for embroidery.
The thread used for embroidery on tulle should be soft and run through the meshes easily without breaking them. Mercerised sewing cotton such as Sylko Perle No.3 or No.5 is suitable for coarse meshed tulle and No.8 or No.12 for finer meshes.

Preparing a pattern
Preparation of tulle for embroidery is very important. The chosen design is copied onto tracing paper, the tulle placed upon it and a piece of firm card placed under the paper. Tack the three layers together so that the design can be seen through the tulle and the card supports the tulle for easy working.

Right: This beautiful traditional design is a form of embroidery called Modano lace. The finely worked pattern is composed entirely of linen stitch, making a crisp, solid contrast to the airy background.

Opposite: Revive the charm of the Thirties with a chairback.

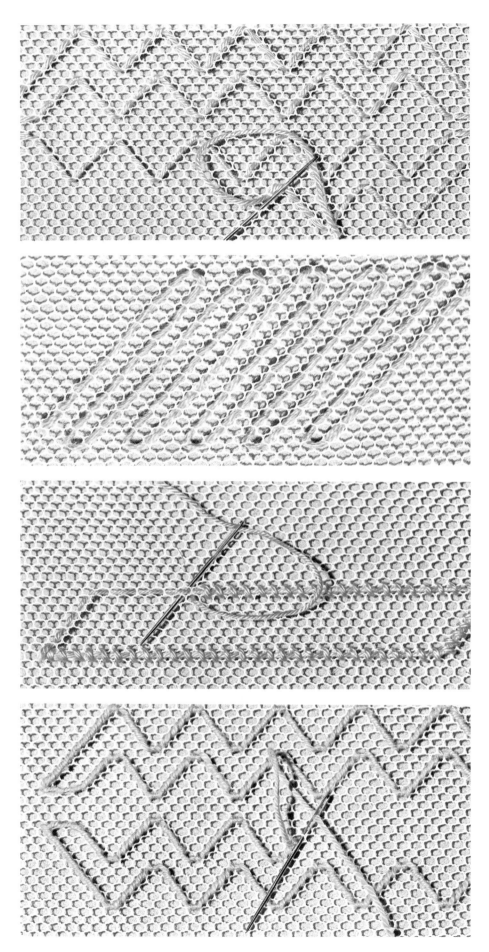

Alternatively, for large areas of embroidery, such as a wedding veil, architect's linen should be used. The design is copied onto the linen and the tulle tacked to it.

The needle used should be blunt, such as a tapestry needle and in proportion to the mesh.

Working method

The outline of the design can be worked in any of the stitches illustrated in this chapter and some of them are also used for filling the pattern. To begin working, run the needle through the mesh, according to whichever stitch is chosen, leaving the end of the thread loose, about 7cm *(3in)* long. After the embroidery work has been completed, darn the end into the back of the work so that it is invisible. Much of the effect of embroidery on tulle depends on even working and care should be taken not to pucker the fabric.

Running stitch

Pass the needle over one mesh of the tulle and under the next, alternately. Running stitch is mostly used for defining outlines but it can also be worked as a filling.

Diagonal running stitch

Pick up every other mesh of the tulle, diagonally. To work this as a filling stitch make several parallel rows up and down, missing one row of holes between each stitched row, and using a thicker yarn.

Cording

First work a running stitch guide line then oversew this as illustrated. This stitch is useful when you want a bolder line than the normal running stitch outline.

Stem stitch

This is worked in the same way as embroidery stem stitch on fabric. For each stitch pick up one mesh of the tulle, always keeping the yarn to the right or left of the needle, depending on the direction of the slope you are working.

The various kinds of stitches used for both outlining and filling-in purposes. Reading from the top of the page they are: running stitch, diagonal running stitch, cording stitch and stem stitch.

Closed filling stitches

Once the pattern outlines have been embroidered onto the tulle, the next stage is to work the decorative filling stitches. Their purpose is two-fold – firstly, to cover large areas of tulle with a solid filling as quickly and simply as possible and secondly, to look attractive.

Darning stitch
This is a very quick and easy way to fill in large areas. Work backwards and forwards, passing the yarn alternately over and under the meshes until the area is complete. Always work two rows of thread in the same meshes so that the return rows fill in the gaps left by the first rows. You can work this stitch in any direction.

Linen stitch
This is another quick way of filling in large areas. Simply work rows of running stitch, diagonally or vertically, and then cross them with horizontal rows of running stitch.

Wavy stitch
Turn the tulle so that the hexagons are vertical.
Work this stitch diagonally taking one thread of the tulle above and one below, missing a hole in between and picking up one thread with each stitch. Subsequent rows are worked by picking up the threads missed on the previous row. Leaving more threads between the stitches makes a gentler wavy line.

Double wavy stitch
With the hexagons horizontal, work a horizontal row of stitches as for wavy stitch, from right to left. Complete the row from left to right, by working over the same threads but picking up the threads left by the first stage of the row, to make a crossed stitch.

Top to bottom: Wavy, darning and staggered running stitches.

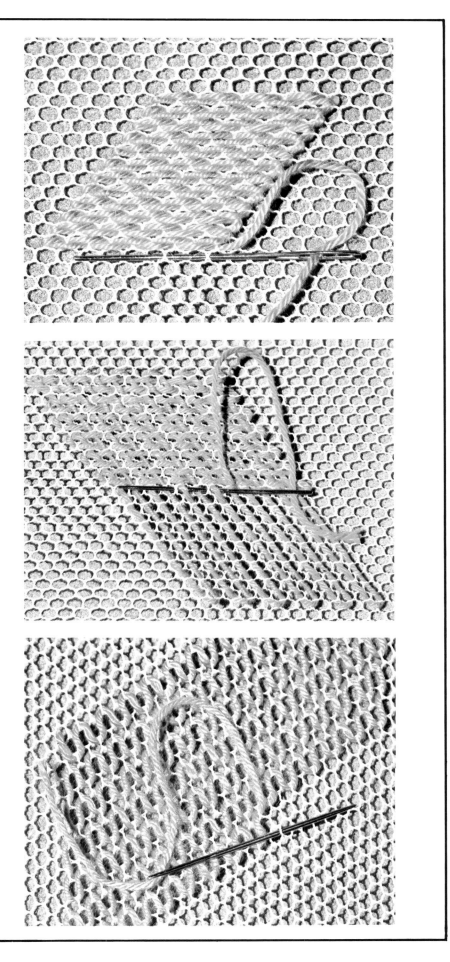

Staggered running stitch

Work running stitch with a double thread, staggering the stitches by moving one thread along on each row, giving the effect of rows of parallel diagonal lines.

Compound stitch

With the hexagons horizontal, work two rows of staggered horizontal wavy stitch. Then work one row of oblique stitches, sloping in alternate directions, each covering one mesh of tulle. Work each oblique stitch twice over to give a double thickness of thread.

Diamond border

Combinations of stitches can make very pretty borders. The one illustrated here, for example, consists of a row of diamonds worked in staggered running stitch. On each side of these diamonds is another row of diamonds worked in cording.

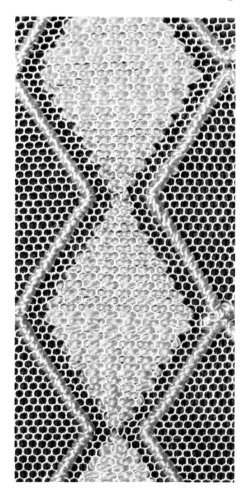

Above: Diamond border stitch

Right, top to bottom: Linen stitch, double wavy stitch and compound stitch.

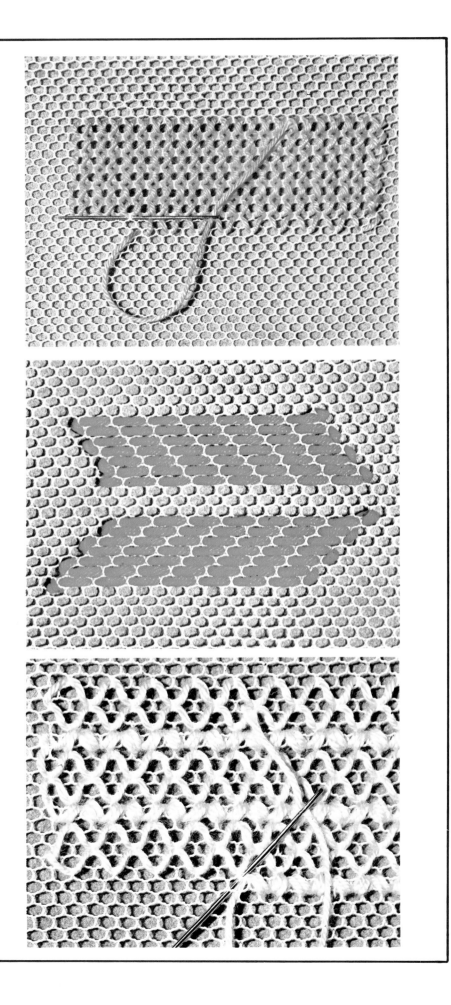

Fancy edgings

When making an item of embroidered tulle it is possible to finish off the edges with something a little more imaginative than just a simple hem. Once the embroidered edging stitches have been worked the surplus is trimmed away, leaving the finished edge which can be either straight or shaped.

There are several ways of finishing off the edges of tulle, and you can make them as decorative as you wish to match the rest of the embroidery on the article.

There are two basic stitch methods for the edge and these can be used in straight lines or following whatever shape is required.

Buttonhole stitch

Pad the edge with a simple running stitch, following the outline of the shape. Embroider over it with one buttonhole stitch for each mesh of tulle.

Darning stitch

Worked as an edging, this stitch is different from the filling darning stitch. Secure the thread to one mesh of tulle, working from left to right. Hold the thread with the thumb of the left hand. Thread the needle through one hole of tulle to the right, pushing it upwards under the top thread of the mesh being covered. Leaving the thread slack, move the needle down under the lower thread of the mesh being covered and over the looped thread. Remove the left thumb from the thread and pull the thread tight. This gives the effect of darning stitch with a small oblique stitch above it. One stitch is worked into each mesh.

Note If yarn is thick enough, one stitch in each mesh will be sufficient for these edgings. However, if the yarn is thin, work two or three stitches into each mesh.

Once the edging stitch, and any embroidery which is to be worked as a border, is completed, trim off the surplus tulle with a small pair of pointed scissors. Nail scissors are ideal. Trim close to the embroidery.

Below left: Working buttonhole edging on the straight.
Below right: Working a zig-zag effect with buttonhole stitch.
Bottom left: Working darning stitch edging on the straight.
Bottom right: The surplus fabric is trimmed away after working a zig-zag darning stitch edging. These illustrations show how simple stitches can look super.

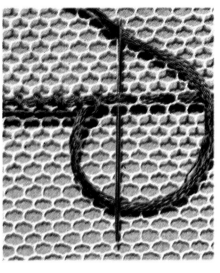

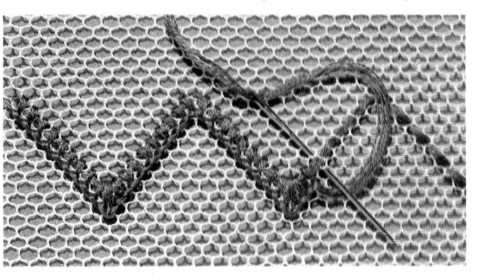

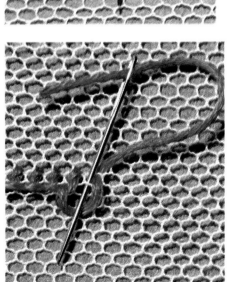

To make a wedding veil

One of the prettiest ways to show off embroidery on tulle is on the top layer of a wedding veil, and such a special item gives you the perfect excuse to show off your skill.

Making the veil itself is a simple matter and you can choose one of two ways. The length of a veil is a matter of choice and is influenced by the wedding dress. A full length veil stops at either floor level or extends to match the length of a train. Alternatively, a veil can be shoulder or elbow length.

Buy tulle 183cm *(72in)* wide and you will need four thicknesses.

First method

For a short veil, all four layers should be of the same length. Measure from the crown of the head to the elbow or shoulder level and double this amount. Buy two separate lengths of this measurement.

For a long veil, measure from the crown of the head to the required length, add 46cm *(18in)* and then double the amount. This gives the measurement for the long underveil. Then measure from the crown of the head to the elbow and double the measurement for the short top veil. For making either a short or a long veil fold the two lengths of tulle in half widthways and pin them together along the fold lines. Work small running stitches along the folded edges which will be gathered up to fit onto the head-dress once the embroidery is worked.

Second method

A romantic, cascade effect is obtained by cutting the edges of the veil in a curve rather than leaving them straight.

For a long veil, add the measurement of the long under veil and the short top veil and buy two lengths of this measurement. By rounding off the corners cut each piece into an oval shape and place them together. Measure the length of the short veil from one end and fold over at this point. Find the centre of the folded edge and measure out 15cm *(6in)* to each side of it. Make small running stitches along the edge of these central 30cm *(12in)* and gather onto the head-dress after working the embroidery. For short veils cut the fabric into two circles and fold them in half. Gather in the same way as for the long version.

Filigree fillings

Embroidering on tulle involves a technique simple enough for you to be able to be your own designer. Therefore, the wider a repertoire of decorative filling stitches you have to draw on, the better. Here are seven more of these fillings to add to your range. Sometimes filling stitches can be used as individual motifs. For example, the star or spot filling given here, as well as making a very pretty filling when worked close together, could be scattered across a design, worked in between the main motifs.

Star filling
Stars are worked by making six stitches over two or more threads of tulle, all meeting in a single mesh in the centre. Secure the ends of the thread by darning them in round the centre mesh on the back of the work.

Spot filling
Work a thread in running stitch round one mesh hole and then work buttonhole stitch over it to form a ring.

Grating filling
This consists of diagonal lines which cross to form a diamond pattern. Each diagonal is two rows of adjacent running stitch.

Fishbone filling
Working over three rows of meshes and from left to right, make a row of stitches which slant from left to right by inserting the needle into one hole in the first row, taking it down vertically and coming out through the mesh in the third row. Miss the next vertical row of meshes before making the next stitch in the same way.
Work a second row from right to left so that the stitches slope in the opposite direction. These two rows form the fishbone pattern.

Interlaced running stitch
The first row of running stitch is worked over as many threads as you wish. Work the second row in waves of the same dimensions, alternating and interlacing with the first row. At the end of each row make a curved line of running stitch down the side as illustrated.

Threaded stitch filling
For the first row start at the right hand side, bringing the thread through a mesh hole from the back. Take the thread down, missing one row of meshes, and insert the needle one hole to the right of the first mesh to form a diagonal line. Take the needle behind the mesh to the left and come out two holes along. Work a back stitch over the mesh hole missed, bringing the needle out at the same place as last time. Take the thread back up to the first hole thus forming a diagonal line sloping to the right. Continue working back stitches over horizontal meshes linked by diagonal lines as in the illustration.
The second row is worked by passing the needle horizontally under two meshes, taking the thread down over two rows of meshes and one hole diagonally to the left, under two horizontal meshes and back up to one hole diagonally to the left.

Four pretty filling stitches to add to your repertoire.
Below left: Star filling
Below right: Spot filling
Both these can be scattered across a design or worked closely together for a more solid filling.
Bottom left: Grating is a much more solid filling
Bottom right: Fishbone filling is also very solid. Notice the downward slant of the needle while working fishbone.

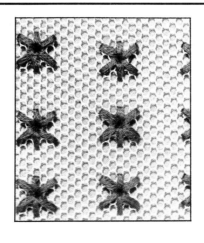

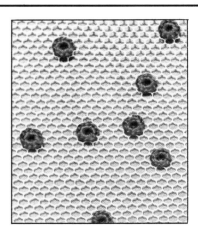

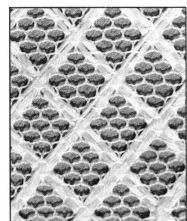

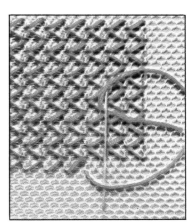

These two rows are worked alternately to form the pattern.

Ring filling

Working horizontally from right to left, begin by taking the thread over one and under one thread of tulle, and thereafter take the thread over one thread of tulle, under one, over one and under one. Then, working in an anti-clockwise direction, outline in running stitch the mesh hole in the row immediately below. The second row is worked three rows of meshes down, the rings worked in a clockwise direction and staggered one hole to the left of those in the row above.

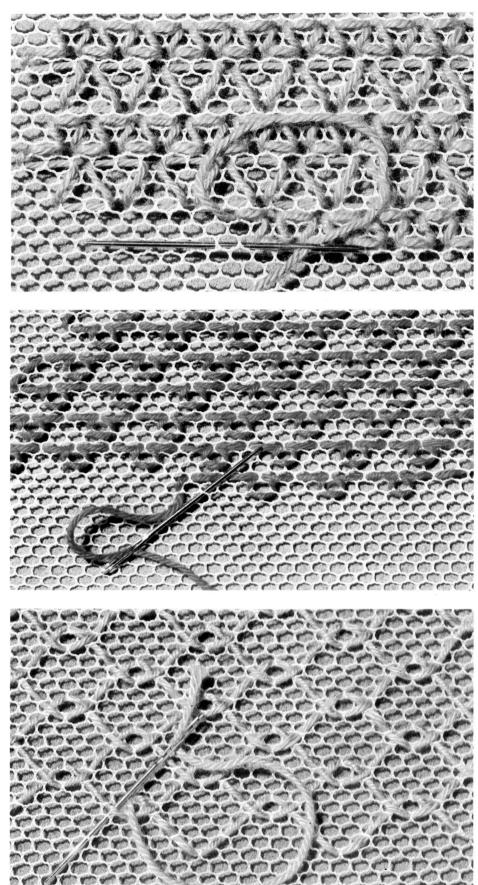

Three more filling stitches to cover large areas. From the top: Interlaced running stitch, threading stitch filling and ring filling.

Handkerchief

Embroidery on tulle gives a fine, delicate effect ideal for handkerchief edgings, This very special one would make a charming gift.

Materials
50cm ($\frac{1}{2}$yd) tulle
50cm ($\frac{1}{2}$yd) lawn
1 skein Anchor Coton à Broder No.18 [4 ply mercerized embroidery thread]
Thin card or stiff paper
Basting thread

Preparing the pattern
Trace outline pattern overleaf, and guide lines. The corner section can either be repeated all round to give the full edging pattern or it can be worked from the one section, moving the pattern round as each corner is completed.
Transfer design to coloured card.

Working on tulle
Because of its transparent quality, embroidery on tulle has to be as neat on the back as on the front. When beginning, work two or three running stitches in the wrong direction and then double back over these to secure. To finish off, darn back into the work with several running stitches and trim the end close to the fabric.

Preparing the fabric
Work in running stitch along a line of meshes to find the straight of the fabric, and then again along another line of meshes at right angles to the first one. Position these threads against the outer guide lines of one corner and pin the fabric in place. Work running stitch along the remaining outer and inner edge lines.

Applying the centre
Place a square of cotton lawn under the centre of the tulle, leaving an allowance of about 2.5cm (1in) round the inner guide line. Baste in position. Work in double buttonhole stitch over the running stitch thread, through the double thickness of tulle and lawn.
Using a fine pair of manicure scissors, trim away the tulle on the inner edge and the lawn on the outer edge.

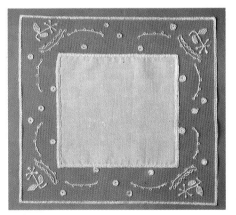

Top: Embroider a fragile border on a handkerchief to show off your work to advantage.

Above: Pattern is transferred to coloured card so it shows through.

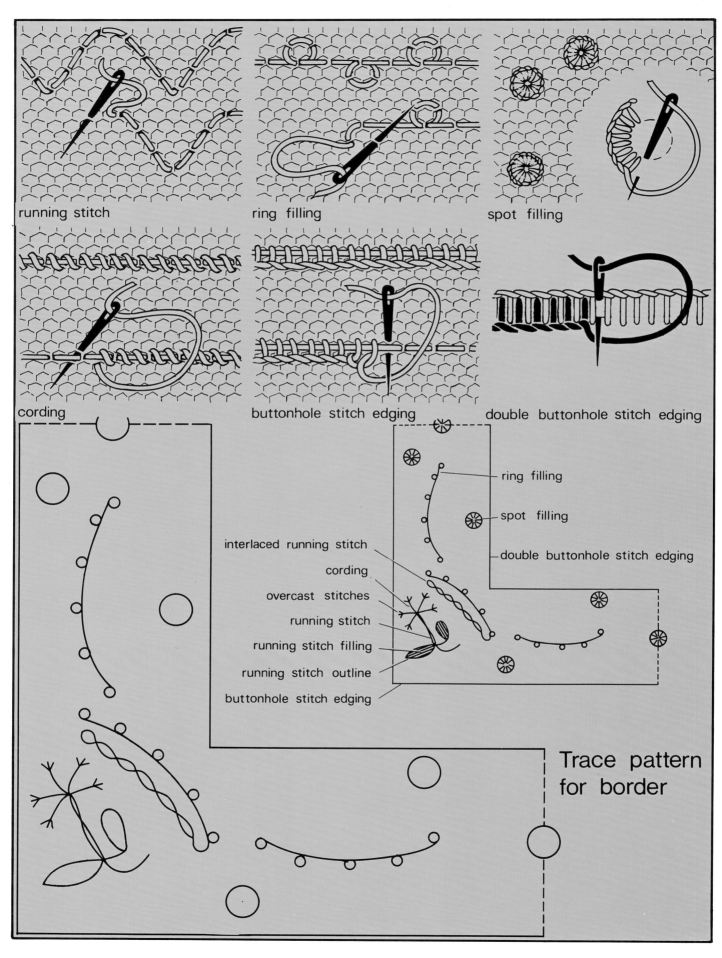

running stitch

ring filling

spot filling

cording

buttonhole stitch edging

double buttonhole stitch edging

ring filling

spot filling

double buttonhole stitch edging

interlaced running stitch

cording

overcast stitches

running stitch

running stitch filling

running stitch outline

buttonhole stitch edging

Trace pattern for border

Embroidery on net

There's hardly a home without at least one net curtain that couldn't be enriched with a little embroidery. White-on-white can look deliciously fresh for a bedroom, or else you may wish to link the curtains to the rest of the colour scheme with matching embroidery. Whichever way you choose, embroidery on net is most effective and simple.

Choosing your net
In some Mediterranean countries girls still make filet lace, knotting the net the way fishermen make nets in any harbour. If you go on holiday in Sardinia, look in the fishing villages – these still produce some of the finest work.

But now that nylon and synthetic square nettings are so widespread, we suggest you take the short cut and start embroidering patterns straight onto a shop-bought net. The advantage is that synthetic net will not shrink, but make sure you use equivalent yarns for embroidery if you want to have a fully washable curtain. If you choose a cotton 'mosquito' netting to embroider with crisp white cotton yarn, just remember to have it dry cleaned or be prepared for shrinkage when it is washed. It is easiest to work on net with 6mm ($\frac{1}{4}in$) or 12mm ($\frac{1}{2}in$) square holes. Smaller squares, of course, take longer to fill, and oblongs do not lend themselves to all the patterns, which are based on square-holed nets usually.

Pattern darning
The curtain shown here is worked the simplest way of all – with pattern darning. All you have to do is to follow the threads on the counted chart. Use coarse creamy thread such as dish-cloth yarn, sandy, soft embroidery cotton, and Pearl cotton to build up the pattern in various colour tones.

Star fillings
These star fillings are easy, and fun to do. If you want to get a long way quickly, use a large mesh and thick thread.

Knot the thread at the bottom left-hand corner of the net.

First row Work diagonal stitches from the bottom left to the top right of each square.

Next row Work back the way you came, intertwining the thread with that of the first row. Working parallel to this, cover the area to be embroidered. Then turn your work and complete another series so that they intersect the first.

Web motifs
Now you can move onto the more intricate web motifs.

Ribbed diamonds
For a bold, relief effect use Pearl cotton No.5. Use the diamonds in vertical or horizontal rows, or build them up in groups.

Start by binding in the tail of the yarn inside one of the ribs as you progress. Weave webs as shown in the illustration which you will find on the next page.

Finish off by slipping the needle through one of the ribs, to the centre of the diamond, and snip off.

Ribbed wheels
Prepare the foundation by running the thread out in four spokes. Overcast the spokes, then work back stitches round and round the centre, over the bars of net and threads, to form a solid wheel, Finish off with a small knot at the back of the wheel. Work ribbed wheels close together as fillings or use as separate motifs.

Flowers
To work petals, stretch the thread diagonally from one corner of a square to the other and overcast it. Then weave under and over bars of the net, and overcast thread. Finish off at back with a knot. Repeat the process in the other three corners of the square, and then decorate the flower centre with loop stitches.

Below: Embroidered net curtain

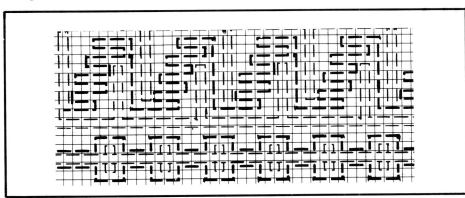

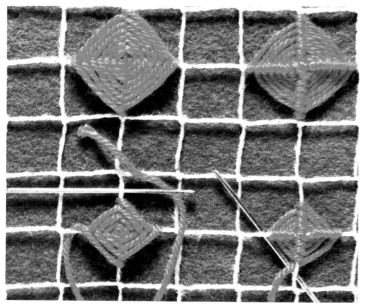

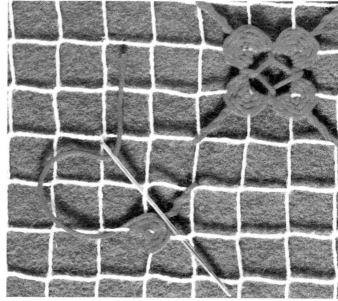

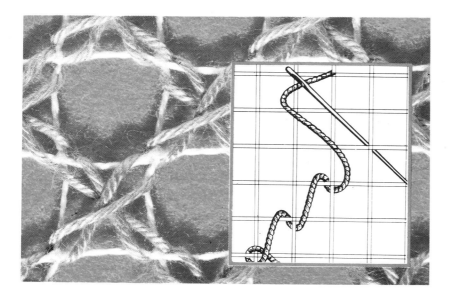

Here are a variety of useful
filling stitches for decorating net
Top left: Pretty spiralled ribbed
diamond shapes are useful for
providing solid relief.
Above: Flower petals, joined
together with loops make a very
delicate motif.
Left and below left: Criss-crossed
star fillings give a light, all
over decorative look. The inset
diagram shows the working method
Below: Ribbed wheels can be part
of a border pattern, or used as
a separate motif by itself.

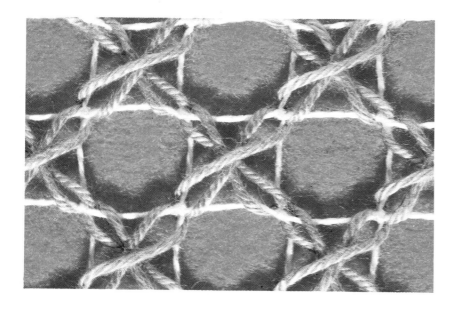

Daisies and spirals

Here are some more fillings which look very effective embroidered in bold, bright colours with heavy thread on coarsely woven net. The motifs can be used as decoration in many ways – on net curtains, bedspreads or ponchos. Alternatively, on a finer net with correspondingly fine thread and more delicate colours, you can work the motifs as borders on cot drapes, a bridal veil or an overblouse.

The geometric filling is quickly done and makes an ideal edging, as each row is worked across three bars of net. It can be made either vertically or horizontally, in one colour or in alternating rows of dark and light thread. One row of spiral filling makes a narrow edging, as well as being an effective filling to cover large areas. The daisy filling is really charming scattered at random over an area of net, as each motif is worked separately.

Geometric filling

This geometric design is made by working a series of diamonds, each one on a base of four knots of net.

Secure the thread to the knot which forms the apex of the diamond, then work over and under the vertical and horizontal bars of net, as shown. When the diamond is finished, wind the thread round the centre bar down to the knot below, to begin the next diamond. This motif is shown worked vertically, but can be worked from left to right.

Daisy filling

Start at the knot which is to be the centre of the flower, then work two diagonal loops as shown in the diagram, working the last one round the centre to pull the petals gently into the middle. If you want a 'random' motif, this type of filling is ideal, as each flower is separate.

Spiral filling

This is worked in rows, left to right. Turn the work after each row so that you are always working in the same direction. Secure the thread with a knot at the left edge of the work. Point the needle downwards diagonally behind the first knot and bring the thread out to the lower right of the knot. Then insert the needle from right to left under the vertical bar above the knot, then from left to right, under the same bar below the knot. Wind the thread two or three times round the centre knot, working under the vertical bars and over the horizontal bars of the net.

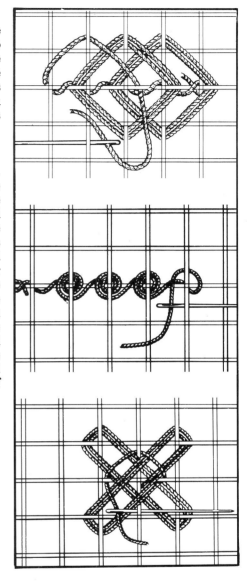

Right, top to bottom: These diagrams illustrate the method of working three very attractive embroidered fillings. They are called geometric, daisy and spiral filling respectively.

Below, left to right: Completed filling stitches for geometric, daisy and spiral embroidery, in bright primary colours.

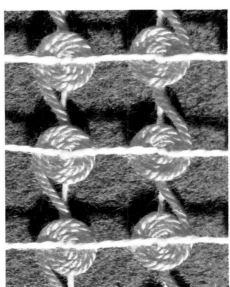

Rustic tray cloth

The loopy filling shown here is a simple way of embroidering on net It can be worked on net curtains, tray cloths, or it would look most effective on a delicate net canopy for a cot. You can make it in several different patterns – in double rows to produce a frogged look, in bands of four rows to make a chain of circles, or in thicker bands to cover large areas of net for a really bold effect.

Fasten the thread with a knot and work a series of loops across the net over the top bar of each square, carrying the thread over all the vertical bars between the loops (fig.1).

When you reach the end of a row, loop the thread round the vertical bar of that square and work back again, making a series of loops over the bottom bar of each square. This time take the thread under the vertical bars between loops (fig.2).

Continue working the pattern taking the new loops through those which you have already worked. (fig.3).

The illustration in fig.4 shows buttonhole stitch worked on netting to form a striking geometric pattern which can be used, very effectively, for edging. First, wind one or two threads of yarn along the line of the design and then fasten them firmly to the net with buttonhole stitch, as shown.

Making the cloth

This unusual rustic tray cloth is worked in white soft embroidery cotton on genuine fishing net which has a unique texture of its own and is worth trying to find.

Right: The three stages of working a loopy filling stitch are shown in figs. 1–3.
1. Work from left to right across the top bar of each square
2. The next stage is to work along the bottom of each square
3. The intricate pattern of circles and loops builds up as you work back and forth across the square of the net.
4. The outline stitch used for the border of the traycloth is called padded buttonhole, and provides a plain contrast.

Materials

You might have to search around if you want to find the real thing (try shipping chandlers or shops selling fishing tackle), but ordinary nylon netting dyed russet will give much the same effect. This cloth has been made with 6mm ($\frac{1}{4}in$) square netting, and the finished size is a 23·5cm ($9\frac{1}{4}in$) square.

How to do it

Either stretch the net over a square frame with drawing pins, or fix it to a thin piece of cardboard with basting stitches. This will keep the squares even and prevent the embroidery threads from pulling too tightly and putting the net out of shape.

First work the loop filling, starting from the centre and working outwards, keeping the loops even and reasonably loose. When the work is completed remove the frame, or cardboard backing, and finish off the edges with padded buttonhole stitch to give a firm, distinct outline to the border. Trim.

Opposite: If you are able to obtain a piece of genuine fishing net, you can use it to make this rustic traycloth in a slightly 'peasant' pattern. Alternatively, buy net with a large mesh and dye it russet.

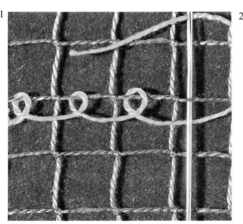

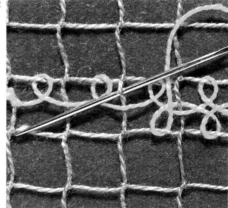

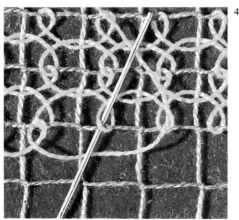

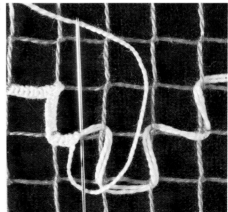

Macramé

Setting on [attaching] threads

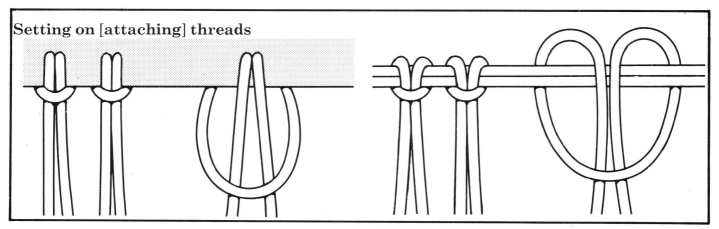

To work onto fabric

Threads must be about eight times the length of the finished work and then folded in half to form doubled threads. Pull the doubled thread through the material with a crochet hook and knot the ends through the loop. Pull the knot firmly up to the edge of the fabric but not so tightly that the fabric puckers.

To work separately

Cut a length of yarn about 15cm (6in) longer than the finished width of the work. Pin to the top of knotting board with overhand knots so that it is taut and running under the setting on [attached] knots.

Cut working threads eight times the length of the finished work. Fold each thread in half and tie onto the foundation thread by holding the doubled strand in front of the foundation thread, fold it over the back and pull the ends through the loop, tightening the knot round the foundation thread. Having the doubled threads four times the length of the finished work is only a guide. The thicker the thread is, the more length will be used up by each knot.

The set on [attached] threads are pushed close together and it helps to prevent tangling if each thread is wound into a small ball secured with a rubber band.

Horizontal double half hitches (DHH)   Double horizontal double half hitches

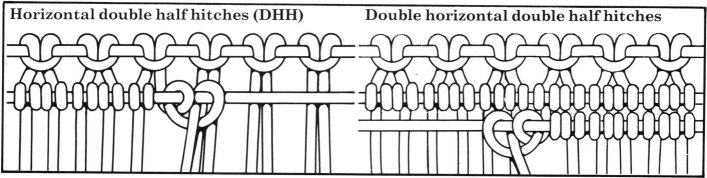

The set on [attached] threads are usually secured with one row of horizontal DHHs which is worked using the basic knot. Each knot is worked over a core [leader] and this can either be a second foundation thread introduced from the side of the work or an outer edge thread. A separate thread should be 15cm (6in) longer than the finished width of the work, the same as the first foundation thread.

The core [leader] is held taut by the right hand, running horizontally under the set on [attached] knots. Working from left to right, bring up each single knotting thread in turn and wrap it round the knot bearer to form a knot. Repeat the same movement to form a double leaf hitch.

Pull the knot tight and repeat with the next thread along.

As well as making a firm base for beginning or finishing a piece of macramé, horizontal DHH's can be used within the design but always using one of the knotting threads as leader and not a separate foundation thread.

Introduce a third foundation thread or use the outer edge thread and work another line of horizontal DHH's from right to left. The knots will be worked in the same way as above but the thread will be knotted round clockwise.

Diagonal double half hitches (stage 1)

(stage 2)

Diagonal double half hitches (stage 1)

(stage 2)

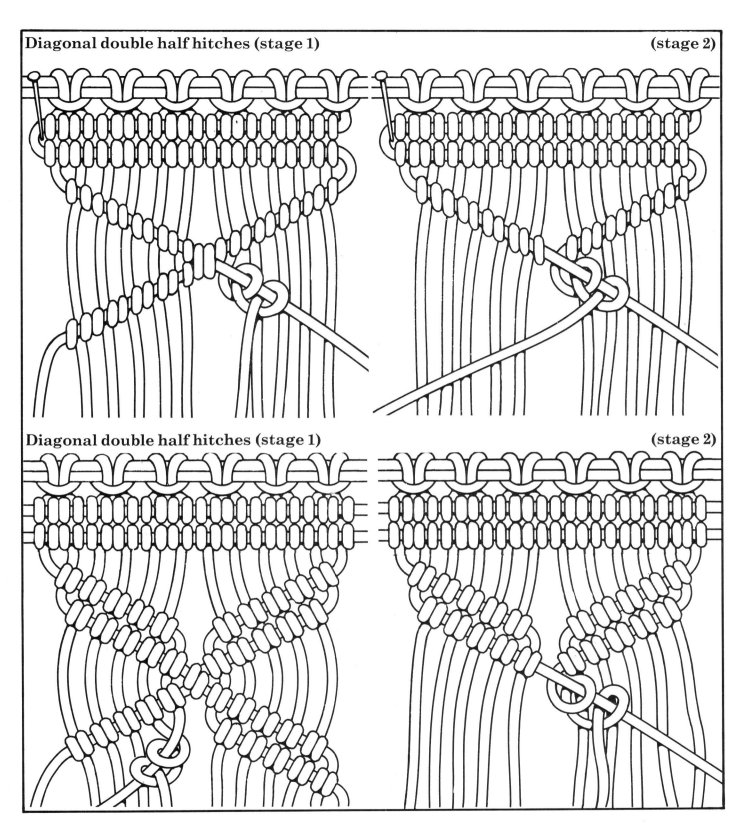

Worked in the same way as horizontal DHH's, using one of the knotting threads as a leader, which is held diagonally downwards to either right or left, depending on which way the work is intended to slope.

The thread next to the leader is knotted round it in the same double knot as for horizontal DHH's. Continue along the row until a diagonal bar is formed.

Cross leaders in the middle as in diagram stage 2.

Work one row of diagonal DHH's on the right and left using the first and last thread as a leader. Take the outside threads and work another row of diagonal DHH'S parallel to rows already done.

DHH the leader on the right across to the left. DHH the next thread in the section on the left, across to the left. Complete the cross by DHH knotting the leader on the left across to the right. DHH the next thread in the section on the right, across to the right.

For flat [square] knots, four

threads, or multiples of four, are required. The two centre threads act as a core and the two outer threads are knotted round them. Hold the centre threads taut by winding them round the third finger of the left hand or by securing them to board with a bulldog clip.

Form the right-hand thread into a loop with the end passing under the centre core and over the left-hand thread. Bring the left-hand thread over the core and thread it through the loop from the front of the work. Pull both ends up until the knot closes tightly round the centre core. This completes first part of knot.

Repeat the process in reverse by forming the left-hand thread into a loop and passing the right-hand thread through the loop. Draw up tight. If only one half of flat [square] knot is repeated continuously the resulting braid will spiral and it depends on whether the first stage or the second stage is used which way the work will spiral.

Turn back the threads and sew them down at the back of the fabric for approximately 6mm ($\frac{1}{4}in$), then trim the ends closely. Do the same with the foundation thread. This method is more practical for macramé than darning in the ends as for knitting or crochet because the tightness of the knots makes too firm a fabric to work into.

If the thread is used up before the work is completed, add an extra length by oversewing one end to the end already incorporated in the work. The threads could also be knotted together providing the knot falls to the back of the work.

Set [attach] knots in multiples of four. Work a flat [square] knot on each group.

In the next row leave two threads and with the next four work a flat [square] knot. Work another knot with the next four and so on until the end of the row when two threads will remain on either side. These will then be incorporated into the work on the next row.

Continue working the rows in this way so that each knot is formed alternately.

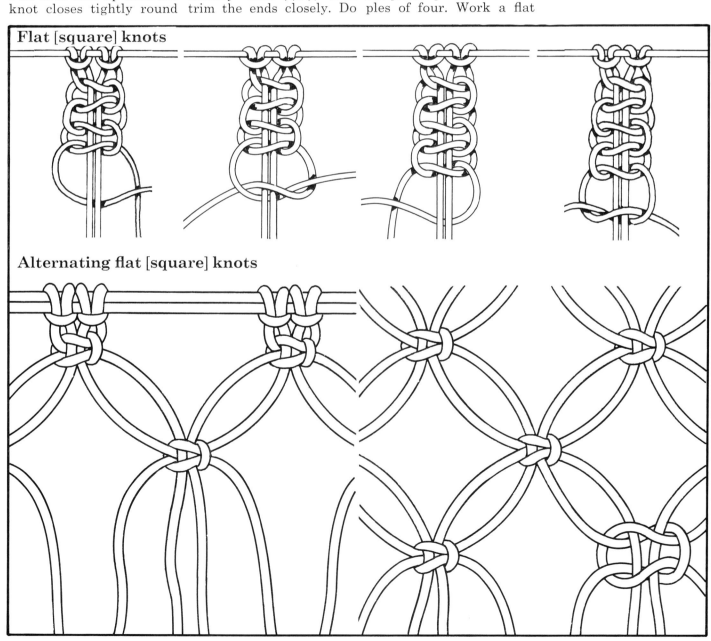

Flat [square] knots

Alternating flat [square] knots

Double half hitch diamond and a flat [square] knot

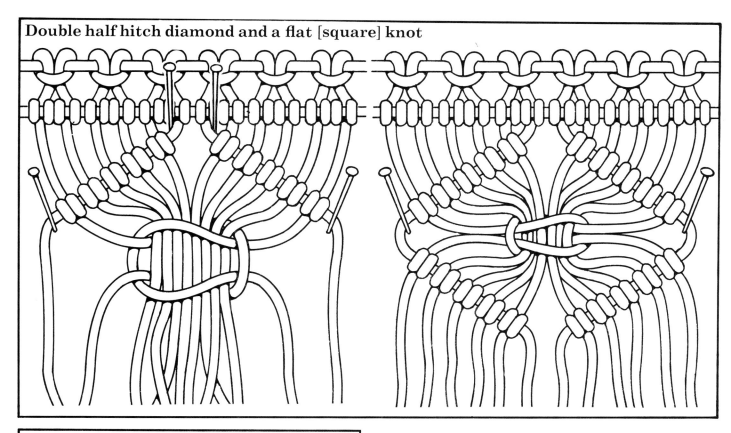

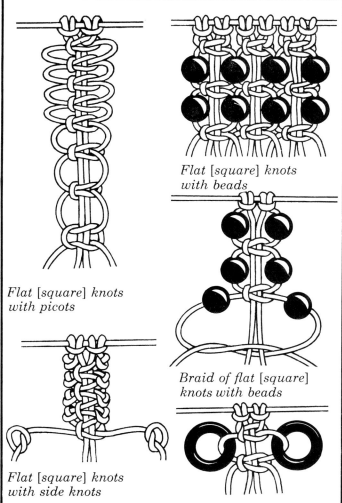

Flat [square] knots with picots

Flat [square] knots with beads

Braid of flat [square] knots with beads

Flat [square] knots with side knots

Cord the centre threads out to the left and right diagonally (see diagonal DHH's).

Omitting leaders on either side, work a flat [square] knot with the central threads. In the diagram eight threads have been used as a core and two threads used for knotting round them.

Insert a pin just inside each outside leader thread, and DHH over the leaders diagonally back into the centre.

Flat [square] knots with picots

Set on [attach] two doubled threads and work one flat [square] knot. Work a second flat [square] knot leaving a space between it and the first one. Push the knot up into place under the first one. The length of thread left between the two knots dictates size.

Flat [square] knots with side knots

Set on [attach] doubled threads and work a flat [square] knot. Tie an over-hand knot on each of the right and left threads using a pin to slide the knots up against the preceding flat knot before finally tightening it. Work a second flat knot.

Flat [square] knots with beads

Set on two doubled threads and work one flat [square] knot. Thread a bead onto each of the left and right-hand threads and work a second flat [square] knot.

Note Choose beads which have large holes so that they are easily threaded. Children's china or wooden threading beads, add an attractive look.

Overhand knot

An overhand knot can be worked with any number of threads. All thicknesses are held together and used as one to form a loop into which the working end is inserted, top to bottom and front to back. The ends are then pulled to tighten.

Blackberry-shaped balls

This decorative bobble is

usually worked over four threads. Work six flat [square] knots, then using blunt ended needle, thread two central threads from front to back through the work above centre of the first knot. Pull up until a little blackberry-shaped roll is formed. The next flat [square] knot which is worked underneath this will then hold ball in place.

Picots and scallops
Setting [attaching] threads onto a foundation cord can be done in more decorative ways than simple knotting by using picots or scallops.
Simple picots. Pin doubled threads behind the foundation cord. Attach to the cord with DHH's.
Scallops. Pin doubled threads as for simple picots but using three threads, one inside the other. Keep the spacing even by pinning. Attach to the foundation cord with DHH's.
Knotted picots. Place three doubled threads side by side behind the foundation cord with the centre thread slightly higher than those on either side. Work a flat [square] knot using the four central threads as a core. Fix with a row of horizontal DHH's to foundation cord.
Knotted loops. Pin two doubled threads, one inside the other. Work two flat [square] knots and attach scallops to foundation cord with DHH's.

Knotted chain
Chains are made by alternating simple knots from left to right. A left and right hand knot make one knotted chain.

Cavandoli
In this technique only two colours and one knot are used. Traditionally, the horizontal DHH's provide the background and the vertical DHH's form the pattern. The result is a smooth, tightly knotted

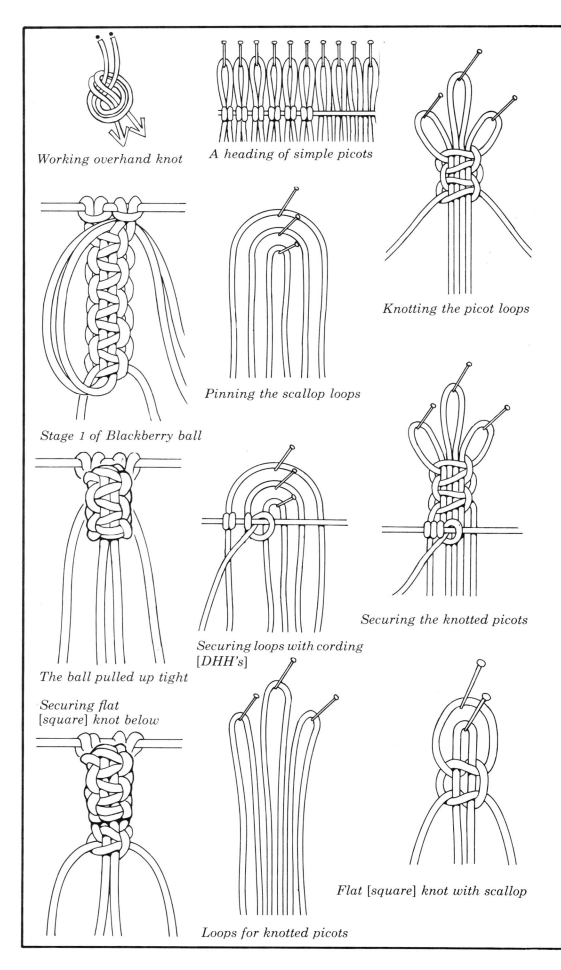

Working overhand knot

A heading of simple picots

Knotting the picot loops

Stage 1 of Blackberry ball

Pinning the scallop loops

The ball pulled up tight

Securing loops with cording [DHH's]

Securing the knotted picots

Securing flat [square] knot below

Loops for knotted picots

Flat [square] knot with scallop

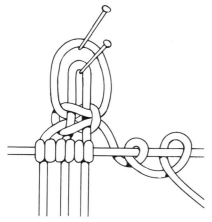

Securing knotted picot with cording [DHH's]

Knotting single thread left

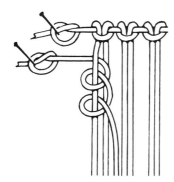

Joining in the picot threads with a vertical knot [vertical DHH]

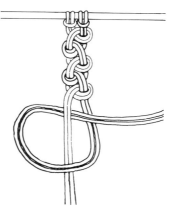

Knotting double thread right

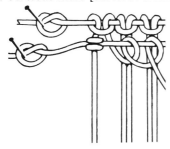

Using the pattern thread as a horizontal cording [DHH] leader

A typical Cavandoli chart

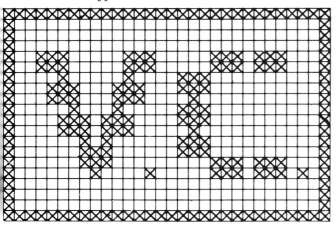

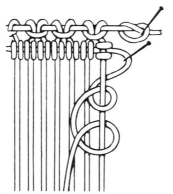

Pinning thread for picot: making first vertical knot [DHH]

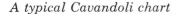

Knotting the pattern in vertical knots [DHH's] as required

fabric.

The horizontal DHH's are as given previously.

The vertical DHH is the same but the hanging thread is used as leader and a second thread is knotted down the length of this leader. The knotting thread always starts by passing behind the leader so that when travelling across the work to the right the knots face to the right, and when returning across the work on the next row the knots point to the left.

The threads in the background colour are set [attached] on the foundation thread, and the ball of thread in the pattern colour is attached to the left-hand corner of the work, from where it is used as a leader for the horizontal DHH's or used to make the vertical DHH's knots which form the pattern.

Designs are worked out on squared paper using crosses or shading for pattern. The resulting work, however, is elongated in comparison to the square shape of the original chart. It is traditional to work the first and last threads in vertical DHH's with a little picot when the thread is turned, thus forming a pretty border. Allow at least eight times the length of the finished article for the background colour threads. The pattern colour is all in one ball and is the same length as the total of all the background threads added together. Roll each thread into a ball.

Child's hammock in macramé

Size
Main section (excluding suspension threads – clew), 99cm *(39in)*
Total length, 174cm *(68½in)*
Width (excluding fringes), 54.5cm *(21½in)*

Materials
5 x 450g (1 lb) balls thick string
2 metal curtain rings, 4.5cm *(1¾in)* diameter
1 120cm *(47in)* broom handle, 2.5cm *(1in)* diameter

Main section
Cut six holding cords each 180.5cm *(71in)* long and 136 lengths each 360.5cm *(142in)*.
Using three holding cords together as one, tie an overhand knot at each end, positioning the knots 106.5cm *(42in)* apart and pin at the knots to the working surface.
Note When working on such a large scale, it may be found more practical to anchor this holding cord between two chairs. Knot each of the 360cm *(142in)* lengths onto the holding cord using a clove hitch as shown in the diagram, placing the knot 14cm *(5½in)* from one end of the working thread and spacing the threads evenly across the 99cm *(39in)* from the left in groups: one of 14 threads, nine of 12 and one of 14 threads. Omit the two outer threads at each end of the holding cord, thus leaving 11 groups of 12 threads. Divide each group into three sets of four threads each and work one flat [square] knot on each set.
Divide each group into two sets of four threads each and alternated with the previous sets and work one flat [square] knot on each set.
Using the four centre threads of each group, work two flat knots.
*From the left, use threads one to three inclusive of each group to work four flat [square] knots with a one-thread core and aligning knots to slant diagonally to the left. Using threads four to six of each group, work four flat knots in the same way, parallel to the diagonal just worked. Complete the right half of each group to corres-

pond with the first side, slanting the two parallel lines of flat [square] knots to the right.
Using the two outer right hand threads of each group together with the two outer left hand threads of the adjoining group, make two flat [square] knots.
Divide the eight threads between the groups into two sets of four threads each and work one flat [square] knot on each set, alternated with those just worked. Using the four centre threads as before, work two flat [square] knots.
At the outer edges of the work, use the two threads previously omitted together with the outer two threads of the edge groups to work two flat [square] knots. Next use the two inner threads of each of these sets of four together with the next two threads to work one flat [square] knot. Then using four threads as before, make two flat [square] knots.
Divide the work into ten groups of 12 threads each alternated with the

first groups and repeat from *, working two extra diagonal parallel lines of four flat [square] knots of three threads each slanting inwards to complete the outer diamonds. Continue alternating the groups until there are six completed diamonds down the outer edges.
Using three 180.5cm *(71in)* threads together as one holding cord, secure each of the 136 working threads to this holding cord with a clove hitch as before.

Opposite: Make your child a special junior garden hammock. It is sturdy enough to stand up to rough games as well as providing a refuge for quieter moments.

Below: Forming the clew. Thread two lengths through the first hole and lace onto the string as shown. Take the strands back and lace onto the pole. Continue until there are six knots on the ring and five knots on the pole.

To finish Cut the broom handle into two equal lengths and smooth down the cut ends.

Drill a hole through each end of both pieces, each placed 3cm *(1¼in)* from the ends. Push the end of each holding cord through one of the holes. Taking the three stranding together as one, secure with an overhand knot.

Clew Cut four lengths each 643cm *(253in)*. Drill a second hole through each end of the poles at right angles to the first and placed 5cm *(2in)* from the end. Take two 643cm *(253in)* lengths together as one and place through one of these holes, securing the end on the inner side of the pole with an overhand knot.

Place the inner edge of one metal ring 31.5cm *(12½in)* from the outer edge of the same pole.

Take the two strands together across and lace onto the ring as shown in diagram. Take the double strand back to the pole and lace on as shown in the diagram, at the same time lacing over the two threads running down the outer edge of the half diamonds.

Continue in this way until there are six knots on the ring and five on the pole. Pass the double strand through the hole in the pole and secure with an overhand knot as before. Form a clew at the other end of the hammock in the same way.

Tie an overhand knot on each fringe thread 11.5cm *(4½in)* from the holding cord and trim close.

Opposite: Add glamour to a plain shawl with a waterfall fringe of elegant macramé. Also included in the pattern is a matching purse which is fun to make.

Below: The completed hammock looks gorgeous hung in a quiet corner of the garden. Add a brightly coloured cushion to make an inviting haven.

Macramé
shawl
and purse

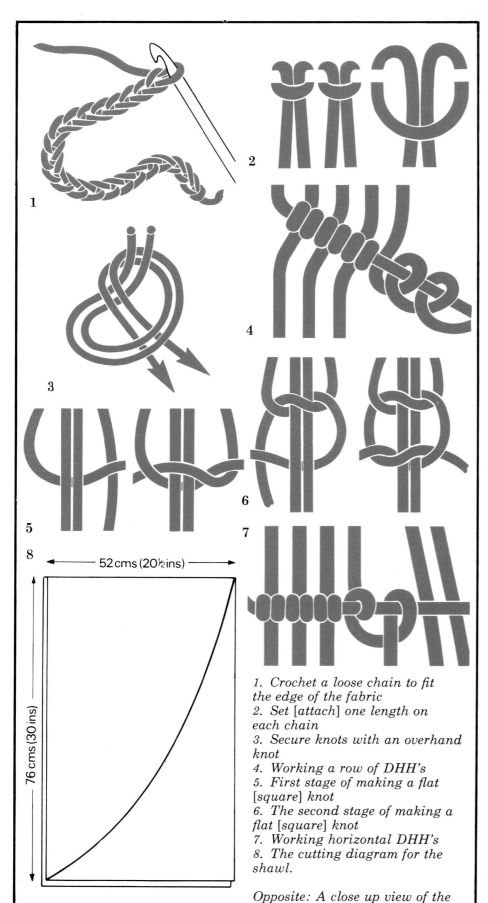

1. Crochet a loose chain to fit the edge of the fabric
2. Set [attach] one length on each chain
3. Secure knots with an overhand knot
4. Working a row of DHH's
5. First stage of making a flat [square] knot
6. The second stage of making a flat [square] knot
7. Working horizontal DHH's
8. The cutting diagram for the shawl.

Opposite: A close up view of the matching purse, showing in detail the pattern of the fabric.

Shawl

Size

Width 152.5cm *(60in)* plus 38cm *(15in)* fringes at each end
Depth including fringes 90cm *(35½in)*

Materials

Rectangle of felt or fabric 152.5cm x 52cm *(60in x 20½in)*
Matching thread
Tailor's chalk
7 x 45m *(50yd)* skeins Atlas Tubular Rayon [Tubular rayon macramé cord] Crochet hook

Cutting out the shawl

Following the cutting layout, fold the fabric in half with the two short ends together and pin. Using tailor's chalk, draw a curve from the fold to the top corner and the raw edges. Pin just inside the curve and cut out the shawl.

The fringe

Crochet a loose chain of 222 stitches to fit the lower edge of the fabric. Cut 222 lengths of cord each 128cm *(50in)* long. Pin the chain to the working surface. Double and set [attach] one length onto each chain. Secure setting on [attaching] knots with an overhand knot on each pair of threads.

Divide the threads into 37 groups of 12 threads each. Counting from the left, with the seventh thread of each group as leader, work one row of diagonal DHH's to the left over the next six threads, then using sixth thread as leader, work one row of diagonal DHH's to the right over next five threads. Omitting these leaders, take the remaining ten threads on each group together as one and make one flat [square] knot. Cross the leaders where they meet between the groups and continue the row of diagonal DHH's to left and right to form a diamond shape. At the outer edges, the leader returns towards the centre. Omitting the leaders, take each of the 36 groups of ten threads together as one and make one flat [square] knot. Omit five outer threads at each end of fringe, cross leaders and complete diagonal DHH's to right and left to complete this row of alternated diamonds.

Knot the right-hand leader over the left-hand leader on each group to complete the diamond.

Omitting the outer thread at each end of the fringe, take the remaining threads in twos together as one and make an overhand knot on each pair, immediately under the diagonal DHH's.

Bringing in the outer threads previously omitted, divide all the threads into pairs, thus alternating with the previous row and make one overhand knot on each pair about 12mm (½in) below.

Take the two threads below the centre of each second row diamond make one overhand knot on each pair about 18mm (¾in) below the previous row.

Trim fringe to about 28cm (11in), matching the curve of the felt shape.

To finish Slip-stitch crochet chain to lower edge of shawl.

Purse
Size
21.5cm x 14cm (8½in x 5½in)

Materials
Rectangle of felt or fabric 23cm x 40.5cm (9in x 16in)
2 x 45m (50yd) skeins of Atlas Tubular Rayon [Tubular rayon macramé cord] Matching thread.

The bag
Cut one holding cord about 23cm (9in) long five separate leaders 23cm (9in) long and 24 lengths each 254cm (100in). Pin holding cord to the working surface. Double and set on [attach] the 24 lengths. Secure each setting on knot with an overhand knot on each pair of threads (fig. 3). Work three rows alternated diamonds as given for Shawl fringe, the first with four diamonds, the second three and the third four again.

Pin one separate leader to the working surface and work one row of horizontal DHH's, immediately below the lowest points of the diamonds.

Taking the threads in pairs, work one row of 24 overhand knots about 6mm (¼in) down.

Pin one separate leader to the working surface and work one row of horizontal DHH's, about 6mm (¼in) down.

Repeat three rows of alternated diamonds as before.

Work one row of horizontal DHH's immediately below the diamond points as before.

Work two rows more each 6mm (¼in) below the previous one.

Work one row of four diamonds, one of three alternated as before, then one row of only two diamonds then one single central diamond.

Using the outer thread as leader, work two rows more of diagonal DHH's along the outer edges, beginning at the outer edge points of the first row of diamonds on the flap. Weave all ends into the back of the work and trim.

To finish Press work lightly. Cut felt to shape of macramé, adding a small seam allowance.

Fold felt in three with pointed section forming flap. Stitch side seams.

Fold macramé in the same way and crochet side edges together with dc [sc], continuing to the widest point of the flap. Work one row dc [sc] across top of setting on [attaching] knots.

Work a small crochet chain loop, threading the length of chain through the point of macramé flap before joining into a ring and fastening off. Sew button to front of bag to correspond with loop. Alternatively, crochet over a small ring ending with a short length of chain.

Knotted pot holders

Here are three ideas for macramé pot holders which can be adapted to fit any size pot. The holders are easy enough for a beginner to make and so quick that they can be used as an experiment with colour and texture.

Materials

Macramé cord in various colours
Different types of cord such as jute, hemp, package cord etc.
Macramé board (pots 2 and 3)
T-pins (pots 2 and 3)
Adhesive
Plant pot (pot 1)

Note The amount of cord needed will vary according to the size of the pot and the design worked.

Pot 1

Pot 1 is worked in cotton macramé cord and two-ply jute. The knots used are flat [square] knots and DHH's.

Measure lengths of cord eight to ten times the length of the pot. The number of sets of cord required will depend on the size of the pot. This number must be divisible by two. Working on the pot for shape, prepare the base of the pot as shown in fig. 1.

Following fig. 3 work in flat [square] knots to the required length. Work an overhand knot with the left and right outer cords of the flat [square] knots as shown in the diagram.

Place a holding cord 12mm to 18mm ($\frac{1}{2}$in to $\frac{3}{4}$in) from the edge of the rim of the pot. Work two DHH's with each cord. Join the holding cord together. Repeat at the rim of the pot. Trim all ends and work in. Glue the macramé to the pot along the last two rows of cording.

Pot 2

This design is worked in four panels using three colours of macramé cord. The number of sets of cords required must be divisible by three.

Measure and cut lengths of cord eight to ten times length of pot.

Base Cut a length of cord to serve as a holding cord. Join the cord together to form a circle which will fit inside the base of the pot. Secure the cords in half and fasten onto the holding cord.

Work series of flat [square] knots in a circular shape until work is as large as the base of the pot. Divide the cords into four sections. Cut a holding cord to fit around the base of the pot allowing extra cord to tie off. Work a series of DHH's to hold the cords in place and an equal distance apart. Work a double overhand knot between each section. Follow part A of fig.2 for Pot 2 on the four sections until they reach the required length. Following part B of the diagram work a row of DHH's, working two knots with each cord. Work three rows of flat [square] knots.

Cut a holding cord to fit around the top of the pot allowing extra cord to tie off.

Work a row of DHH's. Repeat the above step so that the two rows encase the rim of the pot. Trim off the ends, work in and glue down.

Pot 3 (not shown)

Pot 3 is worked with three colours in six panels. The large panels are

Opposite :Macramé pot holders are both decorative and useful. They are very quick and easy to make, and would be ideal gifts. Only pot 1 and 2 are shown here.

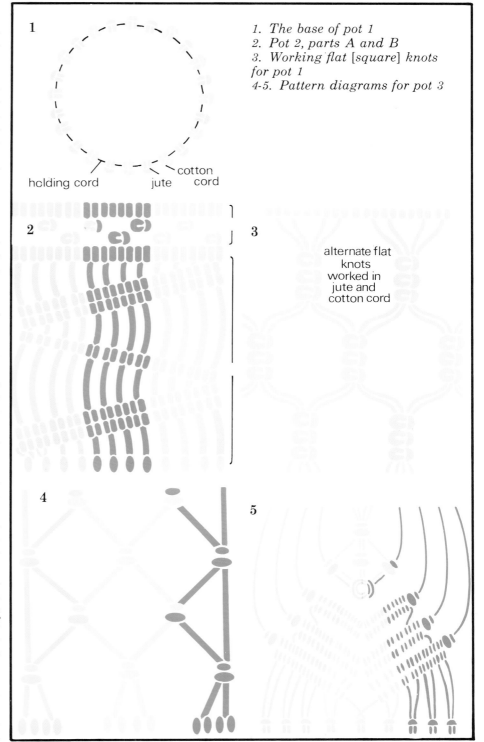

1. The base of pot 1
2. Pot 2, parts A and B
3. Working flat [square] knots for pot 1
4-5. Pattern diagrams for pot 3

holding cord   jute   cotton cord

alternate flat knots worked in jute and cotton cord

worked over nine sets of cords (18 working cords) and the small panels are worked over three sets of cords (six working cords). The size of the panels can be enlarged by adding more cords.

Cut a length of cord the size of the base allowing extra to tie off. Measure and cut the required number of cords ten to 12 times the length of the pot.

Secure the holding cord to the macramé board. Fold the cords in half and fasten onto the holding cord. Follow the diagram given for Pot 3 (fig.5). Join the two holding cords to fit around the base of the pot. Finish off the work in the same way as for pot 2.

Cavandoli watchstraps

Cavandoli is a form of macramé which uses only the basic DHH either vertically or horizontally. This produces a firm, hardwearing fabric. Traditionally two colours are used, the horizontal DHH providing the background and the vertical DHH the pattern. Designs take the form of charts which are extremely easy to follow. These colourful watchstraps combine all these traditions and make a perfect introductory project for Cavandoli.

Sizes
Narrow strap 12mm x 22cm (½in x 8¾in)
Medium strap 2.5cm x 20.5cm (1in x 8in)
Wide strap 4cm x 16cm (1½in x 6¼in)

Materials
Narrow strap Anchor Soft Embroidery Cotton [Medium weight soft embroidery thread] – 1 skein each of colour A and colour B
One buckle to fit
Medium-sized crochet hook
Medium strap As given for narrow strap
Wide strap 3 skeins of colour A, 1 skein of colour B
Felt lining 4cm x 15cm (1½in x 6in)

Narrow strap
Cut three lengths B each 152cm (60in). Wind skein A into a ball and secure with a rubber band. Cut holding cord in B of 5cm (2in) and secure to the working board.
Set [attach] doubled threads in B onto holding cord. Attach the ball of A to the left hand end of the holding cord and work one row of vertical DHH's in A, one over each B thread. Following the chart, working A in vertical DHH's and B in horizontal DHH's, continue to row six, then repeating rows three to six inclusive, continue until work measures 21.5cm (8½in).
Narrow work to a point by omitting centre two threads on next row, keeping remaining pattern correct.
Work two rows on remaining four threads.
Omit centre two threads on next row as before. Work one row more on remaining two threads.
Darn in all ends to back of work and

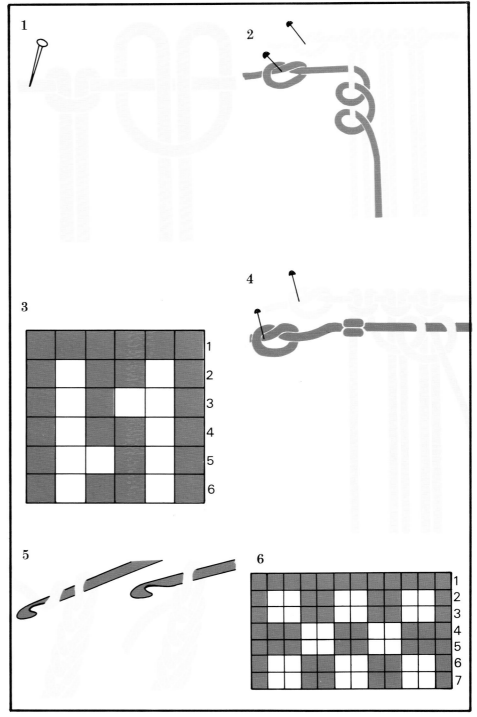

trim.
Using B, sew buckle onto straight end.
Using crochet hook and B, make a small chain loop to hold end of strap in place.

Medium strap
Cut six lengths in B each 152cm

1. Secure the holding cord to the working board
2. Working A in vertical knots [vertical DHH's]
3. Pattern chart for narrow strap
4. Narrowing work to a point
5. With a crochet hook, make a small loop to hold the strap firmly in place
6. Chart for medium strap

Above: These elegant watchstraps are an excellent example of how Cavandoli patterns can be made up quite quickly and easily. They make super gifts, and are suitable for both men's and women's watches.

(60in). Wind skein of A into a ball and secure with a rubber band. Cut holding cord in B of about 6cm *(2½in)* and secure to working board.
Set [attach] doubled B threads onto holding cord. Attach a ball of A to left hand end of holding cord and work one row of A vertical DHH's.
Following the chart, working A in vertical DHH's and B in horizontal

DHH's, continue to row seven, then repeat rows four to seven inclusive until work measures 18cm *(7in)*.
Shape point by omitting centre two threads on next and every alternate row until only the outer two threads remain.
Darn in ends to back of work and using B, sew buckle onto straight end.

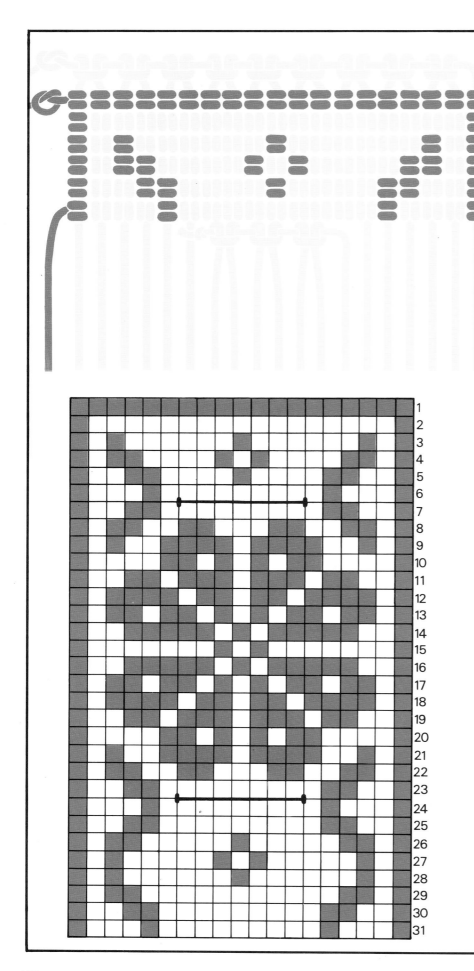

Using crochet hook and B, make a chain loop to hold end of strap in place.

Wide strap

Using B, cut six lengths each 204cm *(80in)*, six lengths each 15cm *(6in)*, one length 213.5cm *(84in)*, four lengths each 25.5cm *(10in)* and three lengths each 40.5cm *(16in)*. Pin one end of the 213.5cm *(84in)* length to the working board and set onto it three doubled 204cm *(80in)* lengths, three doubled 15cm *(6in)* lengths and three doubled 204cm *(80in)* lengths, leaving the remaining part of the 213.5cm *(84in)* thread to make the 19th working thread.

Attach the ball of A to the left-hand end of the holding cord and work one row of A vertical DHH's, one over each B thread. Following the chart, working A in vertical DHH's and B in horizontal DHH's, complete rows one to six inclusive.

Form the first slot by cutting off centre seven threads, leaving 2.5cm *(1in)* ends. Tuck these ends under the work. Pin one end of one 25.5cm *(10in)* length to the working board immediately under left hand side of trimmed threads and set on [attach] three doubled 40.5cm *(16in)* lengths and leave the remainder of the 25.5cm *(10in)* thread to make the seventh working thread, pinning the end of the holding cord so that the tops of the setting on [attaching] knots touch top edge of the slot. Continue following chart, working a second slot in the same way after row 23.

After row 31, turn the chart and work back to row one, making the slots as before except setting on [attaching] three 15cm *(6in)* lengths for the fourth slot. When the work is complete, work one row of horizontal knots in B.

To finish Oversew all ends to the wrong side of the work and trim. Oversew the felt to the back of the macramé, cutting slots to correspond and slip stitch into place.

Top: The method of working the wide strap

Left: The pattern chart

Hanging baskets

Made in 20 minutes these baskets are plain and simple, to set off an attractive plant to best advantage. The hanging basket can be made for a pot of any size.

One size basket
Materials
Twine: plant pot.

Measure from the centre of the base of the pot to the height from which you intend to hang the pot, then add about 30cm *(12in)* to be sure of having enough yarn. Double this length – ie if the measurement from centre of base of pot to hanging point is 75cm *(30in)*, add the 30cm *(12in)*, multiply by two and the total length of yarn will be 210cm *(84in)*. For medium-weight yarn cut five lengths and for rope cut four lengths.
Place all the lengths together, fold the bundle in half and make an overhand knot about 10cm *(4in)* from the fold (fig.1). To make the basket fit the pot, you have actually to work around it. So work where the pot will be safe, possibly by sitting on a thickly carpeted floor if it is an expensive pot.
Place the knot in the centre of the base of the pot. Make an overhand knot (fig.1) with two of the strands at the edge of the pot; if there is no edge, make the knot 7cm *(3in)* from the large knot. Repeat with the remaining strands (fig.2).
Arrange the knots so that they are equal distances from each other around the edge of the base. Hold two of the knots in place and, using a strand from each pair of strands, pinch them together (fig.3). This gives the position of the next row of knots. Remove the pot from the basket. Make an overhand knot where your fingers pinch the strands. Split the other pairs of strands and make overhand knots at the same distance along the length of the strands (fig.4).
Return the pot to the basket and repeat the pinching, taking two strands, one from each pair of neighbouring strands. Remove the pot and tie an overhand knot where your fingers pinch the strands. Split the other pairs and knot them at the same distance along the strands (fig.5).
Lay the basket around the outside of the pot and measure to the top of the pot with a strand from each pair of strands. Remove pot from basket and make an overhand knot which should come just above the rim. Repeat with the other strands.
Return the pot to the basket and check the position of all knots.
Using all the strands, tie an overhand knot near the ends as shown. Trim the ends (fig.5). The basket is now ready to hang.

Hanging plant basket
Size
57cm *(23in)* long and 10cm *(4in)* diameter, to take a flower pot 12cm *(5in)* in diameter.

Materials
18 strands of cotton string, cut into 3.5m *(10ft)* lengths, and a piece 28cm *(11in)* long.
6cm *(2½in)* diameter curtain ring.
Clear glue.

Mount the string on the curtain ring. Overlap the ends of the 28cm *(11in)* length of string by 18mm *(¾in)* and secure them with sticky tape.
Hold the ring between your knees or tie it to an immovable object. Loop the circle of string over the ring and place it just below the knotting strands.

1. An overhand knot
2. First row of knots
3. Position of second row
4. Second row of knots
5. The finished basket

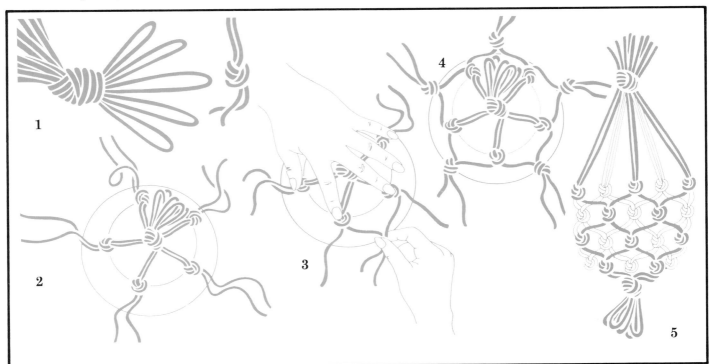

Above: Plants and flowers look even more beautiful suspended in front of a sunny window. Each of these simple knotted baskets can be decorated with brightly coloured beads.

Opposite: Knotted baskets make effective holders for trailers, and an increasingly popular use for them is as hanging fruit bowl containers.

1st row Make a row of DHH's over the string knot bearer (fig.1).

2nd row Arrange the pairs of strands into groups containing four strands (fig.1). Make a chain of four flat knots with each group.

3rd row Take the two right strands from one group and the two left strands from the adjacent group and make a chain of four flat [square] knots with these strands. Regroup the remaining strands and make four flat [square] knots each group.

4th row Regroup the strands again and make four flat [square] knots with each group.

Hold two chains of flat [square] knots together and, using all eight strands, make two flat [square] knots using two strands to make loops and working over four centre strands.

Miss the next chain of flat [square] knots and work two large flat [square] knots with the next pair of flat [square] knot chains. Make a total of three pairs of flat [square] knots with three single flat [square] knot chains between them. Working on the double flat [square] knot chains divide each into the original groups of four strands and make four flat [square] knots. Then, using the centre two strands make a knotted chain. Still working on the same strands, make an overhand knot 10cm *(4in)* from each end. Knot the other strands at the same level and comb the ends to make a fringe. With the remaining three single flat [square] knot chains, make the handle.

To make a handle leave about

immovable object.

1st row Arrange the pairs of strands into groups containing four strands.
Make six flat [square] knots with each group.

2nd row Take two right strands from one group and two left strands from neighbouring group and make one flat [square] knot 5cm (2in) away from chain of flat [square] knots. Regroup remaining strands and make one flat [square] knot with them 5cm (2in) from flat [square] knot chains.

3rd row Regroup strands and make one flat [square] knot 7cm (3in) from the second row.

4th row Regroup strands again and make two flat [square] knots 10cm (4in) from the third row.

5th row Regroup strands again and make two flat [square] knots 10cm (4in) from the fourth row.

Thread a bead over centre two strands of each group of flat [square] knots. If you find this difficult, wrap sticky tape over the ends of the twine so they do not fray.

Make half a flat [square] knot and thread another bead onto the centre strands. Make two flat [square] knots with each group.

Make a spiral using flat [square] knots, 18cm (7in) in length, or until the strands with which you are working are about 2.5cm (1in) long. Using one of the long centre strands cover the other long strand and the short ends with single DHH's for about 10cm (4in). Repeat with all other strands. Cut four more strands of twine each 1.5m (5ft) long. Mount each strand on the top loop of the fourth row of flat [square] knots.

Thread a bead onto one of the strands. Make three single DHH's using the same strand. Thread another bead onto the other strand and make three single DHH's with this strand. Do this three more times using each strand alternately. Finish with a bead. Repeat with the other extra strands. Make a knotted chain with each pair of strands, 38cm (15in) long.

Hold all the strands together that you used for making the spirals and allow the knotted chains to hang. Take one of the long strands that you are holding and cover all the strands for 10cm (4in) with single cording, pulling the knots very firmly. Return to the knotted chains

28cm (11in) of unworked string. Make four flat [square] knots with each group. Using sticky tape bind all strands together for 5cm (2in) immediately above flat [square] knots. Trim away all but three of the longest strands above tape.

Use one of these strands to bind the other two strands with single DHH's for a length of 12cm (5in) from the end of the sticky tape to make the handle. Loop the strand and tape the ends of the two shortest ones to the taped section. Using the remaining strand make a single DHH and then wind it round and round (fig.2) until all the sticky tape is covered. Make a single DHH to secure the strand and trim, leaving a 2.5cm (1in) end. Dab a little glue on the end and, using a hairpin, push the end inside the sticky tape.

A handle can be made in this way with any number of strands as the core. As soon as the glue has hardened, the basket is ready.

Hanging fruit basket

For a hanging basket 90cm (36in) long and 25.5cm (10in) in diameter, to hold a 28cm (11in) bowl or basket up to 12cm (5in) deep. To adjust size add or subtract two extra strands.

Materials

1 ball of parcel or gardening twine.
32 white round, large-eyed beads.
18mm (¾in) curtain ring.
Clear glue.

Cut the twine into eight strands, each 3.5m (11ft) long. Mount the yarn on the ring. Hold the ring between your knees or tie it to an

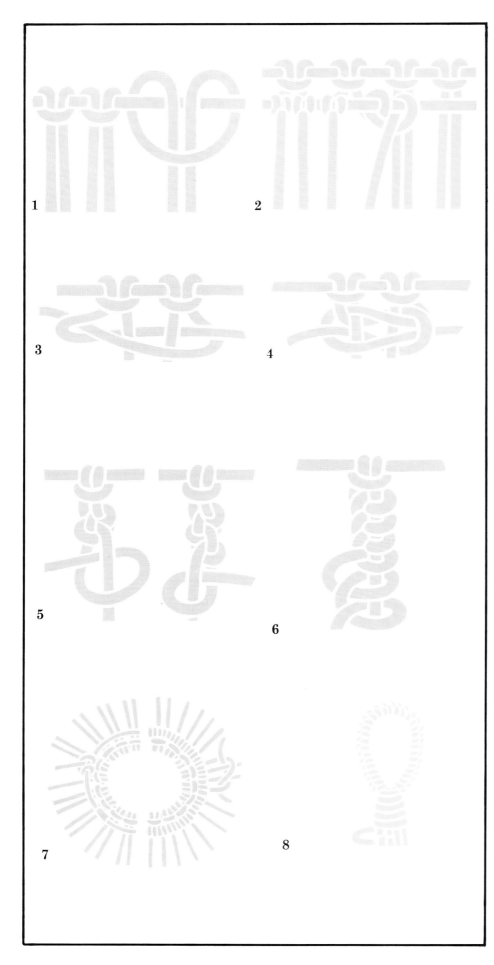

and hold them so that they are positioned between the spirals and held just above the single DHH's. Using the same strand with which you were making the single DHH's, make single DHH's over all the ends and catch in the last knots of the knotted chains.

Make single DHH's until the ends of the knotted chains are covered, trimming them to 5cm (2in) lengths if some are exceptionally long. Make a handle in same way as for hanging plant basket.

1. Mounting the strands on the knot bearer [leader]
2. Double cording knots [DHH's]
3. The first stage of the flat [square] knot
4. Completing the flat [square] knot
5. A knotted chain
6. Single cording [half hitches] over one strand
7. Cording [DHH's] over string knot bearer [leader]
8. Completing the handle

Decorative belts

White belt and variations

The instructions are for a belt to fit a 63.5cm *(25in)* waist. To make the belt larger or smaller, increase or decrease the number of motifs. The motifs are 6cm *(2½in)* long and each motif requires about 30cm *(12in)* of the strands so the yarn can be measured fairly accurately.

Materials

16 strands of yarn each 400cm *(155in)* long for 10 belt motifs, plus 30cm *(12in)* for the tassels at each end; total 460cm *(179in)* each.

Pin the strands of yarn, 30cm *(12in)* from one end, close together to the board or secure them to a firm object (fig.1). The 30cm *(12in)* piece is for making the tassels afterwards.

To make the two-colour belt arrange the strands in the following order: 4 orange, 2 yellow, 2 orange, 2 yellow, 2 orange and 4 yellow.

To make the three-colour belt arrange the strands in the following order: 4 green, 4 orange, 4 yellow and 4 green. The colours are given to tell you the sequence but, of course, you can use any colours.

Use the strand to the right of the centre as a knot bearer and make double DHH's from left to right with all the strands on the right. Repeat on the left, knotting from right to left (fig.2).

Again use the strand to the right of the centre as a knot bearer and make double DHH's with the strands from left to right, varying the distance between the DHH's to form a petal shape (fig.3). Knot the strand that was used as the first knot bearer over the present knot bearer, making seven knots.

Repeat on the left, knotting from right to left, making seven knots.

To make the 'wheatsheaf' effect in the centre, hold together the two strands to the right of the centre with the strand to the left of the centre; these form the knot bearer. Make a loose vertical double DHH with the second strand to the left of centre (fig.3).

Return to the right edge and use the knot bearer used previously, bending it diagonally towards the centre. Make double DHH's over the knot bearer from right to left, stopping at the centre. Repeat on the left.

With the extreme right strand as knot bearer make double DHH's

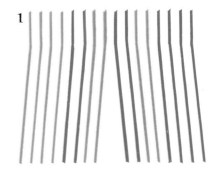

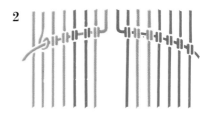

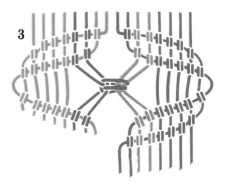

1. This example shows how the strands are mounted for the two colour belt
2. Use the strand to the right of centre as a knot bearer [leader], and then the strand to the left of centre as a knot bearer [leader]
3. Three petals have been made, creating a wheatsheaf effect

Left: A fresh white belt makes a delightful accessory for a colourful dress

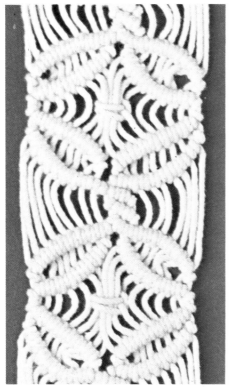

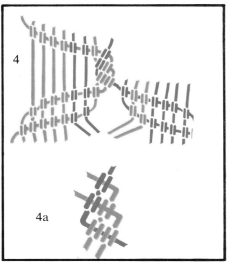

4

4a

*Top: This belt shows the effect
of using 20 strands. Instructions
are given for 16 strands to make
the colour combinations easier*

*4. The fourth petal is now complete.
The strands that are used for the
'knot' in the centre can be seen
very clearly. The last two petals
complete one pattern*

over it, working from right to left, again stopping at centre (fig.3). Repeat on the left, knotting the previous knot bearer over the present knot bearer (fig.4).

Use the same knot bearer and make a double DHH over it with the strand to the right of the centre. Use this strand again and make a double DHH using the strand to left of centre as knot bearer. With the previous knot bearer make a double DHH over the same knot bearer. Using strand previously to right of centre as knot bearer, make two double DHH's over it, using the two strands immediately to the right of it (fig.4a). This is one motif.

When you start the next motif, on the right use the strand that was last used as the knot bearer as the knot bearer again and knot from left to right. On the left knot from right to left in the same way. You have started the first row of the next motif. Make as many motifs as you require.

To finish the white, two-colour and three-colour belts with braiding, use the two centre strands and make a double DHH with one over the other.

Divide the strands at the centre to make two groups. Divide each group into three subdivisions of 3, 3 and 2 and plait [braid] to the end. Use one of the strands to make a double DHH over the others to secure the ends. Trim the ends.

Repeat with the other group of strands and the strands at the other end of the belt. The belt is now complete.

Natural and orange motif

The instructions are for a belt to fit a 63cm *(26in)* waist. The motifs are about 5cm *(2in)* long. Each motif requires about 20cm *(8in)* of the strands so yarn can be measured fairly accurately for whatever size you wish to make.

Materials

8 strands of natural and 6 strands of orange yarn each 300cm *(120in)* long for 13 belt motifs, plus 30cm *(12in)* for tassels at each end. Total 360cm *(144in)* each.

14 strands of natural yarn each 15cm *(6in)* long.

Pin the strands of yarn, 30cm *(12in)*

from one end, to the board, in the following order: 2 natural, 2 orange, 2 natural, 2 orange, 2 natural, 2 orange and 2 natural.

Using one of the 15cm *(6in)* strands as a knot bearer make double DHH's over it, working from right to left (fig.5).

Bend the knot bearer and lay it parallel to the DHH's. Make a second row of double DHH's over the knot bearer. The ends of the knot bearer are sewn to the back of the belt when it is completed.

Divide the strands in half and spread them apart slightly. Take the outside strand on the right and, using it at an angle of 45 degrees as a knot bearer, make double DHH's over it with the other six strands, working towards the centre. With the outside strand on the left as a diagonal knot bearer make double DHH's over it, working towards the centre. Then DHH the right knot bearer over the left one.

Using the outside strand on the right as a knot bearer make six double DHH's over it. Keep the DHH's close to the previous row. Repeat on the left, knotting the strand that came from the right over the left knot bearer.

Using the strands on the right make double DHH's over the knot bearer that came from the left, maintaining the angle. On the left make double DHH's over the strand that came from the right, again maintaining the angle. Keeping close to the previous diagonal DHH's and with the strand to the right of the centre as knot bearer, make double DHH's over it from left to right.

Repeat on left working from right to left. This completes one motif (fig.5). Lay another 15cm *(6in)* knot bearer across the strands and make double DHH's over it. Continue with another row of DHH's and the diagonal DHH until the required number of motifs have been made. Finish with an extra double row of DHH's to make a neat finish.

Trim the horizontal knot bearers to within 12mm *(½in)* of the edge of the belt. Using a needle and cotton, sew the raw ends to the wrong side of the belt so that they are securely held.

Natural coloured belt

The instructions are for a belt to fit a 60cm *(24in)* waist. The motifs are

15cm (6in) long. Each motif requires about 38cm (15in) of the strands so the yarn can be measured fairly accurately for whatever size you wish to make.

Materials
12 strands of yarn each 152cm (60in) for 4 motifs plus 30cm (12in) for each tassel. Total 212cm (84in) each.

Pin the strands to the board. With the outside right strand as a diagonal knot bearer make double DHH's over it, working from right to left at an angle.

With the outside right strand as knot bearer make another row of DHH's close to the previous one. Repeat once more making a total of three rows.

The five strands on the left will now be the knot bearers. Knot the sixth strand from the left over the knot bearer on the left of it. Hold the knot bearer at the same angle as the previous rows of DHH's but in the opposite direction. Knot the other strands to the right of it over the knot bearer.

Knot the strands over the fourth knot bearer from the left, then over the third knot bearer and so on, to make five rows of DHH's from left to right.

The free strands of yarn linking each group of diagonal DHH's could be used as carriers for beads.

The reverse DHH's are achieved by turning the work over and repeating the above motif on the 'wrong side'. When the motif is complete turn the work over again so that you are working on the right side again. Consequently, the back of the DHH knots show on the right side and give a pleasing woven effect. One motif is complete. Make motifs until the belt is the required length.

If you wish to leave the ends free as a fringe, on the wrong side carefully sew through the knots to secure them.

Brown and natural motif
The instructions are for a belt to fit a 72cm (28in) waist. The motifs are 9cm (3½in) long. Each motif requires six strands about 48cm (19in) long and six about 18cm (7in) long, so the yarn can be measured fairly accurately for whatever size you wish to make.

Materials
4 strands of brown and 2 strands of natural yarn each 384cm (152in) long plus 30cm (12in) for the tassels at each end; total 444cm (176in) each; 4 strands of brown and 2 strands of natural 144cm (56in) long plus 30cm (12in) for the tassels at each end; total 204cm (80in); to make 8 belt motifs.

Pin the strands to the board in the following order: 1 long strand, 2 short strands and 1 long strand of brown; 1 long strand, 2 short strands and 1 long strand of natural and 1 long strand, 2 short strands and 1 long strand of brown.

Using one 30cm (12in) strand as a knot bearer, with the raw end on the left, make double DHH's over it working from left to right.

Bend the knot bearer and lay it parallel to the DHH's. Make another row of double DHH's over the knot bearer from the right to left.

Continue with three more rows of DHH's using the extra strand as a knot bearer. The ends from the knot bearer are sewn to the back of the belt.

With the left group of four strands make a chain of 15 flat [square] knots (count loops on left side of the

5. *Diagonal and horizontal cording knots [DHH's] are usually crossed over in this way. The knot bearer [leader] which came from the left passes to the right, and the one from the right passes to left.*

Bottom: Although they look very different, these colourful striped belts are made the same way as the white pattern described previously. You can choose any colour combination.

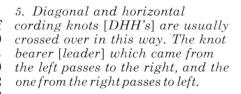

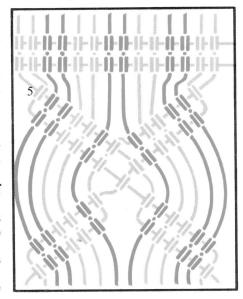

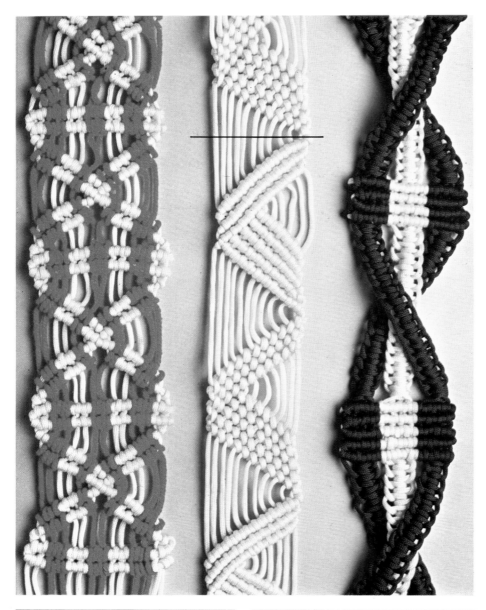

and then chains of 15, 14 and 15 flat [square] knots. Continue in this way, alternately making five and four rows of DHH's until the belt is the required length. Finish with five rows of DHH's.

Trim the horizontal knot bearers to within 2.5cm *(1in)* of the edge of the belt. Using a needle and cotton, sew the raw ends to the wrong side of the belt so that they are securely held.

Belts with a buckle
Double the length of the strands and halve their number. Mount the yarn onto the vertical buckle bar by folding it in half and passing the ends through the loop, and either work the chosen pattern from this point or make the mounting very firm with a row of DHH's before you begin the pattern. Finish off as below.

To finish without tassels
With the left outside strand as the knot bearer, make double DHH's over it towards the centre. With the right outside strand as knot bearer make double DHH's, working towards the centre. Make a double DHH with the right knot bearer over the left knot bearer.

With the left outside strand as knot bearer make one double DHH over it. Pin the strand you have just used to make a knot out of the way. Continue DHH's with the other strands on the left towards the centre.

Repeat on the right.

In the centre make a double DHH with the left knot bearer over the right knot bearer. Ignore the strand pinned out of the way. With the outside right strand as knot bearer, DHH over it to the centre. Repeat on left. Make a double DHH with the right knot bearer over the left knot bearer. Pin the two outside strands out of the way. This finish has an interlocking diagonal effect because the knot bearers are knotted alternately over each other. Continue in this way until only two strands remain and the rest are pinned out of the way. Work the ends into the wrong side of the belt by pulling them through the loops at the back of the pattern. Trim the ends and dab them with a little clear glue to secure. For additional strength, use a fine needle and yarn and oversew the unglued ends to the back of the pattern.

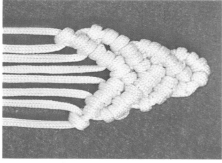

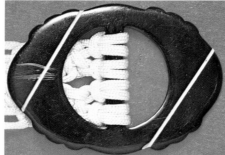

Top, left to right: Two colour belt with a rich texture, in double cording knots [double DHH's]; a belt with an unusual woven effect (to follow the instructions, start at the black line and work downwards); a lightweight belt for wearing with trousers

Above: Attaching the buckle

chain). With the centre group of four strands make a chain of 14 flat [square] knots. Repeat with the last four strands, making chain of 15. Bring left chain to right side.

Lay the centre chain over it, bring the right chain over the centre chain and place it on the left side. One motif is complete.

Using a 30cm *(12in)* strand as a knot bearer make four rows of DHH's

Waistcoat

Here's a waistcoat [vest] that can look casual for daytime with shirt and trousers or glamorous for evening worn with an elegant skirt. It is made by a combination of basic macramé knots.

Materials
3 x 50g (2oz) skeins of Nova Cord Lustre Finish [medium weight rayon macramé cord] in main colour
2 x 50g (2oz) skeins (as above) in first contrast colour
2 x 50g (2oz) skeins (as above) in second contrast colour
Crochet hook No. 4·50 [Aluminium crochet hook G]
Glue
Commercial paper pattern of waistcoat

Measurements
To fit sizes 10 to 12

To make the waistcoat [vest]
Back framework Remove seam allowance from paper pattern. Pin pattern to the macramé board. In the main colour, crochet 32 chain stitches on the crochet hook to form the frame for the waistcoat. Pin the frame into place on top of the paper pattern. Starting at the centre back, pin ten stitches from the centre back to the neck edge of the shoulder point and six stitches to the outer edge of the shoulder. Repeat for other side (fig.1).

Armhole framework At each end of the chain just pinned into position, chain 23 stitches for each armhole. Pin these into place along the armhole edge of the pattern.

Back Cut 30 threads (ten of each colour) 300cm *(118in)* long. Double these in half and hook them into the crochet frame for the shoulders and neck. Place one thread in each stitch of the foundation frame. There are now 60 threads 150cm *(59in)* long with which to work.
1st row Work an overhand knot on

Left: An unusual waistcoat, in an attractive 'chunky' pattern can be made up in various colour combinations. This one is very subtle in its effect, but it would look marvellous in bold contrasting colours

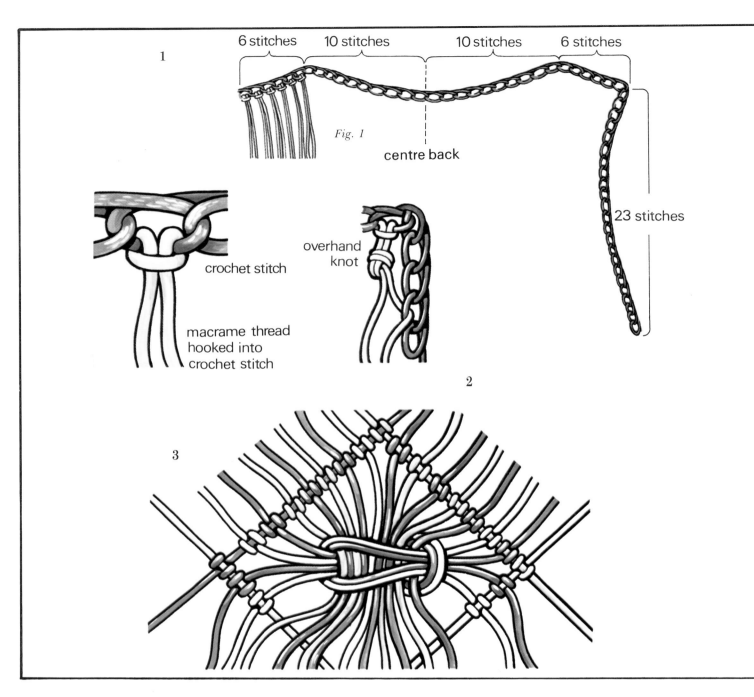

Fig. 1

6 stitches 10 stitches 10 stitches 6 stitches

centre back

23 stitches

crochet stitch

overhand knot

macrame thread
hooked into
crochet stitch

1

2

3

each pair of threads directly below the foundation frame (fig.2).

2nd row Loop the extreme left and right hand cords through the fourth crochet stitch of each armhole frame. Work a row of overhand knots alternately to the first row and 2.5cm *(1in)* below the previous row.

3rd row Repeat first row 2.5cm *(1in)* below the previous row.

4th row Loop outside left and right hand cords through the eighth crochet stitch of each armhole frame. Using the cord thus looped on the left hand side as a holding cord, work a row of horizontal DHH's 12mm *(½in)* below the pre-

vious row.

5th row Loop the last cord worked in the previous row through the tenth chain stitch of the right armhole frame, using this cord as a holding cord work as for row four, with the knots 12mm *(½in)* below the previous row.

6th row Work diagonal DHH's with cords six and seven, 18 and 19, 30 and 31, 42 and 43, 54 and 55. These five sets form the lead cords for the top half of the diamond shapes. Work cords one to five over lead cord seven with diagonal DHH's. Work eight to 12 over lead cord six, 13 to 17 over lead cord 19, 20 to 24 over lead cord 18, 25 to 29

over lead cord 30, 37 to 41 over lead cord 43, 44 to 48 over lead cord 42, 49 to 53 over lead cord 55, 56 to 60 over lead cord 54. The lead cords are then joined together at the base of the V shape with another diagonal DHH. The end lead cords, seven and 54, are then looped through the 14th stitch of the armhole frame on either side.

7th row With the two outside cords of the six cords which form the side of the V shape, work alternate flat [square] knots in the centre of the inverted V shape (fig.3).

8th row Work as for row six, to form the lower half of the diamond (this will also form the top row of

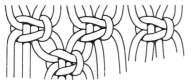

Alternated flat [square] knots

Working an overhand knot

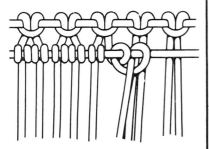

Horizontal cording [DHH's]

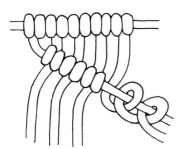

Diagonal cording [DHH's]

the next row of diamonds). These eight rows form the Basic Pattern.

9th row Work as for row seven.

10th row Work as for row eight, looping end cords through the eighteenth chain of the armhole frame.

Additional threads for back underarm Cut ten threads 239cm *(94in)* long. Double the threads in half and hook one through each side of the armhole frames. This gives 20 extra threads.

11th row Using the first new cord on the left hand side as a holding cord work a row of horizontal DHH's.

12 to 17th rows Work Basic Pattern

twice as in rows six, seven and eight using cords eight and nine, 24 and 25, 40 and 41, 56 and 57, 72 and 73 to form the five sets of 16 cords instead of 12 cords as before.

18th row Work as for row 12.

19th row Using the outside cord on the left-hand side as a holding cord work a row of horizontal DHH's.

20th row With sets of four threads work a row of alternate flat [square] knots.

21st row Work as for row 19.

22nd row Work a row of overhand knots 12mm *($\frac{1}{2}$in)* below the previous row.

23rd row Work a row of overhand knots alternately to the previous row, 12mm *($\frac{1}{2}$in)* below row 22.

24th row Using the outside cords on the left-hand side as a holding cord, work a row of horizontal DHH's.

25th row Work diagonal DHH's with cords five and six, 15 and 16, 25 and 26, 35 and 36, 45 and 46, 55 and 56, 65 and 66, 75 and 76, 85 and 86. These eight sets form the lead cords for the inverted V.

Set in four holding cords by doubling each of two cords cut 204cm *(80in)* long and looping them under the end cords of the previous row. Using these holding cords work four rows of horizontal DHH's very close together. This makes a strong neat edge to the work.

Front framework To make the front armhole frames, crochet a chain of 23 stitches on each side of the back outer edge chain at either side of shoulders on the back foundation chain. Pin these chain strips into position on the paper pattern for the front armholes. Insert the crochet hook into the seventh stitch of the back foundation frame. From this, chain 53 stitches to form the front edge. Do this on both sides. This gives the two shoulders and two front edges.

Front Cut six threads (two of each colour, for each side 376cm *(148in)* long. Double these in half and hook them into the crochet frame onto the shoulders. This gives 12 cords 188cm *(74in)* on each side front.

1st row Work a row of overhand knots on each pair of threads close to the foundation frame.

2nd row Work a row of overhand knots on alternate pairs of threads 2.5cm *(1in)* below the previous row.

Opposite: Details of the stitches used to make up the waistcoat

Left, top to botton: Alternated flat [square] knots
Working an overhand knot
Horizontal cording [DHH's]
Diagonal cording [DHH's]

Above: A detail of the front of the waistcoat shows how the pattern is formed and the colours combined to achieve a subtle effect.

Opposite: Favourite nursery rhyme characters, the owl and the pussycat are all ready to set sail in their pea-green boat. As a mobile for the nursery, it can act as a vivid focus for lots of stories.

Loop the outside threads through the fourth stitch of the foundation frame.

3rd row Repeat first row 2.5cm *(1in)* below the previous row.

4th row Work a row of overhand knots 2.5cm*(1in)* below previous row.

5th row Work a row of overhand knots 2.5cm*(1in)* below previous row.

6th row Loop the left hand end cord through the 13th stitch of the foundation frame. Using this as a holding cord, work a row of horizontal DHH's. Loop the holding cord through the 13th stitch of the foundation frame at the end of the row.

7th row With centre cords six and seven as lead cords, work first row of Basic Pattern. Loop lead cords through the 15th stitch of foundation frame on either side.

8th row Work alternate flat [square] knots as for the middle row of the Basic Pattern.

9th row Work as for third row of the Basic Pattern. For each side cut nine cords 259cm *(102in)* long.

Double these and hook into the remaining nine stitches of the armhole foundation frame. This gives 18 extra cords with which to work. With the first six new threads work the Basic Pattern already done in rows seven to nine as one top side of the V shape and the foundation frame of the armhole at the other. In this way they form the equivalent of row seven, so work rows eight and nine again. Cut five threads 295cm *(116in)* long. Double these and attach to the 16th and 20th stitches of the front foundation frame. Pin to the correct angle to form the second side of the V shape already done in rows seven to nine (see detail). Using the first six inside cords work as for rows eight and nine to form the Basic Pattern. With the first outside thread just added to the underarm as a holding cord, work a row of horizontal DHH's across the front edge. Loop the holding cord through the 22nd stitch of the foundation frame. This row is the equivalent of row 11 of the back.

Using 40 threads of the front continue to the end of the piece in the same pattern sequence as the back. Work the second side the same way.

To finish Trim all the threads to about 7.5cm *(3in)* long. Using a crochet hook pull these neatly through the back loops of the last four rows of horizontal DHH's. Glue the ends in place and trim closely. Using Colour two work a row of single crochet along the side seams. Carefully match the patterns on the back and front, along the side seams. With a crochet hook join the two edges with a loose slip stitch. With the main colour, crochet around the whole of the outside edge of the work in double crochet starting at underarm point and increase at corners to keep the work flat. Do not pull the work too tight along these edges especially along front edges. Work a second row outside. Work two rows around the armhole, starting from underarm points. Tuck in and glue any loose ends and trim neatly. Press very lightly and carefully or allow to hang for 24 hours.

Owl and pussycat

Every child who knows the tale of the owl and the pussycat who went to sea in a beautiful pea-green boat will love this ingenious macramé mobile.

Sizes

Owl About 30cm by 20.5cm (*12in by 8in*)

Pussy-cat About 30cm by 12cm (*12in by 5in*)

Pea-green boat About 66cm by 73.5cm (*26in by 29in*)

Materials

Owl 113g (*4oz*) garden string
2 rings, each 3cm (*1¼in*) diameter
2 small beads
2 twigs, one about 18cm (*7in*) and the other about 20.5cm (*8in*) long
Pussy-cat 170g (*6oz*) fine black cotton string; 2 small round beads
Pea-green boat 2 lengths 5mm (*¼in*) cane, one about 90cm (*36in*) long and with the ends bent in an upward curve and the other about 106.5cm (*42in*) long
Thin bamboo rod about 61cm (*24in*)
Thinner bamboo rod (or dowelling) about 30cm (*12in*) long
227g (*8oz*) fine green cotton string
Small ring to fit over larger bamboo rod; Short piece of wire

Owl

Cut string into 6 lengths each 254cm (*100in*), 4 lengths each 228.5cm (*90in*), 4 lengths each 216cm (*85in*), 2 lengths each 279cm (*110in*) and one length of 56cm (*22in*).
Starting at the left of the shorter twig, fold and set on [attach] one of the 228.5cm (*90in*) lengths so that the first thread measures 152cm (*60in*) and the second 76cm (*30in*). Fold and set on another of the same length so that the first thread measures 76cm (*30in*) and the second 152cm (*60in*). Fold and set on [attach] one of the 216cm (*85in*) lengths so that the first thread measures 127cm (*50in*) and the second 88cm (*35in*). Fold and set on [attach] another of the same length so that the first thread measures 88cm (*35in*) and the second 127cm (*50in*).
Double and set on [attach] three of the 254cm (*100in*) lengths.
Fold and set on [attach] one of the 279cm (*110in*) lengths so that the first thread measures 152cm (*60in*) and the second 127cm (*50in*).
Continue setting on [attaching] the threads in reverse order to cor-

respond with the first half. Divide the threads into eight groups of four threads each and work one flat [square] knot on each group. Work a second row of flat [square] knots alternated with the first.
Counting from the left, work the first four threads into a braid of eight flat [square] knots. Repeat on the centre four threads and the last four threads.
Position one ring over each group of omitted threads and DHH all the threads from each group onto the top half of its respective ring. Thread a bead onto the centre thread of each ring and then DHH each thread again round the lower half of the ring. Using the same threads, work two flat [square] knots under each ring.
Including the inner two threads from each outside braid, work a row of three flat [square] knots alternated with the previous row under each ring. Using the centre 16 threads, work 15 rows of alternated flat [square] knots, beginning with a row of four knots.
On each outer group of four threads, work a braid of 16 flat [square] knots. On each inner group of four threads, work a braid of 15 flat [square] knots. Divide all the threads into eight groups of four threads and work one flat [square] knot on each group. Work a second row of flat [square] knots alternated with the first row.
DHH each of threads nine to 12 inclusive in turn onto the longer twig and also threads 26 to 24 inclusive. Divide the threads into two groups of 16 threads each and

tie all the threads together as one in an overhand knot on each group. Trim the threads about 2.5cm (*1in*) below each knot. Take the 56cm (*22in*) length and cord 15cm (*6in*) of each end onto the shorter twig, one end at either side of the setting on [attaching] knots.

Pussy-cat

Cut 14 lengths each 244cm (*96in*), two lengths each 274.5cm (*108in*), one length of 305cm (*120in*) and three lengths each 20.5cm (*8in*).
For left ear, pin the centre of one 244cm (*96in*) length to the working surface and use as a holding cord.
Double and set on [attach] another 244cm (*96in*) length with the knot at the back of the work and then work DHH with each thread. Knot on two others of the same length in the same way.
Fold one 274.5cm (*108in*) length so that the first thread measures 122cm (*48in*) and the second 152cm (*60in*). Pin to the right of the first three lengths and knot on each thread as before.
Using the left-hand thread of holding cord as leader, make horizontal DHH's to the right across the next eight threads.
Using left-hand thread as leader, make horizontal DHH's to the right across the next seven threads.
Continue in this way for six rows more, using each thread in turn as leader until a row of one knot is worked.
For right ear, work as given for left ear but reversing the positioning of the threads and DHH's to the left.

Pin the ears to the working surface with holding cords forming the inner edges and placed about 4.5cm *(1¾in)* apart. Lay a 244cm *(96in)* length underneath as a holding cord with the centre between ears.

Double and knot on as before four of the 244cm *(96in)* lengths between the ears to form the top of the head. DHH nine leaders in turn from each ear onto the holding cord.

Lay the remaining 244cm *(96in)* length as a holding cord immediately under the previous one and DHH central eight threads onto it.

Divide the centre 20 threads into five groups of four threads each and work one flat [square] knot on each group.

Taking in additional threads as required, work a row of six flat [square] knots alternated with the previous row.

Taking in additional threads as required, work a row of seven flat [square] knots alternated with those on the previous row.

Divide the centre eight threads into two groups of four threads each and work one flat [square] knot on each group. Using the centre four threads, work one flat [square] knot.

For upper left eye, use the right-hand core thread of the flat [square] knot at the left-hand edge of row of seven flat [square] knots as leader, DHH to the right across each of the next eight threads.

Onto the centre one of these threads place one or two small rectangular beads to length of 12mm *(½in)*.

Using the left-hand core thread of the same flat [square] knot as leader, DHH to the right across each of the next eight threads, taking the line of knots in a curve under the beads. Work the right eye to correspond.

Using the left eye leaders as core, the left-hand core thread of the central flat [square] knot as left-hand working thread and the left-hand working thread of the central

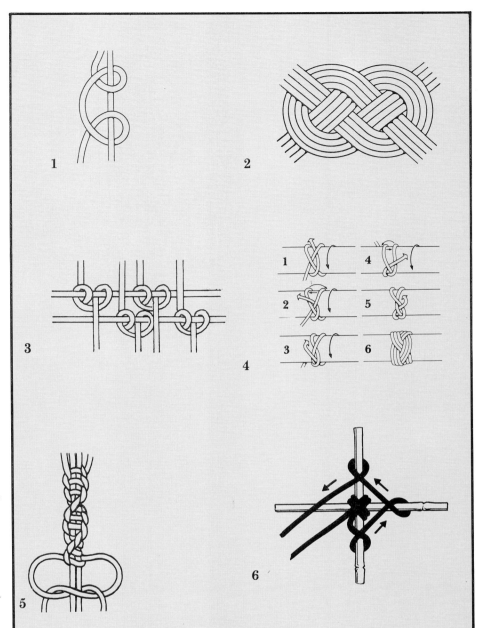

1. Vertical cording [DHH's] with the end taken to the back
2. A Josephine knot
3. Working the fabric pattern for the boat
4. The six stages of working a Turk's head
5. Working a spiral braid
6. Securing the cross piece to the boat's mast
Left: Details of the animals.

flat knot as right-hand working thread, make one flat [square] knot. Work a flat [square] knot under the right eye to correspond.

Using the centre four threads, work a braid of five [square] knots, Turn the braid under to the back of the work and bring the ends out over the top of the braid to form a ball.

Thread the two right-hand threads through the centre of the ball to emerge at the left-hand side and the two left-hand threads to come out on the right to secure the nose. Using the four threads on either side of the nose, work one flat [square] knot on each group. Divide the eight threads under each eye into two groups of four threads and work one flat [square] knot each group.

Make one flat [square] knot alternated with the two just worked.

Make two flat [square] knots alternated with the previous one and in line with the flat [square] knot to the side of the nose. Work a row of two knots alternated with the three on the previous row. Work two rows of alternated flat [square] knots, three and two respectively.

Of the group of four threads at each side of the head, use the inner three to form a core and work over the core with the outer thread.

Beginning at eye level, work vertical DHH's but taking the thread to the back of the work at the second stage of each knot. Take the core over the alternated flat [square] knots round in a curve to a point

135

about 12mm (½in) below the nose and work 11 knots in all.

Take two core threads from each vertical DHH braid and work into a Josephine knot.

Divide all the threads into eight groups of four threads each and work one flat [square] knot on each. Work ten rows more in alternated flat [square] knots.

Using the four outer threads at each side, beginning 12mm (½in) below the last row worked, make nine flat [square] knots each spaced 12mm (½in) below the last.

Divide the remaining threads into two groups of 12 threads each and work ten rows more of alternated flat [square] knots on each group.

Counting from the left, take the first 12 threads together and lay the first 7.5cm (3in) of the 305cm (120in) length with them to form a core and then work over the core with the 305cm (120in) length in vertical DHH's as before. Continue along the base of the cat, taking the remaining central threads into the core as they are reached. Once past the central threads, curve the core round as illustrated and taking the vertical DHH's through the alternated flat [square] knots at the end of the tail to secure. Fasten off and trim the core to about 7.5cm (3in).

Curve the right-hand group of four threads to correspond with the other side, darn into back of the tail and trim.

Glue a small bead to the rectangular beads in each eye.

Thread the three 20.5cm (8in) lengths through the nose for whiskers. Turn the top two upwards and glue in place. Cross the lower ones under the nose, curve the ends downwards and glue in place.

Pea-green boat

Cut 26 lengths each 50cm (20in), 16 lengths each 72cm (28in), 16 lengths each 90cm (36in), 6 lengths each 122cm (48in), 13 separate leaders each 90cm (36in), one length of 610cm (240in) and two lengths each 45.5cm (18in).

Double and set [attach] the cords onto the 90cm (36in) cane with the knot at the back and then work one half DHH with each thread, beginning from the left with 13 50cm (20in) lengths, eight 72cm (28in) lengths, eight 90cm (36in) lengths, three 122cm (48in) lengths and then

Above: A detail of the boat shows the texture of the fabric.

place the remaining threads in reverse order. Tie an overhand knot on the end of the right-hand thread of the third 122cm (48in) length to mark the centre.

Lay the 90cm (36in) length immediately under the cane and use as a separate leader for one row of horizontal DHH's across all threads. Divide the centre 12 threads into three groups of four threads each and work two flat [square] knots on each group.

*Omit eight threads on each side of these braids and divide the next 12 threads into three groups of four threads and work two flat [square] knots on each group. Repeat from * once more.

Lay another separate leader immediately below the flat [square] knots and work one row of horizontal DHH's across all threads except the 16 outer threads at either side. Lay across a separate leader.

1st pattern row Omitting a further six threads at either end, *DHH the first thread round the leader, lay the second over the leader, repeat from * to end. Lay across a separate leader.

2nd pattern row Omitting a further five threads at either end, *DHH the first working thread round the leader, lay the second over the leader, repeat from * to end. Continue in this way, laying in a new leader for each row and alternating between DHH's and laying over both across the row and from row to row, at the same time omitting a further three threads at either end

on each of the next five rows, five threads on the next row, seven on the next and nine on the next.

Lay across a separate leader and beginning and ending at the same place as the previous row of horizontal DHH's work a row of horizontal DHH's all round the base of the boat.

Place the 106.5cm (42in) cane round the base of the work and crossing the ends with the first cane. DHH each thread onto it in turn. Use the ends of the separate leaders to weave through the threads to fill any gaps.

Work a Turk's head knot to hold the two canes together at either end. Trim all ends to 2.5cm (1in), turn to the back of the work and glue in place.

Tie the centre of the 610cm (240in) length to the small ring and then unravel the strands to make four finer threads. Using the first two stages only of a flat [square] knot, work a spiral braid.

With a red hot piece of wire, make a hole through the longer bamboo cane near the top and secure the ring to the mast with wire, continuing the wire into a hanging loop. Secure the spiral braid at either end below the Turk's head knot.

Place the 30cm (12in) cross-piece in position and wind a length of string round each arm in turn in an anti-clockwise direction to secure.

Divide one 45.5cm (18in) length into three thinner strands, double each strand and set [attach] onto a 7.5cm (3in) piece of wire as before. Place the end of the second 45.5cm (18in) length along a wire and work four rows of horizontal DHH's.

Continue in rows of DHH's but omitting one knot on each until the work comes to a point. Darn in the omitted ends down the back of the work and bind all the ends together at the point. Trim ends and glue. Bend 2.5cm (1in) of the wire down against the cording to secure and hooking on the hanging loop. Insert the other end of the wire into the top of the mast.

Make a long hanging loop of thread and hook it into the bent wire. Make two holes in the foot of the mast and use them to sew the mast to the back of the boat behind the central flat [square] knot braid.

Balance the cat and the owl, one from each crossbar.

Bobbin lace

Bobbin lace is the art of twisting or weaving threads together to form a pattern. Traditionally, the pattern is first pricked out on parchment which is pinned to a pillow. The thread is wound on bobbins – hence the name – which are hung in pairs from pins.

Lace made on the principle of twisting threads is known to have been produced in Ancient Egypt. It was not until the fifteenth century that bobbin lace was developed. It is thought to have originated in Italy, and quickly spread to France and the Low Countries and, in the late sixteenth century, to England. As demand for lace from the Church and the wealthy aristocracy of Europe increased, so the art of bobbin lace grew to be a fine and well-established art by the end of the seventeenth century. The importance of the tradition is reflected in the words of Dr Samuel Johnson in 1780: 'Greek, Sir, is like lace; every man gets as much of it as he can.'

Although all bobbin lace is formed from the same basic stitches, the stitches were combined in different ways in different areas, and the resulting varieties of lace were often named after their place of origin such as Brussels, Bruges and Chantilly. The lace produced in each area had a special pattern of its own – thus Cluny lace is characterized by leaves, Maltese lace by a cross, and so on. The three main English laces, still made today, are Honiton, Bedford and Buckingham. There is no hard and fast rule as to which lace should be learned first. The following chapters describe the basic stitches and give instructions for making Torchon lace. This lace is so called from the French word for rag, and is sometimes also known as 'dish-cloth' lace.

The materials for bobbin lace are inexpensive and easy to obtain or to make oneself.

Bobbins

Thread is wound onto bobbins in pairs. The bobbins act as reels for thread, as handles to manipulate the threads and as weights so that the threads remain taut.

Since bobbin lace is a craft that has been practised for centuries, many old bobbins can be found in antique shops. They are usually expensive, however, since they have now become collectors' items.

Just as different regions developed their own lace patterns, so they made their own types of bobbin, from the simplest to heavily carved ones inlaid with silver or brass. They were usually made of wood, bone or ivory and often had beads or 'spangles' threaded onto the end for extra weight to increase the tension of the thread and to stop them from rolling around.

Modern bobbins made of wood and plastic are inexpensive and can be obtained both with and without spangles. If they are unbeaded, simply push a thin wire through the hole at the end of the bobbin to make a loop and thread on five or six beads.

The size and weight of the bobbins needed depend on the thread used. For the work described in these chapters it is only necessary to buy medium-sized bobbins. To begin with, for the basic stitches used here, 12 bobbins are sufficient.

Making bobbins

It is also possible to make your own bobbins from dowelling. Use 6mm ($\frac{1}{4}in$) dowelling and cut off a piece about 11.5cm ($4\frac{1}{2}in$) long for each bobbin. Whittle out a space with a sharp knife about 2.5cm ($1in$) long near one end. Smooth this section with fine sandpaper as this is the part onto which the thread is wound. (This is called the long neck.) Drill a small hole near the other end and thread on beads as for commercial unbeaded bobbins.

Below: Lace and lace-making accessories, old and new
Left: Modern Torchon prickings
Centre: Old Buckingham parchments
Right: Honiton, Torchon and Maltese

Pillows

Pillows used for bobbin lace making must provide a very firm surface into which pins can be stuck. A pin must remain in position when weighed down by bobbins.

Again, different areas developed their own types of pillow depending on the kind of lace being made. There are now three basic kinds of pillow used for bobbin lace – flat pillows, bolster pillows and round Honiton pillows.

As these are not easily available, and it is not possible to improvise with an ordinary pillow since this

Above: Bobbins are available in a wide variety of designs, many of which are regionally 'ethnic'. They are often highly decorated with beads and spangles, and the antique ones are collectors' items in themselves, The top and middle illustrations show lace-making in progress with the bobbins attched to the work. The ones in the illustration above are old Honiton (left) and chunky Buckingham (right).

would be too soft, it is necessary to make a flat pillow.

Materials

46cm *(18in)* of strong cotton fabric or unbleached calico, 90cm *(36in)* wide. 40cm x 40cm *(16in x 16in)* of 6mm *(¼in)* plywood or hardboard.

Stuffing – chopped hay or straw is the best kind of stuffing to make a really hard cushion. If you cannot obtain hay or straw, you can use sawdust, or bran which is available from pet suppliers. Bear in mind, however, that the latter kinds of stuffing produce a heavy cushion.

Make a fabric bag – finished size 40cm *(16in)* square, allowing generous turnings of about 2.5cm *(1in)* and leaving one side open.

Push the piece of plywood or hardboard into the bag and stuff on one side only. Pack the bag as full as possible.

Turn in the seam allowance on the open side and slip-stitch part of the opening to prevent stuffing from falling out. Leave a small gap in case you need to add more stuffing.

Knead the pillow or hammer it with a mallet until it is very hard and even. You will probably need to add more stuffing as you work, until the bag will hold no more.

Slip-stitch remainder of opening. It is a good idea to make a removable cover for the pillow. This can then be washed easily whenever necessary to keep it clean.

You will also need two cover cloths about 30cm *(12in)* square. They should be made from a smooth fabric such as poplin, and preferably in a dark colour. One cloth is pinned over the lower part of the pricking not in use, over which the bobbins lie, to protect the threads. The other cloth is used as a dust cover when you are not working.

Pins

Pins are used to keep the bobbins in order and to hold the threads in place as the pattern is worked. They should be of brass so that they do not stain the lace, and preferably as long and as strong as possible, so that they can be pushed into the cushion without bending and can bear the strain of several bobbins. It is a good idea to use a pin cushion to store pins. This is usually pinned to the pillow for easy access.

Pricking card

The pattern is pricked out on pricking card which is pinned to the pillow.

Traditionally, lacemakers used parchment, but today a special tough waxed card is used. To begin with, you can use two thicknesses of thin card glued together.

Photocopied sheets of lace pricking are obtainable for different patterns. Patterns can also be transferred onto graph paper from diagrams and pricked out in this way.

Pricker

This is useful for pricking out the

Bobbin lace is a relaxing and highly rewarding craft which can be practised both indoors and out.

pattern on the card. It can be made by forcing the eye of a needle into the end of a piece of 6mm (¼in) dowelling. Alternatively, you can use a pin vice (from hardware stores or lace-making suppliers).

Thread
Almost any size and type of thread may be used depending on the kind of lace and the desired effect. For the purposes of the work described in the following pages, it is advisable to use fairly thick thread. This is more easily obtainable than the fine linen lace thread, and is also more manageable for a beginner than the very fine thread necessary for more delicate patterns.

Above: A handkerchief in fine linen fabric is the ideal size and shape to display your skills in lace-making. The border on this one is made in an exquisite pattern in Bedfordshire lace.

Below: Bedfordshire lace has many distinctive patterns, ranging from the ornate to more simple designs as shown in these examples.

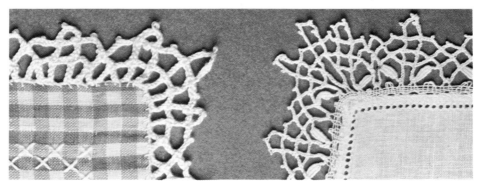

Basic stitches

You have been introduced to the materials required for bobbin lace. Now here are the instructions for working the two basic stitches – cloth stitch and half stitch.

Cloth stitch and half stitch are the rudimentary stitches for all lace making. As in knitting, once you have learned the basic stitches, there are no patterns that cannot be built up. The particular pattern simply depends on the combination of these stitches or the addition of an extra 'twist' of the threads.

Materials
12 bobbins
Flat lace pillow and two cover cloths
Pricking card
Graph paper with eight squares per 2.5cm *(1in)*
Pencil
Pricker
Brass pins and pin cushion
Thread – begin by using a fairly thick thread such as DMC coton perlé No.8 [DMC pearl cotton No.8] or Anchor pearl cotton No.8

Winding bobbins
Bobbins are wound in pairs.
Hold a bobbin in the left hand with the narrow end or 'long neck' – the section on which the thread is wound – pointing towards the right hand.

With the right hand, wind the thread onto the bobbin, starting at the left-hand side of the long neck. Wind the thread over and away from you in a clockwise direction (fig.1). The thread must be wound evenly and tightly.

When you have wound about 1m *(1yd)* of thread onto the bobbin, pull out another 1m *(1yd)* of thread from the ball of yarn, and cut off.

Wind the thread onto another bobbin, starting at the cut end of the thread, and winding it in the same way as the first bobbin.

When there are about 15cm *(6in)* of thread left between the two bobbins, make a 'hitch' on the thread of each bobbin (fig.2).

This secures the thread in that it prevents it from unravelling freely, but you can pull out more thread as you need it.

Wind six pairs of bobbins in all.

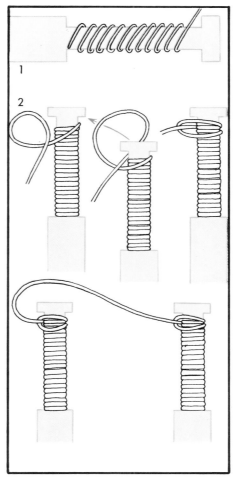

The pattern
Cut out a piece of pricking card about 23cm *(9in)* by 2.5cm *(1in)*.

Cut out a piece of graph paper with eight squares per 2.5cm *(1in)* to the same size.

Transfer the pin marks shown in fig.3 to the graph paper with a pencil. Pin the graph paper on top of the pricking and onto the pillow. Holding the pricker vertically, prick out the holes where marked. Remove the graph paper. The pricking is now ready for use. The pricking should be pinned firmly to the pillow lengthwise. It should be central widthwise and only about 5cm *(2in)* to 7.5cm *(3in)* from the top of the pillow.

Cover the lower half of the pricking with a cover cloth to protect the threads as you work, and pin the cloth tightly to either side of the pillow.

1. Wind the thread onto the long neck of the bobbin.
2. Wind and hitch bobbins in pairs as shown here

Below: A sumptuous border made entirely of bobbin lace makes a beautifully romantic garment

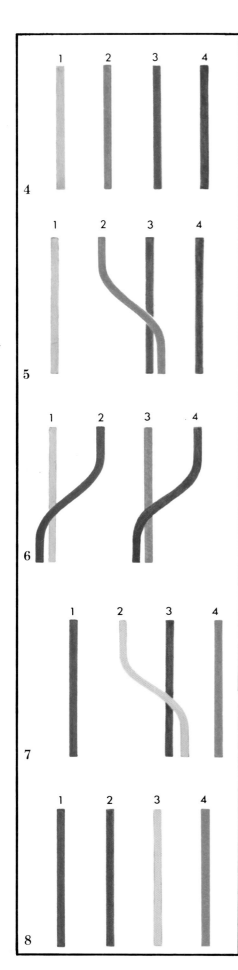

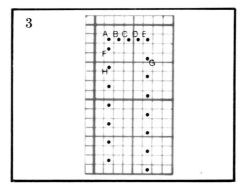

3

3. Pin-holes for pattern are marked on graph paper as a guide
4-8. Working cloth stitch

Cloth stitch

Following fig.3, put a pin in each of the holes A to F and hang a pair of bobbins on each pin.

Begin by working with the pairs hanging from pins F and A. The pair from pin F should be on the left of that from pin A. Number the positions of the four threads in your mind from left to right as 1, 2, 3 and 4 (fig.4). Note that these numbers represent the positions of the threads and not the threads themselves.

Using one hand, lift the thread in position 2 over that in position 3 (fig.5).

Using both hands simultaneously, lift the thread in position 2 over that in position 1, and the thread in position 4 over that in position 3 (fig.6). Using one hand, lift the thread in position 2 over that in position 3 (fig.7).

These three moves constitute a cloth stitch. Note that the two pairs of threads from pins F and A have completely changed places (fig.8). Push the left-hand pair of threads aside to the left and take the pair hanging from pin B from the right. Work another cloth stitch using the pairs from pins F and B in exactly the same way.

Then push the left-hand pair aside to the left as before.

Continue working in cloth stitch, taking the pairs of threads from C, D and E in turn.

The pair from pin F has now travelled right across the pattern to the right-hand side of the work, weaving through all the other pairs. It is this pair that does all the work and it is called the 'weaver', while the other threads, which lie straight down the pillow, are called the 'passives'.

Twist the weaver threads twice by lifting the right-hand thread of the weaving pair over the left-hand one and then repeating the move.

Insert a pin in hole G to the left of the weavers.

Make another cloth stitch with the weavers and the pair of threads from pin E exactly as before, but this time push the right-hand pair to the right before taking the next pair from pin D.

Continue working back across the pattern from right to left in cloth stitch, taking the threads from D, C, B and A in turn.

When the weavers reach the extreme left of the pattern, twist the weavers twice as before.

Put a pin in hole H to the right of the weavers and work back across the pattern to the right.

Note In whichever direction you are weaving, the cloth stitch and the twists at the ends of rows are worked in exactly the same way. Only the side to which you push each pair aside as you have finished working with it, and the side from which you take the fresh pair, will alter.

It is important to obtain good tension in lace making. A useful working hint is to hold the weavers firmly at the end of each row when you have worked the twists and inserted the new pin and to stroke the passives downwards.

Work a sample length of lace in this stitch, until you can work it automatically.

Cloth stitch and twist

This is a variation on cloth stitch which produces a very firm stitch. Work each cloth stitch as before but then repeat the second step of the cloth stitch each time, twisting each pair of threads once, right over left (see fig.6). Thus each stitch is made up of four, rather than three, moves.

At the end of each row, before inserting the next pin, twist the weavers once more only. (Since they have just been twisted once already, this makes two twists in all.)

Practise this stitch until you can work a neat length of the pattern.

Half stitch

Half stitch is the only other basic stitch. As its name implies, there are fewer movements involved than in

cloth stitch.

Each half stitch is made up of the first two movements only of the cloth stitch (see figs.5 and 6). Work across the row towards the right as before. Before inserting the next pin at the end of the row, twist the right-hand pair once more only (since they have just been twisted once in the last move, this makes two twists in all). You should soon realize that, in fact, only one of the original weaving threads is travelling across the work and that all the other threads are travelling diagonally.

This is rather a loose stitch when used on its own. When you have gained confidence in working this and the previous stitches, try working cloth stitch and twist with the first and last pairs of each row (from A and E), and half stitch with the middle three pairs (from B, C and D).

Note When you reach the bottom of the pricking, secure each loose thread carefully to the cover cloth with a pin to keep them all in their correct positions. Fold the cover cloth over the threads and the bobbins to take the tension off the threads, and remove all the pins from the pricking card. Lift the lace very carefully to the top of the pricking card and replace the side pins (F, G, H and so on) along the first 2.5cm *(1in)* or so of the lace. Remove the pins holding the loose threads in place, and carry on working, being careful at first not to pull too hard on the passive pairs of threads.

Work a length of lace in each of these stitches until you can do them automatically, watching the threads just below the pins rather than the bobbins.

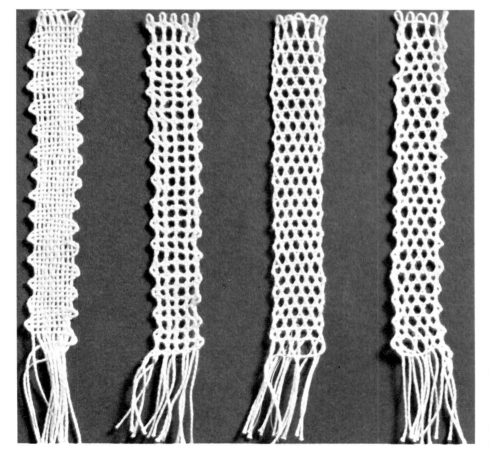

Top: Work in progress on a piece of Spider and Fan lace. This is a kind of Torchon pattern, and instructions are given later
Left to right: Cloth stitch; cloth stitch and twist; half stitch; half stitch with cloth stitch and twist at the edges.

Ladder and Little Torchon Fan

You should by now be familiar with the basic techniques and stitches for working bobbin lace. Once you have practised these sufficiently to work them with confidence, you are ready to start your first pattern. This section gives instructions on two of the simplest patterns – the Ladder and Little Torchon Fan. You will need the same basic materials for both patterns as for the basic stitches. 12 bobbins are required for the Ladder and 16 for the Little Torchon Fan.

The Ladder
Wind six pairs of bobbins using a fairly thick thread such as DMC coton perlé No.8 [DMC pearl cotton No.8] or Anchor pearl cotton No.8. Prepare the pricking card as for the basic stitches using graph paper with eight squares per 2.5cm (1in) and the pattern given in fig.1. Following fig.1, put a pin in holes A and B.

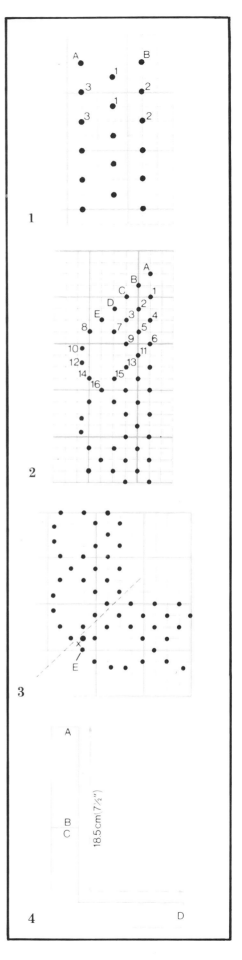

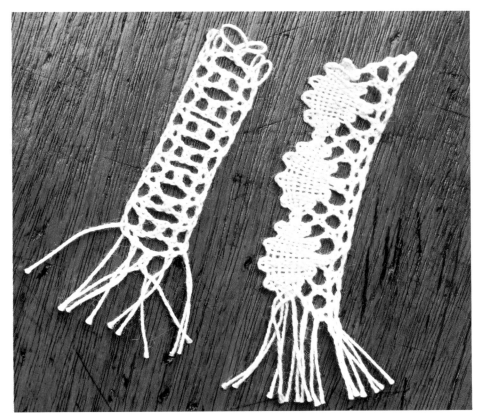

Opposite: Lace hairband in the Ladder pattern is an easy way of making up this fragile design.
1. Pricking chart for the Ladder pattern
2. Pricking chart for the Little Torchon Fan pattern
3. How to work a corner
4. Cutting the pricking
Left: Ladder and Little Torchon.

Hang three pairs of bobbins from pin A, one pair from pin B, one from pin C, two from pin D and one from pin E. Following fig.2, work pattern as follows:

Pin-hole 1

The pin in pin-hole 1 is a foot pin. With the third pair from the right (from A), work cst with each of the two pairs to the right of it in turn. Insert a pin in pin-hole 1 between the second and third pairs from the right and work a cst with these two pairs.

Pin-hole 2

With the left-hand pair from pin 1 and the pair from pin B, work half stitch (hereinafter hs).

Place a pin in pin-hole 2 between these two pairs and work another hs with the same two pairs.

Pin-hole 3

With the left-hand pair from pin 2 and the pair from pin C, work hs. Insert a pin in pin-hole 3 between these two pairs, and work hs with the same two pairs.

Take out pins A, B and C, and carefully pull down loose loops.

Pin-hole 4

Work as pin-hole 1.

Pin-hole 5

Work as pin-hole 2, using the left-hand pair from pin 4 and the right-hand pair from pin 3.

Pin-hole 6

Work as pin-hole 1.

Pin-hole 7

Work the pair from pin E (weavers) to the right in cloth stitch (hereinafter cs) through the next three pairs. Twist the weavers right over left twice and put a pin between the weavers and the last pair passed through.

Pin-hole 8

Work back through the same three pairs in cs. Twist the weavers right over left twice and put a pin between the weavers and the last pair passed through.

Pin-hole 9

Work as pin-hole 7 but work

Hang three pairs of bobbins from pin A and three pairs from pin B so that each bobbin of each pair lies next to its partner.

Pin-hole 1

Take the two centre pairs – ie the right-hand pair from pin A and the left-hand pair from pin B – and work them together in cloth stitch and twist (hereinafter cst).

Put a pin in pin-hole 1 between these two central pairs, and work another cst with the same two central pairs.

Pin-hole 2

Using the right-hand pair from pin 1, work cst through each of the two pairs from pin B in turn.

Put a pin in pin-hole 2 between the second and third pairs from the right. Leave the pair on the extreme right aside, work cst with the other two pairs.

Pin-hole 3

Now take the left-hand pair from pin 1 and work cst through each of the two remaining pairs from pin A in turn. Put a pin in pin-hole 3 between the second and third pairs from the left. Leave the pair on the extreme left aside, work cst with the other two pairs. These last moves (with pairs from pin A) match those on the right-hand side (with pairs from pin B) to make a completely symmetrical pattern.

The three pins – 1, 2 and 3 – complete a pattern repeat. Continue working the pins in the same order until the desired length of pattern is reached. Pins 2 and 3 are called 'foot pins'. The straight edge formed outside these pins is called the 'foot edge'.

This pattern looks most attractive when the lace is threaded with a narrow velvet ribbon for use as a hairband or choker, or even to trim a dress.

If you wish to make a finer lace, reduce the size of the graph paper and the thickness of the thread. For example, use graph paper with ten squares per 2.5cm (1in) and a finer thread such as DMC coton perlé or Anchor pearl cotton No.12.

Little Torchon Fan

Wind eight pairs of bobbins using pearl cotton No.8.

Prepare the pricking card using graph paper with eight squares per 2.5cm (1in) and the pattern given in fig.2. As this pattern is more complicated to follow than the previous one, it is helpful to mark pin-hole numbers on the pricking card for quick and easy reference. Use a fine felt-tipped pen or ink rather than a ballpoint pen or a pencil as these will soil the lace. Following fig.2, insert pins in pin-holes A, B, C, D and E.

through four pairs.

Pin-hole 10
Work as pin-hole 8 but work through four pairs.

Pin-hole 11
Work as pin-hole 7 but work through five pairs.

Pin-hole 12
Work as pin-hole 8 but work through five pairs.

Pin-hole 13
Work as pin-hole 7 but work through four pairs.

Pin-hole 14
Work as pin-hole 8 but work through four pairs.

Pin-hole 15
Work as pin-hole 7, working through three pairs.

Pin-hole 16
Work as pin-hole 8, working through three pairs.

Take out pin D and carefully pull down loops of thread.

Put one twist, right over left, on each of the pairs hanging from pins 11, 13 and 15.

This completes a pattern repeat.

A corner

If you wish to make enough Little Torchon Fan lace to trim a handkerchief, it is advisable to work proper corners for a more professional finish, rather than gathering a straight length of lace around the corners.

To work a corner, make another pricking, using corner pattern (fig.3). It is better to plan your work so that the join in the lace will be along one side of the handkerchief. Thus the length of the straight pricking, from the starting point, plus the whole inside edge length of the corner pricking should measure the same as the edge of the handkerchief to be trimmed. For example, if the handkerchief measures 18.5cm *(7½in)* square then following fig.4, the length from A to D should also measure 18.5cm *(7½in)*. In order to achieve the desired length of pricking, the prickings will have to be cut. It is best to do this when you have worked about 10cm *(4in)* of the straight pricking.

Cut the bottom of the straight pricking, at B (see fig.4) horizontally immediately below the pin-hole which completes a fan (pin-hole in position 16). Cut the top of the corner pricking, at C (see fig.4), horizontally immediately below the first pin-hole of a fan ie pin-hole in

position E.

As the last pin-hole of a fan is equivalent to the first pin-hole of the next fan, these two prickings will butt one against the other, so that the pattern is continuous.

Bearing in mind the length of handkerchief and the desired length of the pricking, cut the bottom of the corner pricking, at D (see fig.4), in exactly the same way as at B.

You will later also have to cut the top of the straight pricking, at A (see fig.4), in the same way as at C, but do not do this yet as the first pattern repeat of lace is lying on top of the pricking and is in the way. Pin the corner pricking onto the pillow, so that B butts against C (see fig.4).

To work the corner, following fig.3, work all the pin-holes before the dotted line.

To work pin-hole X, work the weavers to the right in cs through two pairs. Put a pin in pin-hole X and work back in cs to the pin-hole at the top of the next fan (pin-hole in position E). Now turn the pillow around through 90 degrees so that you can work down the next straight side, and you will see that you must work another fan in cs before returning to the foot edge. When you have worked around the corner, you will find that you have very little room to work on the pillow. To move up the corner pricking, first remove all the pins from the first straight pricking.

Pin the loose threads carefully to the cover cloth as when moving up a straight pricking (explained on page 143) but, instead of removing all the pins, lift the corner pricking, pins and lace all together and move the entire work to the top of the pillow in the same position as the original straight pricking.

Push all the pins carefully back into the pillow.

You now have room to replace the original straight pricking. First, cut the top of the straight pricking in the same way as the top of the corner pricking, as described previously. Pin the straight pricking directly below the corner pricking, so that they butt together, and continue working down the pillow along the second side of the lace edging.

Work around all four sides, with the pieces of pricking leap-frogging over each other, until you meet the

first pattern repeat on the first side.

Finishing off

When all four sides have been completed and the last pattern repeat has been worked, pin the very first pattern repeat back into place onto the pillow, inserting pins into all the original pin-holes. It is helpful to push these pins right down so that the heads are flush with the pillow.

Each pair of bobbins must now be linked to the hole in the lace at the pin-hole to which it would normally travel.

To make this link, take the relevant pin out of its pin-hole. Push a fine crochet hook through the little hole in the lace where the pin was and draw one thread of the corresponding pair of threads through the hole to form a loop. Pass the partner bobbin of the pair through this

loop in the thread so that the two threads are linked.

Tighten the loop and replace the pin to hold the lace firm.

Tie the two threads together with a reef knot against the pin.

There are eight pairs of bobbins, hanging from pins 6, 11, 13, 15 and 16. The linking should be done as follows: The pair from pin 11 would normally travel through the two pairs from pin 6 to pin-hole 1 (pin 1 is a foot pin). In order to preserve the foot edge, work as pin-hole 1 until the point at which you would normally insert the pin. Make a link between each of the two right-hand pairs and the hole at pin 1. The third pair from the right does not naturally travel to another pin, so make this link with the bar between pins 1 and 2. This also preserves the vertical line of the pattern.

The pair from pin 13 is linked to the hole at pin 2.

The pair from pin 15 is linked to the hole at pin 3.

The pair on the extreme left-hand side from pin 16 (weavers) is linked to the hole at pin E.

The two passive pairs of threads, hanging between pins 16 and 15, can also be linked to the hole at pin E. It is neater, however, if they are darned into the work by hand after the lace has been taken off the pillow, in which case the bobbins should be cut off and the loose threads left for the time being.

When the linking is complete, cut off all the bobbins and take out all the pins. Remove the lace from the pillow. If you are darning in the two passive pairs of threads, take each thread in turn and, using a fine needle, make a couple of tiny darning stitches into the fan of the

first pattern repeat. Cut these threads off flush with the lace. To neaten the join, using one of the weaving threads on the extreme left and a fine needle, neatly oversew all the other loose ends of thread along the diagonal line. Alternatively, if you find this difficult, you can simply cut all the loose threads close to the knots. Whichever way you choose to work, this side will obviously be the wrong side of the piece of lace when you come to sew it to the handkerchief.

Stitch the lace to the handkerchief by oversewing edge to edge. Take the thread alternately into the hole where the foot pin was and into the gap between the foot pins. Ensure that your stitches are neat and small. Try to avoid pressing the lace, but, if this is absolutely necessary, press on the wrong side, using a soft pad, such as a folded towel

Spider and Fan; Little Fir Tree

You are now ready to learn two more patterns for Torchon lace. The first is the Spider and Fan pattern which provides a suitable sequel to the Little Torchon Fan as parts of the pattern are similar.

The second pattern given in this section is Little Fir Tree and is completely different from any of the patterns covered so far. Instructions are given for making a round mat. The basic requirements for these two designs are the same as those for the basic stitches. For detailed instructions on all the stitches used, turn back to the previous pages.

Spider and Fan

This pattern is wider than any learned previously – 26 bobbins are required. Wind 13 pairs of bobbins, using a fairly thick thread, such as DMC coton perlé [DMC pearl cotton No.8] or Anchor pearl cotton No.8. Prepare the pricking card as for the basic stitches using graph paper with eight squares per 2.5cm *(1in)* and the pattern given in fig.1. Mark

Above: The deep border on this handkerchief is made up in a really exquisite lace pattern in a combination of Torchon designs. Once you are more confident, you'll find that you can combine and create your own ideas.

the pin-hole numbers with ink or a fine felt-tipped pen on the pricking card for easy reference.

Note If you wish to make a finer lace, use a finer thread and graph paper with ten squares per 2.5cm *(1in)*. If you prefer to make lace that can be easily machine washed – for a pillow-case border or tray cloth edging for example – use No.20 crochet cotton. This thread has a much higher twist than is normally used for lace making and is not usually considered to be very suitable since it produces a rather hard, stiff lace. It will, however, stand machine washing.

Following fig.1, put a pin in each of the holes A, B, C, D, E, F, G, H, J and K.

Hang three pairs of bobbins from pin A, one pair of bobbins from each of the pins B, C, D, E, F, G, H, two pairs from pin J and one pair from pin K.

Work pin-holes 4, 5, 6, 7 and 8 in the same way as pin-holes 2 and 3, each time taking the left-hand pair of the two pairs used for the previous pin-hole, and one new pair. For example, pin-hole 4 uses the left-hand pair from pin 3 and the pair from pin D, and so on.

When all eight pin-holes have been worked, take out pins A, B, C, D, E, F, G and H and carefully pull down the loops of thread.

Pin-hole 9

Work as pin-hole 1.

Pin-holes 10, 11 and 12

Work as pin-holes 2, 3 and 4.

Pin-hole 13

Work as pin-hole 1.

Pin-holes 14 and 15

Work as pin-holes 2 and 3.

Pin-hole 16

You are now ready to work the spider, the basic construction of which is shown in fig.2. This will be worked with the pairs hanging from pins 6, 7, 12 and 15.

Put two more twists, right over left, (making three in total) on each of the pairs hanging from pins 6, 7, 12 and 15. The spider's body is worked entirely in cloth stitch (cs).

Work the pair directly to the left of centre (from pin 6) in cs through the two pairs to the right of centre (from pins 12 and 15).

Work the other pair to the left of centre (from pin 7) in cs through the same two pairs.

Put a pin in pin-hole 16 so that two of the four pairs hang on either side of it.

Make sure that the threads are taut. Work the pair directly to the left of centre in cs through the two pairs to the right of centre.

Work the other pair to the left of centre in cs through the same two pairs. Put three twists on each of the four pairs.

This completes the spider.

Spiders occur frequently in Torchon lace and may have any number of

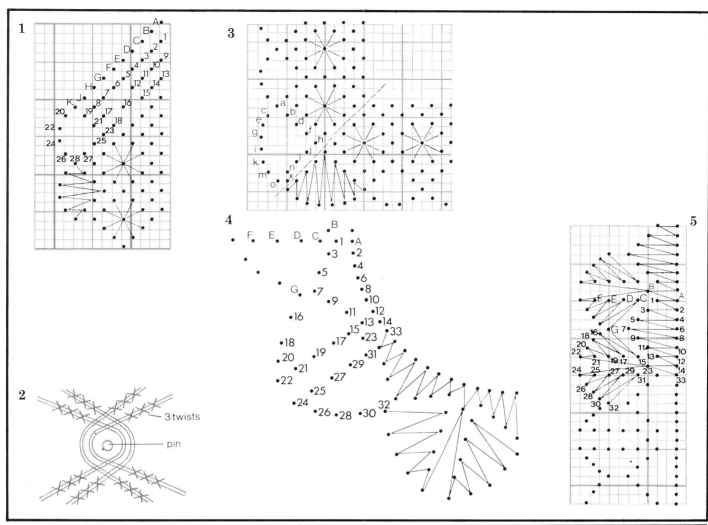

1. Graph pattern for Spider and Fan
2. Basic construction of the Spider design
3. Spider and Fan corner
4. Quarter circle Little Fir Tree trace pattern
5. For a square handkerchief border, work the Little Fir Tree pattern using this pricking for a straight border.

Right: This unusual example of coloured Torchon lace was made in Russia.

legs. The method of working is, however, always the same.

Pin-hole 17
Work as pin-hole 2, using the right-hand pair from pin 8 and the first of the spider's legs.

Pin-hole 18
Work as pin-hole 2, using the right-hand pair from pin 17 and the second of the spider's legs.
Pin-holes 19, 20, 21, 22, 23, 24, 25, 26, 27 and 28 constitute the fan. This is worked in exactly the same way as the fan in the Little Torchon Fan (see page 139).
Take out pin J and carefully pull down the loops.
Put one twist on each of the pairs hanging from pins 23, 25 and 27. This completes a pattern repeat.
It can be seen that this pattern falls naturally into three sections – the Torchon net, the spider and the fan.

Corner
If you wish to make a lace edging for a handkerchief or mat, it is advisable to work a proper corner as for the Little Torchon Fan (see previous pages). Follow the general instructions for working a corner given for the Little Torchon Fan, using the corner pattern given here (fig.3). Note that the fans immediately before and after the corner are larger than those in the rest of the pattern so as to accommodate the spiders.
If pin-holes A to O (see fig.3) are worked in order, it will be seen that an extra pair of bobbins must be brought into the pattern from the right at pin H to keep the threads running correctly. Also, note that you must work four extra rows of the fan pattern to complete the fan.

Little Fir Tree
The fan in this pattern is highly typical of Torchon lace, although quite unlike that used in the previous pattern. A narrow edging with this type of fan is thought to have trimmed Oliver Cromwell's baby clothes.
A pattern and instructions are given for making an edging for a round mat (fig.4). There is no reason, however, why this pattern cannot equally well be worked for a straight edging – a pattern is also given for this (fig.5).
To make the round mat edging, trace the pattern (see fig.4) very

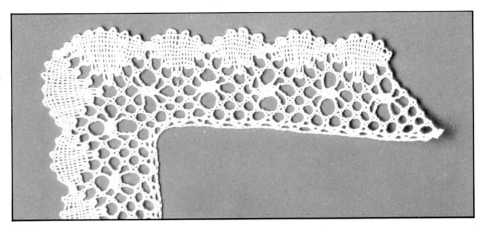

carefully and make an accurate pricking from the tracing. It is easier to prepare the pricking in this way because it is round and does not lend itself well to graph paper.
Mark the pin-hole numbers for at least one pattern repeat for easy reference.
Wind nine pairs of bobbins with pearl cotton No.8 [DMC pearl cotton No.8] (or crochet cotton No.20 if the finished article is to be frequently machine washed).
Following fig.4, put a pin in each of the holes A, B, C, D, E, F and G. Hang one pair of bobbins from pin A, two pairs from pin B, one pair from each of the pins C, D, E, F, and two pairs from pin G.

Pin-hole 1
Work the pair from A (weavers) to the left in cs through three pairs. Twist the weavers twice, right over left, and insert a pin in pin-hole 1 between the weavers and the last pair passed through.

Pin-hole 2
Work back through the same three pairs in cs.
Twist the weavers twice and insert a pin between the weavers and the last pair passed through.

Pin-hole 3
Work as pin-hole 1, but work through four pairs.
Pin-hole 4
Work as pin-hole 2, but work through four pairs.
Pin-hole 5
Work as pin-hole 1, but work through five pairs.
Pin-hole 6
Work as pin-hole 2, but work through five pairs.
Pin-hole 7
Work as pin-hole 1, but work through six pairs.

Top: Sample of Spider and Fan
Above: Circular Little Fir Tree border

Pin-hole 8
Work as pin-hole 2, but work through six pairs.
Pin-hole 9
Work as pin-hole 1, but work through five pairs.
Pin-hole 10
Work as pin-hole 2, but work through five pairs.
Pin-hole 11
Work as pin-hole 1, but work through four pairs.
Pin-hole 12
Work as for pin-hole 2, but work through four pairs.
Pin-hole 13 Work as pin-hole 1, through three pairs.
Pin-hole 14
Work as pin-hole 2, through three pairs.

Then work the weavers to the left in cs through two pairs.
Twist the weavers once and leave.
Put one twist on each of the pairs hanging from pins 7, 9, 11 and 13.
Take out the pins B, C, D, E and F and carefully pull down the loops of thread.
Note It will be seen that there is no foot edge on this pattern. If one is preferred, work as follows:

For the last stitch before all the pin-holes on the right-hand edge, ie pin-holes 2, 4, 6, 8, 10, 12, 14 and 33, twist the weavers once and work cs. Then put a pin between the second and third pairs from the right. Leave the extreme right-hand pair aside on the right. Pin-holes 3, 5, 7, 9, 11 and 13 are then worked in the same way as described previously, but through one pair less each time.

For example, pin-hole 2 would read as follows: work back through the first two pairs in cs. Twist the weavers once and work cst with the next pair on the right (ie the last of the three). Put a pin between the second and third pairs from the right and leave the right-hand pair aside on the the right.

Pin-hole 3 would now read: work back across the row to the left in cs with the second pair from the right, working through three pairs only. This will produce the same pattern as above but with a foot edge.

Pin-hole 15
You are now ready to work the fan.

Work the left-hand pair from pin G (weavers) to the right in cst through five pairs.

Twist the weavers once more and insert a pin between the weavers and the last pair passed through.

Pin-hole 16
Work back through the same five pairs in cst.

Twist the weavers once more and insert a pin between the weavers and the last pair passed through.

Pin-hole 17
Work as pin-hole 15, but work through four pairs.

Pin-hole 18
Work as pin-hole 16, but work through four pairs.

Pin-hole 19
Work as pin-hole 15, but work through three pairs.

Pin-hole 20
Work as pin-hole 16, but work through three pairs.

Pin-hole 21
Work as pin-hole 15, but work through two pairs.

Pin-hole 22
Work as pin-hole 16, but work

through two pairs.

Pin-hole 23
Work as pin-hole 15, but work through six pairs.

Pin-hole 24
Work as pin-hole 16, but work through six pairs.

Pin-hole 25
Work as pin-hole 15, but work through two pairs.

Pin-hole 26
Work as pin-hole 16, but work through two pairs.

Pin-hole 27
Work as pin-hole 15, but work through three pairs.

Pin-hole 28
Work as pin-hole 16, but work through three pairs.

Pin-hole 29
Work as pin-hole 15, but work through four pairs.

Pin-hole 30
Work as pin-hole 16, but work through four pairs.

Pin-hole 31
Work as pin-hole 15, through five pairs.

Pin-hole 32
Work as pin-hole 16, through five pairs.

Pin-hole 33
Work the pair hanging from pin 23 to the right in cs through two pairs. Twist the weavers twice and insert a pin between the weavers and the last pair passed through.

This completes a pattern repeat. Work right around the mat in this way, moving the cover cloth when necessary.

When you get about half-way around, you will find that the first pins get in the way. Push down flat all the pins on the right-hand edge and around the first triangle of cloth stitch. Then, in the remainder of the pattern, take out two pins in every three and push the third flat into the pillow as you continue round. In this way, the bobbins and threads will be able to lie over the completed work when you near the end.

To finish off, cut a circular piece of linen slightly larger than the inside edge of the lace. Place the lace edging centrally on top of the circle of linen and sew with a buttonhole stitch.

Index

Photographers and Illustrators:
J. Ahlberg 94;
Malcolm Aird 6; 9;
Theo Bergstrom 80;
Mike Berkofsky 70;
Beta Pictures 12;
Steve Bicknell 11; 68/9; 123; 148; 149B; 150;
Tony Boases 113; 114; 115;
John Carter 34;
Martin Chaffer 122;
Roger Charity 28BL;
courtesy J & P Coats Ltd. 46/7; 60; 61; 63; 64; 65; 86/7; 88;
Bob Croxford 99; 100;
Victoria Drew 121;
Alan Duns 29; 145; 146; 147;
Fratelli Fabbri 89;
Jean Paul Froget 116;
Geoffrey Frosh 151;
Melvin Grey 74; 76; 83; 143;
Diane Groves 91; 92; 101;
Charles Holdgate 27; 28TR; 31; 35;
Geoff Howes 138/9;
Paul Kemp 137; 140;
Mary Konier 84;
Trevor Lawrence 125; 126;
David Levin 79;
Chris Lewis 21; 36; 37; 39; 41; 42; 125;
Dick Miller 128B;
Ena Milton 97;
Coral Mula 75; 76; 77; 78; 81; 82; 141T; 142; 144R; 149;
David Newsome 90;
Julien Nieman 44; 133;
Tony North 129;
Alisdair Ogilvie 127; 128TL;
Roger Phillips 119;
Peter Pugh Cook 67; 110;
Julien & Renee Robinson 19; 20;
courtesy Shetland Industries 73L;
Lynette Stock 10;
Jerry Tubby 141BR; 143; 144BL;
Peter Watkins 73R;
Rupert Watts 59;
Paul Williams 24;
Endpapers by courtesy of the Victoria and Albert Museum/
Photograph Rodney Todd-White.